£15 9⁹

CINEMA OF INTERRUPTIONS

Action Genres in Contemporary Indian Cinema

Lalitha Gopalan

 Publishing

For Appa,
the first cinephile I knew

First published in 2002 by the
British Film Institute
21 Stephen Street, London W1T 1LN

The British Film Institute promotes greater understanding of,
and access to, film and moving image culture in the UK.

Cover design: Jürgen Miller

Set in Italian Garamond by Wyvern 21, Bristol
Printed in the UK by Bell and Bain, Glasgow

British Library Cataloguing-in-Publication Data
A catalogue record for this book is available from the British Library
ISBN 0 85170 922 2 pbk
ISBN 0 85170 923 0 hbk

Contents

Acknowledgments

Although this book has been a post dissertation project, I owe a great debt to my teachers Mieke Bal and Sharon Willis for continuing to serve as my ideal models of scholars and colleagues. I wish my first teacher Josef James who drew connections between economics and art was still alive to see a different ordering of his story. In a similar spirit, I hope my own students can hear echoes of our discussions on films and theory.

A Rockefeller Residency Fellowship at the University of the Chicago in Spring 1992 provided the ideal beginning for this project. I wish to acknowledge Bernard Cohn, Ronald Inden, the late A.K. Ramanajum, and Sandhya Shetty for their encouragement and sharp questions. The *Screen* Prize for the chapter on 'Avenging Women' provided a much needed boost to the project plus the funds for a laptop computer. A fellowship from the American Council for Learned Societies in 1997–98 made it possible for me to conduct research in India and have uninterrupted time for writing. Walsh Research Grants from the School of Foreign Service at Georgetown University in Summer 1996 and Winter 2000 made possible additional trips to Bombay, Madras, and London. Kim Hall, Leona Fisher, Jeff Peck, Henry Schwarz, and James Slevin have been wonderful mentors at Georgetown University.

Several chapters in this book have benefitted from queries and comments raised at seminars and conferences. I wish to particularly thank Carla Petievich, Gina Marchetti, Gyan Prakash, David Ludden, Indira Peterson, John Caughie, Kathryn Hansen, Mustapha Pasha, Nicholas Dirks, Sankaran Krishna, Susan Hayward, Shelly Feldman, and Valentine Daniel not only for these invitations to present my work but for their intellectual generosity and support.

This book was written in New York and owes a great deal to persons and institutions in the city that I claimed as home for several years: Librarians at the Performing Arts Library of the New York Public Library and David Magier at Columbia University readily spring to mind. I am grateful to Faye Ginsburg and Barbara Abrash for inviting me to their Center for Media, Culture and Society at New York University. Discussions at the Columbia Film Seminar fueled my enthusiasm for films during the darkest moments of writing. The movie theaters and video stores in Queens and on Lexington Avenue were most inviting after a long day at the computer.

I have been fortunate to have the company of other scholars of Indian cinema – Parag Amladi, Ira Bhaskar, Sumita Chakravarthy Teja Ganti, Sheila Meehan and Jyotika Virdi. Telephone calls to Parama Roy helped me navigate through many an intellectual impasse during the writing process. Many thanks to Ravi Vasudevan for innumerable discussions on films and theory via telephone, e-mail, and in person. Comments and suggestions from Ayisha Abraham, M. S. S. Pandian, Pritham Chakravarthy, and Venkatesh Chakravarthy in Madras and elsewhere enriched this project.

I am grateful to several last minute rescues: Barbara Ramasuck generously mailed copies of her essays on Rajasthan; Jake Gerli was the ideal research assistant who located essays on Avid; Katie Kinski and Stephanie Frontz copied and mailed essays from the Art Library at University of Rochester after a postal disaster; Prema Koshy copiously copied many pages of *Trade Guide* from the BFI Library; Svati Lelyveld carefully composed the bibliography; Ashish Rajadhyaksha directed me to the Film Stills Librarian at the National Film Archives in Pune, who in turn, promptly sent me much needed slides. Thanks to Jürgen Miller for coming through on DVD grabs and for designing the cover.

This book would have been poorer without conversations with many filmmakers. I wish to thank my oldest interlocutor T. B. Srinivas for discussions on the form of popular films and for encouraging me to look at J. P. Dutta's films. Despite his tight shooting schedule, J. P. Dutta was always available for my questions on his cinematic style. Thanks also to Vidhu Vinod Chopra and his assistant Promod, and K. Parthepan for locating the relevant production stills. Conversations with P. C. Sriram and Thotta Tharani sharpened my understanding of the production process. An interview with Mani Ratnam fortified my reading of his cinematic style.

I am extremely fortunate to have had careful readings on earlier drafts from Corey Creekmur, David Desser, and Madhava Prasad whose suggestions vastly improved the structure and argument of the book. Patricia White and Sumita Chakravarthy's comments as respondents helped guide my revisions on Dutta's films and Mani Ratnam's *Nayakan*. I owe a huge debt to Alan Tansman for his detailed comments on the Introduction that helped tighten and improve the argument. Thanks to Carl Bromley for proofreading the manuscript and for sharing his cinephiliac knowledge of gangster films. I wish to thank Jane Hoehner, Editor of the 'Film Studies Series' at Wayne State University for her enthusiastic support during a very trying period. Many thanks to my editor Andrew Lockett for his consistent support.

I am glad to have the opportunity to thank friends whose support continues to be immeasurable: Ajit Subramaniam, Alan Tansman, Amy Robinson, Anne Cubilié, Barbara Miller, Bhaskar Chakravarthy, Christina Joseph, Elissa Marder, Gita Rao, Kim Hall, Jeff Peck, Ram Ranganathan, Ritu Vij, Robert Cagle, Scott Redford, Sean

Miller, Sangeeta Tyagi, and Veena Siddharth. Meena Alexander, David Lelyveld, George Robb, and Promita Sengupta for their conviviality during months of writing in Washington Heights.

My parents and parents-in-law have offered various forms of sustenance during this project and I am as relieved as they are that this book project is finally over. Many thanks to my brother Murali Gopalan for always responding to my telephone queries on obscure film details, for reading a draft of this book, and for sustaining me with humour during this long process. My other brother Krishna Gopalan was not only forced to proofread two chapters but over the years subjected to a litany of questions on Indian cinema. After all, what are brothers for!

It is no exaggeration to say that this book would not have been written without Itty Abraham who remains not only my favorite film date but has also played the parts of director and producer. Despite the narrative of interruptions that has governed our lives for many years, he made sure that intervals and songs were long pauses to listen to my half-baked formulations, to read several rough drafts, to challenge my film taste, and to travel to distant suburbs for a film. Although the usual disclaimers hold, the best parts of this book bear the indelible mark of his incisive suggestions and intellectual generosity. Sorry folks, we have a film to see.

I

Introduction: 'Hum Aapke Hain Koun?' – Cinephilia and Indian Films

Consider a scene from Ram Gopal Varma's Hindi film *Rangeela/Colourful* (1995). Muna walks into the film studio to apologise for his uncouth behaviour at the movie theatre the previous evening. He sees Mili practising her dance moves and cannot fathom her stories of studio grandeur emanating from this ordinary, dark space. She rises to his challenge: the lights beam on her, music streams in, and Mili gyrates to 'Jo mangta hai'/'What you want'. Dumbstruck, Muna imagines joining Mili in a song and dance sequence that includes a virtual journey through New York and Hyderabad. In short, Muna falls hopelessly in love with Mili. Until this moment, the film insists on a bantering relationship strengthened by their mutual love for films: he is a ticket tout outside Bombay film theatres; she, a chorus girl in a Hindi film. Each is trying to get closer to the magic of cinema. Occurring in the first half of the film, as seasoned viewers of the Hindi film love story, we expect him to run into troubled waters, thus delaying his union with Mili. As he struggles to confess his love, to get what he wants (jo mangta hai), a triangular economy of desire unfolds: the hero of the film within the film, Kamal, also falls in love with Mili when he watches her practise dance on the beach. Unlike Muna, Kamal is motivated in his desire for Mili by her exuberance outside the studio. In a fortunate turn of events, Kamal recommends Mili to replace the heroine in his film. They finally produce their film, and the audience declares Kamal and Mili a successful pair on the screen. Intimidated by their success, Muna flees Bombay, assuming that Mili's rise to stardom squeezes him out of her life. However, Mili, with Kamal's help, tracks him down. In the final moments of the film, she confesses her love for Muna.

Their union remains credible within the film's own internal logic favouring cinephilia over film-making, a preference dictating the difference between Muna's and Kamal's desire for Mili. Even as the film struggles to preserve Muna's love as independent of Mili's meteoric rise to stardom, we *know* that it orchestrated his love from the point of view of a film-going fan, a cinephile, and only later as somebody outside the play of light and sound. He falls in love with Mili's image in the studio, the film star, not his pal on the streets. Mili, on the other hand, expresses her desire only at the very end of the film, but her unstated reasons and indecisiveness drive the narrative logic of the love story. In other words, we wait eagerly for Mili to decide between her star-struck devotion for Kamal and her love for films that leads her to Muna. The film implies that Kamal loses because of his inability to participate in the correct triangulation – he loves only Mili, whereas Mili's first love is the cinema. It is Muna and Mili's love for cinema that dictates their love story, the preferred triangulation in the film.[1]

Rangeela, like Varma's other films, summons cinephilia, reminding us that both film-makers and viewers share complicity – their films can 'read' our desire as much as we can marshal our critical machinery to read their creations. Obviously, *Rangeela* is not a first in this genre: Ketan Mehta's comic film *Hero Hiralal* (1988) revolves around an auto rickshaw driver's obsession with a film star; casting Kamal Haasan in four different roles, Singeetham Srinivasa Rao's Tamil film *Michael Madan Kama Rajan* (1990) plays with thematic and visual conventions in Tamil cinema; and Ram Gopal Varma's *Daud/Run* (1997) uses the caper to highlight the frustrations of a hermeneutic reading of Indian popular films. Reading back our insights to us, analysing stereotypical endings and stock details, these films showcase a cinema that can confidently parody its own conditions of production while fine-tuning certain genre tendencies. Parading conventions as comic interventions – the wet sari, the sad and loving mother, song and dance sequences – each of these films strikes an

Poster for *Hum Aapke Hain Koun..!* (courtesy of the National Film Archive, Pune)

ironic posture that, as critics, we are reluctant to accord the commercial industry. Even Sooraj Barjatya's Hindi film *Hum Aapke Hain Koun..!/Who Am I to You..!* (1994), a smash hit advertising itself as wholesome family entertainment with four-teen songs, does not shy away from a comment on spectatorship.[2] The opening credit sequence has both leads, Madhuri Dixit and Salman Khan, looking straight at us and singing 'Hum aapke hain koun?'/'Who am I to you?'; asking us to reflect on our relationship to cinema, the film draws us into a triangular economy of desire, making us an integral part of its love story.[3]

We can fully appreciate the verve of these films if we recall that in each filmic instance they maintain a respectful distance from Indian cinema's tragic tale of film-making narrated in Guru Dutt's *Kagaz Ke Phool* (1959), in which the hero as film director suffers a tortured relationship to both film-making and love. Dutt's film interpolates us as voyeurs looking at the unfolding narrative of doom, a relationship to the screen ideally suited to reaffirming the negative potential of cinema. In sharp contrast, the playful and ironic commentary on film-making cited in the above films depends on our familiarity with cinematic conventions, familiarity cultivated through our long relationship with Indian popular cinema. More often than not, by calling attention to our viewing habits within the diegesis and naming it love, con-temporary Indian films have closed the gap between the screen and spectator. Whether or not we accede to the proposal of love and familiarity from the screen, these films signify a confidence in film-making we have not been privy to for the past twenty-five years.

This confidence signals changes in aesthetic, technical, and reception conditions, simultaneously nudging us to acknowledge a shift in our critical engagement with cinema. To account for the changing conditions of production and conditions satis-factorily, between the screen and the spectator, we should read popular Indian films from the point of view of a cinephiliac, one that is based on an ambivalent relation-ship to cinema: love and hate.

Whereas cinephilia colours the selection of genre films in this book, the task of this introductory chapter is to map the theoretical and methodological issues implicit in my reading of films. Starting with the place of cinephilia in film theory, I move to consider the different changes in production and reception of Indian films, both locally and globally, that inspire the love of this cinema. Encouraged by its ability to entertain beyond national boundaries, this book places popular Indian cinema within a global system of popular cinema to account for its simultaneous tendency to assert national and local cinematic conventions, and also to abide by dominant genre principles.

Identifying the strength of certain conventions unique to Indian cinema as a *constellation of interruptions* allows us to consider national styles of film-making even as Hollywood films assert their global dominance. By bearing in mind this constellation of interruptions, we should reconsider the direct importation of film theory as ideal reading strategies for Indian films, even though they have been productive in understanding the structure of pleasure and anticipation of Hollywood genre films. The introduction, in short, suggests that, just as popular Indian films rewrite certain dominant genre principles, film theory, too, needs to undergo revisions in order to read adequately the different structuring of anticipation and pleasure in this cinema that also has a global application and circulation.

Even the most casual tourist in India resorts to hyperbole to describe the potency of this cinema that produces a thousand films in more than twelve languages each year. For instance, in his travelogue *Video Nights in Kathmandu*, Pico Iyer declares in a significant synecdoche that spills over its own rhetoric, 'Indian movies were India, only more so.'[4] Other writers, such as Salman Rushdie, Alan Sealy, and Farrukh Dhondy, have used various aspects of Indian film culture to spin fabulous narratives of success and failure, stardom and political life, love and villainy.[5] For the uninitiated, most commentators will list implausible twists and turns in plots, excessive melodrama, loud song and dance sequences, and lengthy narrative as having tremendous mass appeal, but little critical value. However, the films cited above belie such judgments and are symptoms of seismic changes between cinema and society that have seeped into the ways in which we read, think, and write about Indian cinema, thus initiating our love affair with it.

However expansive the influence of cinema, Indian film-makers are acutely aware that most films fail at the box office. Their financial anxieties have increased in recent years with the rise of adjacent entertainment industries that threaten to diminish the power of films, even if cinema as an institution is not waning in the public imagination. Trade papers from the 1980s record the industry's fears of the growing video industry that many believed would eventually discourage audiences from going to theatres. Nevertheless, the arrival of video shops in India also exposed the film-going public to world cinemas, an opportunity previously afforded only by film festivals and film societies. Suddenly films from other parts of Asia, Europe, and America were easily available to the film buff. Film-makers were also very much part of this video-watching public, freely quoting and borrowing cinematic styles: for instance, director Ram Gopal Varma started his career as a video-shop owner. While a section of the urban rich retreated to their homes, trade papers reported an increase in film attendance in small towns and villages. Instead of assuming that one mode of watching would give way to the next evolutionary stage, we now find films coexisting alongside a robust video economy and satellite or cable television. Ironically, both cable television and video shops are also responsible for creating nostalgia for older films. Together, these different visual media have changed reception conditions by generating an audience that has developed a taste for global-style action films while simultaneously a cherishing a fondness for the particularities of Indian cinema.

In addition to video and satellite saturation of the visual field, American films (sometimes dubbed in Hindi) started reappearing in Indian theatres after a new agreement was signed between the Government of India and Motion Picture Producers and Distributors of America, Inc. (MPPDA) in April 1985, ending the trade embargo that began in 1971.[6] Initially, Indian film-makers protested against this invasion, but slowly reconciled themselves to their presence after recognising that American films did not pose a threat to Indian film distribution.[7] Occasionally we find characters in Indian films taking potshots at American cinema: in Ram Gopal Varma's *Satya* (1998), protagonists purposely misread *Jurassic Park* (1993) as a horror film starring lizards; in Tamil films, cross-linguistic puns abound around James Cameron's *Titanic* (1997). These playful engagements with American culture confidently acknowledge that Indian cinema audiences belong to a virtual global economy where films from different production sites exist at the *same level* – a democratisation of global cinephilia. Perhaps I am exaggerating the dominance of Indian cinema, but the confidence of some Indian film-makers does hold out hope for unsettling the inequalities of the global marketplace where we are all too aware of American films unilaterally expanding into newer territories.

While economic liberalisation opened Indian markets to a range of television programmes and videos, it also facilitated, however slowly, access to state-of-the-art film technology for film-makers. Within the industry there were discernible changes in the production process. According to Manmohan Shetty, who runs a film processing business, Adlabs, a sea change occurred in 1978 when Kodak introduced a negative film that could be processed at high ambient temperatures (105°F), improving colour resolution.[8] At about the same time, professionally trained technicians in editing, cinematography, and lighting began entering the commercial industry from film institutes in Pune and Chennai (Madras), vastly improving the quality of film production, as well as increasing its cost. Manjunath Pendakur notes that the rising costs of film production since the 1980s not only includes huge salaries for film stars, but also higher wages for directors and technicians.[9] Audiences seem attuned to these changes on screen: in Chennai, the crowds become hysterical when cinematographer P. C. Sriram's name runs across the screen; directors have fan-supported websites competing with those of movie stars.

The profusion of film-making talent strengthened the Malayalam, Tamil, and Telugu industries. Since 1979, film production in Tamil and Telugu continued to keep pace with Hindi films, each producing about 140 films annually.[10] Increased production from regional industries has weakened the stranglehold of Hindi films as the largest commercial industry in the nation, while improvements in dubbing facilities have ensured a national audience for Tamil and Telugu films. Additionally, film-makers from the south such as S. Shankar, Sashilal Nair, Priyadarshan, Mani Ratnam, and Ram Gopal Varma have been making inroads into the Hindi film industry, once a prerogative of female stars.[11] The migration of directors also means that narratives focusing on national themes – inter-communal love story, war, and terrorism – are no longer a prerogative of Hindi cinema, but also surface in regional cinemas. Concurrently, narratives in Hindi films have receded from national secular themes addressing an urban audience, dabbling instead with regional stories resonating with preoccupations of the Hindi belt: Rajputs, Biharis, and Punjabis now crowd the Hindi film screen.

Technical and aesthetic improvements in mainstream Indian cinema remind us that commercial film-makers benefited from narrative experiments introduced by independent film-makers in the 1970s. Consciously setting themselves apart from commercial cinema, films by Adoor Gopalkrishnan, G. Aravindan, Mrinal Sen, Girish Kasarvalli, Kumar Shahini, and Mani Kaul focused on social and political antagonisms to narrate their tales of disappointment with the post-colonial state while also conveying hopes for a different society.[12] Screened at film societies or special shows in large movie theatres, their films drew the urban elite to cinemas and shaped film-viewing habits by encouraging the audience to focus more intently on the screen. A substantial number of commercial films made in the late 1980s borrowed from these film-making practices while continuing to improve on conventions of entertainment. Not unlike independent cinema, we now find directors gaining currency as auteurs in commercial cinema, controlling the production of their films and characterising them with a unique cinematic style. In turn, the National Film Development Corporation (NFDC, the state body that finances independent films) started producing films that liberally incorporated mainstream stories and stars.

Further, Indian films have, on occasion, internationalised the production process: S. Shankar's Tamil film *Kaadalan/Lover* (1994), for example, had its special effects enhanced in a Hong Kong film studio. Critics rightly focus on the film's playful commentary on upper-caste hegemony and its attendant economies of taste, but we cannot ignore how globalisation of the production process also influences the narrative of caste contestations.[13] The more conventional representation of the world in Indian popular cinema – song and dance sequences set in foreign locales – is not only spruced up to arouse the spectator's interests in tourism, but also aggressively participates in the movement of global capital. These sequences not only bring the world home, but also acknowledge a loyal audience abroad that wishes to see its own stories of migrations and displacement written into these films. A number of Hindi films – *Pardes* (1997), *Dilwale Dulhaniya Le Jayange* (1995), *Dil to Pagal Hai* (1998), *Kuch Kuch Hota Hai* (1998) – index an audience straggling between national identities, harbouring longings for an original home, or possessing the capital for tourism. Considered together, these narrative and production details place the viewer of Indian films in a global cinematic economy, finally catching up with a long history of global reception.

Since Independence, Indian films have travelled to the former Soviet Union, Latin America, Africa, and Southeast Asia, entertaining audiences whose personal histories have few ties with the subcontinent.[14] Sometimes, these travel routes are visible on video copies – Arabic subtitles on Hindi films, Malay on Tamil films – telling us of a global set of viewers who watch other national cinemas besides Hollywood. More recently, *Newsweek* reported that Japan is spellbound by Tamil films, especially those starring Rajnikanth, because 'Indian films are filled with the classical entertainment movies used to offer.'[15]

Although Indian films now enjoy a crossover audience, extra-filmic events nudge us towards other readings of popular films. It is now commonplace to find the loyal Indian diaspora cultivating appreciation by sponsoring stage shows of film stars, events that read popular films as star-studded texts. However, it is film-makers in the diaspora who have been openly engaging with, and in the process teaching us a lesson or two in, defamiliarising Indian film conventions. In both Srinivas Krishna's Canadian production *Masala* (1992) and Gurinder Chadda's British film *Bhaji on the Beach* (1994), we find lengthy quotations from Indian cinema: protagonists express desire by resorting to song and dance sequences. Inserted in films working with small budgets and relying on art-house distribution, such sequences serve as fabulous strands expressing immigration fantasies born out of travel and displacement. In a more abrupt manner, Rachid Bouchareb's French–Algerian film *My Family's Honour* (1997) uses Hindi film songs on the soundtrack and even splices an entire musical number from *Hum Kisise Kum Nahin/We Are Number One* (1977) into its narrative on North African immigrants living in France. Displaying no diegetic link to the narrative, the jarring disjunction of this sequence conveys the disruption brought about through immigration and displacement in Bouchareb's film. Terry Zwigoff's *Ghost World* (2000), narrating traumas of the summer after high school, opens with a song and dance sequence, 'Jab jaan pechachan/'When we got to know each other' from *Gumnaam* (1965), intercutting with the main narrative. The feverish cabaret and twist number offers the bored teenager the requisite degree of exotic abandon. Baz Luhrmann confesses to not only having seen Indian popular films, but also being mesmerised enough to deploy several song and dance sequences in his film *Moulin Rouge* (2000). Benny Torathi's Israeli film *Desparado Piazza*, also called *Piazza of Dreams* (2000), splices in a song sequence from *Sangam* (1964) to map a different history of migration for ethnic Jews.[16] All these films celebrate these interruptions as a way of accounting for cinephilia even when the protagonists have to adjust to arduous conditions imposed through transnational migration, ennui-ridden teenagers, or a courtesan's love story. These unexpected sites of reception allow us to see, from without, how Indian films are available for a wide range of readings, including camp and cult possibilities, based on their multi-plot narratives and multiple disruptions.

Within India, critical writing on cinema has blossomed in the past two decades, reporting a serious, sometimes cinephiliac, relationship to films. Published from Bangalore, *Deep Focus* combines interviews with directors from different parts of the world, film reviews, and lengthy critical pieces. *Cinemaya*, based in Delhi, follows the festival schedule in Asia, brings its readers news of the latest films and interviews with directors, and addresses a pan-Asian audience from Turkey to Japan. These two magazines locate Indian cinema, both popular and alternative, and its audience within a global network of cinematic styles.

The short-lived *Splice* was published from Calcutta with an exclusive focus on alternative cinematic practices, and it explored the correspondences between avant-garde practices in India and those in the former Soviet republics. For a brief time *Splice* was an integral part of a thriving film scene in Calcutta, which now includes a film archive at Nandan and a brand-new film studies department at Jadavpur University. The *Journal of Moving Images* from the Department of Film Studies at Jadavpur addresses an emerging academic audience in India. *Lensight*, published by the Film and Television Institute of India (FTII) in Pune, addresses itself to film-makers with reports on state-of-the art lab processing techniques, editing equipment, and cameras, and also carries lengthy interviews with film-makers on their craft. Although pitched exclusively at film-makers, *Lensight* carries a wealth of information on sociological conditions of production that are not widely available to a film critic.

Finally, the publication of *Encyclopaedia of Indian Cinema* (1994, revised edition 1999) stamped the scholarly seal of approval on Indian cinema. Expansive in its scope, Ashish Rajadhyaksha and Paul Willemen's opus strings together biographies, film lists, and plot summaries, providing a road map on different features of Indian cinema from genres to independent film movements and regional cinemas. Considered together, these publications both expanded and variegated the scope of cinephilia in India beyond the standard fanzines celebrating the star system.

These disparate details form the bedrock of material changes in the production and reception of Indian popular cinema. Spelling out these details undercuts a series of archaic oppositions that we find steadfastly held in film studies: between national and international cinemas, overlooking alternative routes of film distribution; between Hollywood and other national cinemas, casting the latter as bad copies instead of examining them as a rejoinder to a hegemonic cinema; between national and regional cinemas, placing Hindi cinema at the helm of the national imaginary and ignoring a simultaneous move towards regional nationalisms; between national and global audiences, by not anticipating audiences that also endow Indian popular cinema with meaning that exceeds its own intended horizon of address; between art and commercial cinema, repeating a high-modernist division between high and low cultures without admitting to a more variegated terrain of taste. Naming these mobile processes speaks to a post-colonial condition that according to Stuart Hall marks a 'critical interruption into that whole grand historiographical narrative which, in liberal historiography and Weberian historical sociology, as much as in the dominant traditions of Western Marxism, gave this global dimension a subordinate presence in a story which could essentially be told from within European parameters'.[17] In other words, this book reads popular Indian films as an interruption in film theory, a film theory that, although generated from engagements exclusively with Euro-American cinemas, assumes a trans-regional durability.

Sholay and Reading Strategies

More than any of the above material conditions effecting our relationship to the screen, Ramesh Sippy's *Sholay/Flames* (1975) was a landmark in Indian cinema, for ever changing the production and reception of popular cinema in the past twenty-five years. Coinciding with the state of emergency declared by Prime Minister Indira Gandhi in 1975, *Sholay* was emblematic of a number of films feeding off what political theorists refer to as a crisis of legitimacy of the Indian state.[18] Film critics, media activists, and film scholars agree that the unrest in civil society marked by communal riots, police brutality, violent secessionist movements, and assaults against women and minorities seeped into film narratives.[19] Stacked with gangsters,

Wall poster for *Sholay* (courtesy of the National Film Archive, Pune)

avenging women, brutal police, and corrupt politicians, these films resolve their narratives through vigilante actions that repeatedly undercut the authority of the state.[20]
Activist organisations such as Delhi's Media Advocacy Group argue that representations of brutality in contemporary commercial cinema have a direct and
reinforcing effect on the level of violence in civil society.[21]

However, *Sholay*'s iconic status exceeds a mimetic relationship to reality, drawing in large part from its reconfiguration of the Western.[22] Mixing a host of
conventions from Indian popular cinema such as song and dance sequences, *Sholay*
successfully produced an Indian riposte to the classic American Western. Fans of
this cult film extensively quote Salim Khan and Javed Akhtar's script back to the
screen; rumours abound on the existent variations of the closing sequence; and
overnight the actor Amjad Khan, playing the villain Gabbar Singh, became one of
the most popular stars of the film. Anupama Chopra's book *Sholay: The Making of
a Classic* – required reading for a fan – revives cinephiliac obsession with this film
by journeying to the origins of production.

The film also spurred the first psychoanalytical critique of popular Indian cinema.
In a much neglected essay, Madan Gopal Singh evaluates the tremendous success
of this film by picking one scene as a symptom of the changing relationship between
screen and spectator: the 'Mehbooba! Mehbooba!' song and dance sequence.[23]
According to him, in this sequence the camera gropes the dancer's body and, by
extension, provides us a point of view that was hitherto unavailable in popular Hindi
cinema. Singh uses voyeurism as a conceptual tool to describe the altered relationship between screen and spectator in the film, an idea that draws extensively from
certain cinematic principles found in Hollywood – omniscient narration, continuity
editing, internally coherent narrative, and the ideal spectator's identification with
the camera – leading to the argument that the camera's groping mechanism fragments the female dancer's body and generates viewing pleasure. But he glosses over
the fact that song and dance sequences explicitly distract the viewer from narrative
flow and contradict the conventions of continuity editing. Overtly exhibitionistic,
song and dance sequences break the codes of realism on which psychoanalytical
voyeurism relies.[24] Nevertheless, Singh's cryptic formulation prods us to consider
how even the most superficial and entertaining song and dance sequences carry an
ideological charge, heightening our viewing pleasure.[25]

Singh's essay also tells another story, a story of the intellectual context of his critical engagement with Hindi films. Originally published in the Left avant-garde
Journal of Arts and Ideas, Singh's essay echoes the opinions of alternative film-makers
such as Kumar Shahini, Mani Kaul, and John Abraham, who were both writing and
making a different kind of narrative cinema. Accounting for the hegemonic potential of Hindi commercial cinema, especially its ability to throttle radical film-making,
Singh bemoans the loss of freshly minted student film-makers from the Film and

Television Institute of India (FTII) to the commercial industry, a move, he argues, that turns them into technicians of special effects. Whereas *Sholay* affords Singh the occasion to critically assess the ideological manifestations of the consumerist cinema, his theoretical speculations helped shape an entire generation of film theorists working on Indian cinema.[26]

In sharp contrast to Singh's critical essay, *Sholay* is a revered master text of success for film-makers: Ram Gopal Varma confesses to knowing every shot of two of his favourite films – *Sholay* and *The Godfather* (1972); more recently, Rajkumar Santoshi allegedly watched *Sholay* every morning while shooting his own *China Gate* (1999).[27] *Sholay* is the legendary source that spurred an entire generation of film-makers to borrow from globally circulating genres, yet also to reincorporate conventions from Indian popular cinema with great aplomb.[28] Spawning a number of B films throughout the 1980s, the full impact of Sippy's innovative cinematic style on popular Indian cinema – accommodating Indian cinematic conventions within a Hollywood genre – was fully developed a decade later by J. P. Dutta, Mani Ratnam, Mukul Anand, Ram Gopal Varma, Rajkumar Santoshi, and Shekhar Kapur.

These divergent readings of *Sholay* demonstrate a gap between critics writing on popular Indian cinema and film-makers. Simply put, critics tend to take a moralistic view of mainstream cinema, seeing very little of the 'popular' in them, whereas commercial film-makers see themselves as entertainers and regard critics as elitists whose opinions rarely count in the workings of the industry.[29] This stand-off between critics and commercial film-makers is as old as the practice of narrative cinema itself and has little new to add to debates on the differences between highbrow and lowbrow, mass and popular cultures, which as cultural critics we have learned to make and then unmake. In the end we have settled on 'popular culture' as the most viable concept that absorbs the paradoxes of our trade: we can read resistance in its form, even as we continue to be mesmerised by it.[30] This rather tenuous definition seems vastly superior to the polarised definitions of cultural taste that plague readings of Indian films. There is no doubt that we learn a great deal from vigilant readings of cinema's hegemonic influence that reveal its power to affirm ethnic stereotyping, sexism, and jingoism, and caution us against being taken in by its dazzling surface. But all too often we tend to pay little attention to questions of pleasure. Inasmuch as we assume that commercial films maintain the status quo, suppressing all radical possibilities in their viewers, we must also admit that film-makers are constantly inviting us to return to the movies through novel cinematic approaches.

Cinephilia and Film Theory

Cinephilia, as Paul Willemen reminds us, suffers from considerable neglect in film theory, even though it once dominated the writings and films of the French *nouvelle vague* directors.[31] What distinguishes cinephilia from its more lofty cousin, film criticism, is its attention to a system of signs beyond the central narrative – gestures from actors, *mise en scène* details, and even throw-away shots – that the obsessive film-viewer reads as special signals from the film-maker. Suggesting that the eclectic use of psychoanalysis was one of the reasons cinephilia has a shifting presence in film theory, Willemen speculates:

> Even though the recourse to psychoanalysis did allow the questions of cinephilia to be addressed, the importation of psychoanalytic terminology was a costly business both for film theory and for psychoanalytic theory. The cost was erasure of concepts such as transference and resistance from both theoretical discourses. Since the practice of psychoanalysis is inconceivable without these two terms, the psychoanalytical theory mobilized by and for film theory was seriously flawed, to say the least. On the other hand, the absence of these two key concepts allowed critics freely to delegate their neuroses to the films where they would be 'read'. In effect, this reduced the films to the reader's screen memories. Since then, the relation between psychoanalysis and film theory has been reversed: instead of using random bits of psychoanalytic theory to generate readings of films, now bits of films are used to introduce readers to psychoanalytic theory. [p. 225]

Willemen does not offer a clear definition of cinephilia, but his discussion on the discourse of cinephilia proposes at least a proper name to grasp the incoherence of 'loving cinema'. Several ideas, associations, and relationships that crop up in Willemen's discussion I find particularly instructive for my own reading of Indian cinema.

> Cinephilia doesn't do anything other than designate something which resists, which escapes existing networks of critical discourse and theoretical frameworks. What is this thing that keeps cropping up in all these different forms and keeps being called cinephilia? [p. 231]

> Cinephilia being designated in cinema is an activation of complicity. Cinephilia is a component of a film culture which is then recycled in the film and which therefore bonds viewer and film in a particular moment of complicity. [p. 241]

> Actually the cinephiliac moment is my preferred description because of its overtones of necrophilia, of relating to something that is dead, past, but alive in memory. So there is a kind of necrophilia involved, and I don't mean that negatively. [p. 227]

> It's a theory premised on notions of revelation, on the notion of excess.... So it is no accident, indeed, from what is highly necessary, that cinephilia should operate particularly strongly in relation to a form of cinema that is perceived as being highly

coded, highly commercial, formalized, and ritualized. For it is only there that the moment of revelations or excess, a dimension other than what is being programmed, becomes noticeable. [pp. 237–8]

Describing cinephilia variously as resistance, complicity, necrophilia, and excess, Willemen prescribes it as an antidote to the usual theoretical practice of subsuming, even smothering, films under a formal theoretical edifice. In tandem with Willemen's formulation, discussion of cinephilia or its death has filled the pages of film criticism: Susan Sontag's essay lamenting the death of cinema; French film journals *Vertigo* and *Cahiers du cinéma* devoted complete issues to cinephilia; *Film Quarterly* used the genre of letters between Jonathan Rosenbaum and a group of younger critics to generate discussions on cinephilia.[32] Christine Keathley glides through these discussions foregrounding the overlaps and incommensurable links between film theory and cinephilia.[33] What these essays capture is a disenchantment with certain strands of film theory that repudiate the love of films as a primary condition; reading symptoms has overtaken the love-struck moments that brought many of us to film studies. A glance at critical work in film studies in the past two decades confirms Willemen's and his fellow travellers' suspicions of waning cinephilia; thankfully, there are a couple of exceptions that deserve mention. Even if these writers do not completely incorporate ideas of transference, they provide us with tools to help us grapple with our complicity when analysing films we love but rarely admit to in our writing. Richard Dyer's essays time and again address various contradictory reasons for studying popular culture, by insisting that we cannot spend our time imagining why it is pleasurable to 'others' if we do not understand how we as critics may find popular culture pleasurable.[34] Not forgetting the Frankfurt School's warnings that dazzling entertainment reels us into pure appearances, Dyer walks a tightrope between critical positions to suggest that we crack the common-sense assertion that it is 'only entertainment':

Yet entertainment offers certain pleasures not others, proposes that we find such-and-such delightful, teaches us enjoyment – including the enjoyment of unruly delight. It works with the desires that circulate in a given society at a given time, neither wholly constructing those desires nor merely reflecting desires produced elsewhere; it plays a major role in the social construction of happiness. We have to understand it itself, neither take it as given nor assume that behind it lies something more important. [p. 7]

Dyer's assertion that we consider entertainment *qua* entertainment bears an uncanny resemblance to the more negative dismissal of cinema as 'pure appearances', but with a difference. Incisively using Gramsci's concept of 'common sense', Dyer leads us to de-familiarise the obvious aspects of entertainment, whose meaning appears settled, before using his critical scalpel.

Admitting that we as critics are very much subjects of entertainment also echoes in Sharon Willis's readings of race and gender in contemporary Hollywood film.[35] In *High Contrast*, she argues that films rely on the visibility of race and gender, categories resonating with our own theoretical preoccupations with difference:

> So powerful is our cultural wish to believe that differences give themselves to sight that the cinema is able to capitalize, both ideologically and financially, on the fascination that dazzling visual contrasts exercise upon us. At the same time, *as films read our social field*, they may both mobilize and contain the conflict, uneasiness, and overwrought affect that so often accompany the confrontation of differences in everyday practices. Cinema seems to borrow and channel these energies through a volatile affective range, from terror, panic, shock, and anxiety to titillation, thrills, excitement, fascination, pleasure, and comfort, while it proliferates representations of social difference as a central or peripheral spectacle. [p. 1. My emphasis]

Both Dyer and Willis not only demonstrate a dialectical relationship between viewer and screen, but also uncover our complicity in the circuits of pleasure generated by mass culture – a contrast from the usual refrain that popular cinema numbs, leaving us few options of resistance. Their positions extend Willemen's cinephilia by suggesting that our investments in popular cinema can yield changes in the public sphere through more watchful yet playful reading strategies. In all three positions we find a marked tendency towards seizing filmic details and revealing symptoms in our cultural imaginary, whether racist, sexist, or, more positively, queer possibilities. In an analogous fashion, Roger Cardinal argues for pausing over peripheral detail in films, a mode of looking associated with 'non-literacy':[36]

> The mobile eye which darts from point to point will tend to clutch at fortuitous detail (the chicken) or to collect empathetic impressions of touch sensations (the bare feet in the dust) … . The act of pausing over the peripheral detail can have more than trivial implications … the whole screen is acknowledged as a surface which is, so to speak, *detailed all over*, like a mosaic, available to the gaze as an even field of rippling potency and plenitude. [pp. 124, 126]

In a not so dissimilar manner, Naomi Schor elegantly argues in *Reading in Detail* that reading details betrays an investment in the ornamental, the useless, and, by extension, the feminine, even if details are routinely recruited to serve realism.[37] Reading details emerges as a space of memory for the reader as she travels through various intertextual details triggered by an image. Schor asserts that, despite the rather long association between detail and femininity, reading details is very much a feminist project.

If today the detail and wider semantic field it commands enjoys an undisputed legitimacy, it is because the dominant paradigms of patriarchy have been largely eroded. Eroded, but not eradicated. By reversing the terms of the oppositions and the values of the hierarchies, we remain, of course, prisoners of the paradigms, only just barely able to dream a universe where the categories of *general* and *particular*, *mass* and *detail*, and *masculine* and *feminine* would no longer order our thinking and our seeing. [p. 4]

These critical positions suggest in a roundabout way that cinephiliac readings – the fetishisation of details – open film texts to other scenes of contestations in public life towards which master theoretical tools broadly gesture in their proclamations of progressive and regressive meanings of films. Willemen's insight into the symbiosis between cinephilia and 'highly commercial' cinema, in particular, instructs my own reading of contemporary Indian popular films, where one of the pleasures of working on contemporary Indian cinema surfaces when films read our desires back to us, both regressive and Utopian.

Undoubtedly this relationship to Indian films emerges from my own location in American academic life, where on the one hand I am constantly translating Indian films into the established paradigms of film theory and, on the other, circumscribing a discrete theoretical domain for reading Indian cinema. But the translations are far from perfect. At film conferences in America, for instance, one finds a polite interest in Indian cinema – alternative or popular – but little enthusiasm. The same small clutch of listeners migrate from one international panel to another – Russian, Italian, Chinese, Indian, Iranian – with hordes of American film scholars crowding into auditoriums for papers on the latest Hollywood blockbuster. In spite of film studies' self-representation as a marginal field, there is no doubt that the dominant American imaginary, where its own interests are at the centre, influences my colleagues who find *difference* in international cinema a difficult idea to come to terms with. All too often as students of Indian cinema, we spend too much time imparting basic information to an audience whose standard question begins: 'Although I have not seen an Indian film …' Unlike my colleagues in the field, my students are more open to international films, more agreeable to expanding their film taste beyond the canon of genre films. In all honesty, however, unequal power dynamics in the classroom cannot be entirely discounted as a proximate cause for their enthusiasm. Yet there are limits to their cosmopolitan film taste. For instance, in my course on postwar Westerns, I decided to show Ramesh Sippy's *Sholay*. My students were already well prepared for international responses to the American Western and had only recently discussed Paul Smith's essay on Sergio Leone. But they seemed rudely shocked by Sippy's film. Leaving aside the problem of a bad video copy, the students were indignant that they had to watch such a long film. Whereas some of them were genuinely interested in a different national cinema, others were not keen on going down this politically correct route, complaining that it did not merit the attention that they accorded even to kung fu films. Since we had not seen the singing cowboy Westerns, singing in a Western, especially two men singing to each other, was the last straw for them. I had no choice but to confess that this film changed my viewing experience when I was a teenager growing up in India with an ambivalent relationship to popular cinema. Having internalised a middle-class disdain for popular cinema, I did not care for it, but seeing *Sholay* changed all that. It was not pedagogical authority that changed their attitude to the film, but rather a peek into my cinephiliac obsessions as well as my nostalgia infused with diasporic longings for Indian cinema. Instead of disabling me, admitting to enjoying Indian cinema a long time ago sharpened my reading of differences between films instead of seeing them as an amorphous form of mass culture the ideological content of which is transparent. We ended our class discussion with a renewed interest in Christian Metz's famous formulation:[38]

> To be a theoretician of the cinema, one should ideally no longer love the cinema and yet still love it: to have loved it a lot and only have detached oneself from it by taking it up again from the other end, taking it as the target for the same scopic drive which made one love it. [p. 15]

Genre and Interruptions

Sholay exemplified the possibility of very deftly combining dominant genre principles developed in Hollywood films with conventions particular to Indian cinema. Recasting the linear trajectory of genre films to include several local cinematic conventions, Indian popular films often render the former illegible to the outsider. For example, my students' initial reaction to *Sholay* was based on how song and dance sequences distracted them from the structuring of anticipation in a Western, rather than on asking how the film rewrites the genre so as to shore up our investments in a linear narrative. What I am suggesting is that it seems presumptuous to think that, when Hollywood genres are appropriated by other national cinemas, we should find a straightforward application of dominant genre principles instead of reading how local contexts of production and reception intervene and prevail over genre. The end product of this encounter between global and local features can, at times, be read as a subordinate response to Hollywood, a strategy forwarded by Paul Smith in his reading of Leone's 'spaghetti Westerns', or we can simply read them as a riposte that simultaneously reveals how Hollywood genres are also built around certain national cinematic styles.

Some clarification of the concept of film genre is in order before I launch into the particularities of Indian cinema. Identified as a narrative form developed by classical Hollywood commercial cinema, film theorists have developed a barrage of theoretical and methodological tools to understand the narrative structure, cinematic specificity, and viewer's relationship to genre films. For instance, cinematic genres are differentiated by iconography: frontier landscapes in a Western, city spaces in gangster films. At other times, we understand how genre verisimilitude derives from details in the *mise en scène*: monsters in horror films and horses in a Western. Genre theory continues to benefit from psychoanalytical theories by allowing us to see how our viewing pleasures are dictated by a structuring of repetition and difference in films. Research on advertising and distribution practices of Hollywood films reveals that film producers were deeply involved in using genre categories to target and consolidate their audience: women's films, summer action films, etc. Instead of considering genre in either–or terms, Steve Neale suggests we see genre films as a dynamic among the industry, films, and viewers to better understand cinema as a modern commodity form.[39] In his book on American genre films and theory, Rick Altman proposes that, far from being particular, Hollywood films are constructed as multiple, overlapping genres to reach a wider audience.[40] Discrete genres as a predilection of critics only surfaces after the fact. Whatever particular features film critics or film-makers deploy to differentiate one genre from another or see multiple genres in one film, American genre films broadly obey certain cinematic principles perfected in classical Hollywood cinema that frame the unfolding narrative: continuity editing, omniscient narration, internally coherent diegesis, and character-motivated plot.

In contrast to the internally coherent narrative form generated by Hollywood genre films, genres in Indian popular cinema display a set of features that are akin to pre-classical cinema, especially several extra-diegetic sequences or sequences of attractions. Instead of concluding that these films stage the underdeveloped aspects of capitalism in the Indian economy, a different set of concerns nurtures this narrative form, including a desire to domesticate cinematic technology and develop a national cinematic style. For instance, writing on Dadasaheb Phalke's *Raja Harishchandra* (1913), Ashish Rajadhyaksha argues that the prevalence of frontal address in this film points to how narrative strategies in early cinema borrowed from painting, theatre, and traditional arts lured the viewer into this new technological apparatus. In a similar vein, Geeta Kapur suggests through her reading of *Sant Tukaram* (Damle/Fattelal, Marathi, 1936) that frontal address in this 'saint film' was a calculated move by the film-makers to draw in viewers accustomed to watching theatre, while the sequence of miracles mandatory in a saint film highlighted cinema's ability to produce magic. Both Kapur and Rajadhyaksha alert us to how cinema in India developed in a whirl of anti-colonial struggles that included an impulse to forge an independent cultural form by both reinterpreting tradition and making technology developed in the West indigenous.

Besides the direct address, other features of Indian popular cinema similarly undercut the hermetic universe developed in Hollywood films by interrupting it with song and dance sequences, comedy tracks, and multi-plot narratives. Spectacular, at times excessive, the elaboration of these attractions in this cinema has invited critics to dub them 'masala films' – a culinary term that seeks to define a medley of narrative strands in popular cinema. Naming the films made in the 1950s and 1960s as the 'feudal family romance', Madhava Prasad argues that this super genre asserts its dominance through narrative strategies of annexations whenever new sub-genres emerge.[41] In short, Prasad suggests that instead of discrete genres, a megalomaniac genre cannibalises the formation of sub-genres. In a more generous tone, Ravi Vasudevan sees popular Hindi film as a discontinuous form that includes attractions such as song and dance sequences and comedic sub-plots.[42] Instead of skipping over these moments that either break the diegetic universe or disrupt the linear trajectory of the narrative, we must simply face the fact that the most persistent narrative form found in Indian popular cinema includes several interruptions bearing a more or less systematic relationship to the narrative. In other words, we should start to heed production details that concentrate on how Indian film-makers expend considerable energy experimenting with the choreography and location of these sequences, and in the process acknowledge how our viewing pleasure arises from these interruptions and the novel ways in which a popular film strings together these sequences.

Identifying these interruptions encourages us to start in the reverse direction, that is, by exploring how these films experiment as well as strengthen Indian cinematic conventions, rather than mulling over how these films are derived from Hollywood genres. Moreover, attending to these interruptions throws light on how the concept of a national cinematic style emerges at the conjuncture of state interests in quality cinema, the film industry's interests in profits, and the global circulation of popular cinemas. To account for how these disparate interests in production and reception shape the textual make-up of popular films, this book looks at three different kinds of interruptions that brand the narrative form of Indian cinema: song and dance sequences, the interval, and censorship.

Song and Dance Sequences

One of the most common and popular features of Indian films are its song and dance sequences. According to Barnow and Krishnaswamy, Indian talkies always had songs: the first sound feature, Ardeshir Irani's *Alam Ara/Beauty of the World* (1931), had more than seven songs; another early Hindi film had forty songs; and, not to be outdone, a Tamil film had sixty.[43] By the 1950s, 'the film song had become a key to successful film promotion'.[44] Film-makers continue to release audio tracks before the film's release, and it is widely believed that those sales alone can recover the production costs of a movie.[45] Music directors, choreographers, and singers receive

awards, and these sequences often outlast the film's own story in the popular memory. Over the years, commercial film-makers have tried experimenting with their
absence with varying commercial success: K. A. Abbas's *Munna/Lost Child* (1954),
the Tamil film *Antha Nal/That Day* (1954), B. R. Chopra's *Ittefaq* (1969), P. C. Sriram's *Kurudhippunal/River of Blood* (1995), and Ram Gopal Varma's *Kaun/Who?*
(1998) are some examples. But, as song and dance sequences guarantee a definite
income, it has been difficult to dispense with them altogether. Song and dance
sequences traverse radio and television, independently of the films themselves, a
phenomenon encouraging critics to rush to the conclusion that they are inserted into
films only as entertaining spectacles with tangential links to the narrative.

In contrast to these assumptions that promote their extra-diegetic relationship to
the narrative, or dismiss them as 'sequences of attractions' reminiscent of early cinema, song and dance sequences deserve another look, differentiating their
relationship to the diegesis: delaying the development of the plot, distracting us from
the other scenes of the narrative through spatial and temporal disjunctions, and
bearing an integral link to the plot. Even in one film, there can be different articulations of these sequences, thus complicating the idea of a single diegesis or the value
of the extra-diegetic. The lack of uniform temporal sequencing across different films
alerts us to consider genre differences and auteur signatures inflecting the choreography of song and dance sequences.

In addition to attending to the ways in which song and dance interrupt the narrative in various ways, the iconography of these sequences of attractions calls our
attention to other interests that bolster a spectator's interests in Indian cinema. For
instance, the abrupt cut to exotic locations sparks the tourist interests of the viewer,
and similarly the object-laden *mise en scène* endorses consumerism. Not unlike the
commercial imperative towards product placement in contemporary American cinema, song and dance sequences draw in a whole host of adjacent economies such as
tourism and consumerism that are not so easily compartmentalised in Indian cinema.

Interval

The 'Interval' is the ten-minute break in every Indian popular film after eighty minutes of film screening. Lights are turned on, the projector is turned off, and viewers
step out of the theatre to smoke a cigarette, eat a snack, or visit the restroom. Unlike
the strong imprint of song and dance sequences in the filmgoing experience, the
location of the interval remains an elusive detail in the memory of even the most
avid film viewer. It is simply seen as a brief respite from the long screening. Trade
papers, however, make passing references to which halves of the film were more, or
less, interesting.

The interval weighs in as a crucial punctuation, adjusting both opening and closing strategies of the film – in effect, producing two opening and closing sequences

in every Indian film. As with the song and dance sequences, I suggest the interval is not randomly located, but is regulated by genre constraints and directorial style. Breaking the spell of the dark auditorium, the interval reminds us of early cinema's exhibition practices when a film was one of many instalments of the evening's entertainment. In its current form, the interval is a cinematic device that organises the dose of cinematic attractions mandatory in Indian cinema as well as serving as a punctuation mark that continually directs our anticipation in surprising ways by opening and closing certain narrative strands.

Both song and dance sequences and the interval attune us to their structural function in popular Indian films, particularly their play on spatial and temporal disjunctions. Their articulation in specific texts highlights how films imbibe both global and local conventions: genre films adjust to song and dance sequences, and the interval doubles the structuring of anticipation and pleasure found in genre films. In each case, they call attention to interruptions in the convention of the linear narrative with a single diegesis dominant in Hollywood or other commercial industries, with their attendant assumptions of realist codes.[46] The ideal spectator of film theory, cloistered from adjacent consumer economies, surfaces as a phantom figure in Indian popular cinema; the Indian spectator, in contrast, travels several circuits of pleasures generated by a multi-diegetic narrative.[47]

Censorship

In addition to these two kinds of interruptions, viewers of Indian films are aware that the state monitors the relationship between cinema and society most visibly through film censorship. The most glaring manifestation of state intervention in film production is the Board of Censors' certificate that precedes each film. This inaugural moment of every film publicly released in India, imported or indigenous, informs the spectator that the film has been approved by the state and carries with it traces of censored cuts. Although a carry-over from the colonial period, the postcolonial state, too, perceives films as having a tremendous influence over its citizenry and thus directs its regulations towards the production and control of 'quality' films.[48] However, instead of seeing censorship as *post facto* interference from the state, I suggest that film-makers spend considerable energy in incorporating censorship regulations *during* film-making, in an attempt to pre-empt sweeping cuts that would drastically effect the flow of the narrative. Moreover, over the years, the relationship between the state and the film industry reveals a spectrum of negotiations – from an obedient nationalism to a flagrant flouting of regulations – that fuels the production of images on the screen.

Although the obscenity codes governing Indian cinema address a wide range of issues affecting both image and dialogue, in practice the object of greatest scrutiny is the female body. I use the term *coitus interruptus* to exemplify the different ways in which the film industry negotiates the code to finally produce the female body on screen. This is not a gratuitous evocation of contraception, but rather a play on the structural similarity between two mechanisms – contraceptive regulations and censorship – suggesting how the state isolates the female body as the prime site of control and regulation in the public sphere. Among the several manifestations of *coitus interruptus*, the withdrawal-of-the-camera technique is instantly recognisable in various Indian films: the camera withdraws just before a steamy love scene ensues, and the film replaces it with extra-diegetic shots of waterfalls, flowers, thunder, lightning, and tropical storms. The varying configurations and recurrent use of *coitus interruptus* demonstrate how the film industry, despite its laments about state control, has been preoccupied with the withdrawal-of-the-camera technique as a crucial source of surplus pleasure. With its focus on dodging censorship prescription as well as maintaining its interest in the female body on screen, *coitus interruptus*, as a cinematic convention, captures an intimate and tense relationship between the state and the film industry predicated on attempts, however contradictory, to align the *national* subject with the film spectator. Far from perfectly aligning with the interests of the state and the film industry, the viewer is drawn into a fetishistic scenario where she or he oscillates between a cinephiliac mourning over lost footage on the one hand and, on the other, acknowledges that the state employs patriarchal laws to produce limits on seeing.

I maintain, however, that these sequences of attractions do not completely override attempts to construct an internally coherent narrative, as some critics have implied. Song and dance sequences are not randomly strung together in the Indian films I look at, but both block and propel the narrative in crucial ways. The interval, the halfway stopping point, obviously upsets the image of the dream chamber, but by not acknowledging its presence we fail to see it as a punctuation that binds and disperses narrative energies in Indian popular cinema. Censorship regulates representations on screen, but the innovative sequences that are inserted as replacements afford not only a commentary on the relationship between the state and the film industry, but also on the contours of the extra-diegetic. Just as continuity in classical Hollywood narrative offers us both pleasure and anger, in this cinema, too, we find pleasures *in* these interruptions and not *despite* them. Indian cinema is marked by *interrupted pleasures.*

These interruptions do not carry equal weight across the terrain of popular cinema. Depending on directorial style or genre pressures, each film measures these interruptions differently in such a way as to suggest a *hierarchy* of interruptions. For instance, song and dance sequences are better elaborated in a love story than in a gangster genre. In a Mani Ratnam film, irrespective of the genre, we expect an elaborate choreography of song and dance sequences, flattening the temporal disjunctions of other interruptions.

Although the presence of numerous interruptions warrants Madhava Prasad's claim that Hindi cinema, at least in the 1950s, took the shape of the 'supergenre' that absorbed any hint of a reformist tendency, I would suggest that a characteristic feature of contemporary popular cinema in India has been its ability to balance strict genre features with the conventions of attractions peculiar to this cinema. In the process, the structuring of anticipation and pleasure in Hollywood genre films is rewritten. For instance, *Sholay* revises the Western by mixing a series of local features: song and dance sequences, the interval, censorship, and the idea of a 'multi-starrer'. Ram Gopal Varma's *Satya* (1998) elaborates on the interrelationship between the globally circulating gangster genre and local conventions, fully aware that its audience is habituated to global television and video programmes. In contrast to the typical ensemble found in the multi-starrer, Varma raided television and regional cinema for its actors. The most significant detail that haunts the public reception of the film is the relevance of the song and dance sequences. Apparently, Bharat Shah, the producer, did not approve of the initial rough cut, which had no songs; the final version has four songs developing the romantic sub-plot, as well as celebrating the fraternity of gang members.

Film-makers are constantly at work finessing the alchemy of conventions and at times generating a commentary on the sequencing of these codes. Parthepan's Tamil film *Housefull* (1999), for instance, remarks on the function of these interruptions.

K. Parthepan directing actors in *Housefull* (courtesy of K. Parthepan)

The plot involves a bomb scare at a movie theatre in Madurai. The police and the bomb squad try to surreptitiously control the situation by asking the projectionist to keep the audience's attention on the screen, thus preventing them from leaving the theatre. Complying with the police request, the projectionist skips two crucial reels – one with song and dance sequences, which he claims will bring the men out in large numbers; the other, which marks the interval, will open the floodgates for the entire audience. While the audience in the film is transfixed on the unfolding story of the film within a film, our film also responds to the police dictate: although we have a clearly defined 'Intermission', the film has dispensed with song and dance sequences. At one level, Parthepan's film comments on the rash of bombings that mark Indian public life by intimidating the Utopian community of moviegoers – people from different communities, classes, and religions – that venture to see a film at a movie house aptly called the 'Bharat Theatres'. Yet what I find compelling about the film is its ability to articulate police work as a method to discipline the narrative – bombs and attractions are managed simultaneously. *Housefull* exemplifies the conditions of contemporary film production: a film leaning towards an internally coherent narrative yet continuously commenting on its textual production, and at the same time maintaining the intermission as a local condition of reception. These

Production stills from *Housefull*: (top left) The owner of the Bharat Theatre checks for song and dance sequences in the projection room; (top right) the audience watching the film; (above left) the audience leaving the theatre after the bomb threat; (above right) the bomb explodes in the theatre (courtesy of K. Parthepan)

examples reveal how we cannot simply import one theoretical paradigm over others to account for non-Hollywood narrative styles, but must work through the ways in which they address a spectator who is at the crossroads of several intersecting cinematic styles.

The peculiar conditions of Indian commercial film narrative are constantly shifting, undoing our assumptions concerning some of its constituent elements. Defying making sense by importing reading strategies inspired from classical, early, or contemporary American cinema, contemporary Indian cinema compels us to employ several of these theoretical positions simultaneously to read *one* film. Despite being far removed from the central engine of capitalism and its accompanying realist narrative, Indian cinema mimics, copies, and rewrites these forms while simultaneously maintaining a local quotient of attractions. In a curious twist in the history of appropriation and application of film theory across national cinemas, certain ontological questions surrounding narrative cinema – questions that Eisenstein raised in his famous essay on 'montage of attractions' – find a fertile ground in contemporary Indian cinema.[49] Amalgamating different interruptions in Indian popular cinema also bears an uncanny resemblance to Peter Wollen's conceptualisation of the 'multi-diegesis' in Jean-Luc Godard's *Vent d'Est/Wind from the East* (1969), a film that he claims undoes the narrative conventions of both Hollywood and Soviet films.[50] We might be hard-pressed to see an immediate link between an overtly avant-garde practice and popular Indian cinema, but, not unlike Wollen, viewers of Indian films do see its digressions and interruptions as intrinsic to enjoying and understanding these films, as well as the place of intense ideological struggles.

Film Theory and Interruptions

Although suggesting that only a cinephiliac relationship to Indian cinema reveals a constellation of conventions peculiar to that cinema, I do not wish to overstate the case for the privileged point of view of the native viewer who implicitly knows all the plots and their temporal sequences. Such a claim overlooks how film-viewing habits are also shaped by globally circulating genres and that one does not have to be a connoisseur of Indian popular cinema to understand the narrative logic of this cinema. In fact, a film buff familiar with both pre-classical and avant-garde cinemas in America will recognise, with little difficulty, this cinema's difference from Hollywood, as well as its points of contact.

At the same time, I believe that a simple transposition of film theory developed through readings of Hollywood films cannot adequately account for local features. Instead of putting forward a separate theoretical paradigm for reading Indian cinema, I suggest calibrating film theory through a reading of *interruptions* in Indian films, thus rupturing the provincialism surrounding film theory and, in the process, rejuvenating it. In turn, certain aspects of film theory are ideally suited to cracking the ideological underpinnings of this cinema that appear so obvious to the familiar viewer. Inasmuch as this book dwells on interruptions and principles of continuity in Indian cinema, it equally seeks correspondences with film theory by investigating particular disruptive moments that have periodically shifted the terms of debate.

Film theory, especially the semiotic and psychoanalytical paradigms of the 1970s, argues that classical Hollywood films seem particularly pliable to conceptualisations of fetishism and scopophilia, given their impulse towards an internally coherent narrative where we are encouraged to identify with the cinematic apparatus while sitting in a dark room. These near-perfect conditions of film viewing wedded to the studio system do not hold up so well even when transported to early cinema in the same region. For instance, Tom Gunning describes early narrative cinema as a series of several 'attractions' loosely strung together – a far cry from an internally coherent narrative typified in classical Hollywood narrative.[51] He speculates that traces of these attractions later surface in underground cinema, which by intention works against conventions of mainstream narrative cinema. Similarly, Miriam Hansen reminds us that recalling early cinema tempers the notion of the ideal spectator that psychoanalytical film theory depends upon; in the process, she encourages us to consider the historical conditions shaping film viewing.[52]

To the credit of psychoanalytical film theory, it should be pointed out that Christian Metz did raise the issue of exhibitionism in his essay on 'two kinds of voyeurism', but for the most part film theorists have ignored narrative cinema's overt attempts to create spectacles by preferring to focus on conventions of realism.[53] Laura Mulvey's classic essay 'Visual Pleasure and Narrative Cinema' raises a number of issues concerning sexual difference, but we often overlook one of the crucial insights of her work: the moments of *disruption* in classical Hollywood that we have habituated ourselves not to notice, in particular the excessive focus on a woman's body that often breaks the diegesis.[54] Mulvey identifies a particular tendency in narrative cinema to fetishise parts of a woman's body in excess of narrative needs, a process that merits our naming those moments as *spectacle*. In other words, Mulvey's essay should have urged us to look for other ideologically charged disruptions – the focus on coloured bodies for comic relief, on ethnic faces for stereotypes of fear and loathing – instead of exclusively salvaging conventions of realism in cinema. What I am suggesting is that, before the onset of critical work on early cinema, there were moments in psychoanalytical film theory that cast doubts on the internally coherent realist narrative, but this was a road not taken until film historians started marshalling empirical evidence from another period to remind us that questions of spectatorship need to be located within historical contexts of reception.

Critical work on early cinema is not the only challenge to a film theory developed by coupling semiotics and psychoanalysis. Increasingly, we find work on contemporary Hollywood springing from a dissatisfaction with premises of ideal spectator-ship. Timothy Corrigan's *A Cinema without Walls* exemplifies this trend by alerting us to changing reception conditions, including 'the media politics of the Vietnam war, the restructuring of the movie industry through conglomerate takeovers, the widespread effect of technologies such as the VCR, and the contemporary fasci-nation with different kinds of nostalgia'.[55] Commenting on the collapse of the fixed walls of the movie theatre (Plato's cave or 'dream chamber' in film theory), he sug-gests that 'audiences remove images from their own authentic and authoritative place within culture and disperse their significance across the heterogeneous activity that now defines them'.[56] Corrigan remarks on the links between fragmented audi-ences and post-studio production conditions:

> As a powerful revision of Baudrillard's 'mirror of production' model, the fluidity and unpredictability of the international market has made, it would seem, the structures of production less and less determinant, and so force films increasingly *to anticipate the volatility of their reception as a textual determinant*. [p. 23. My emphasis]

According to Corrigan, in contrast to Euro-American cinema's preoccupation with classical notions of an integrated film text, which generated an industry of readers who expended critical energy in deciphering the secret of the text, we now confront 'illegible films' that test the limits of 'intelligibility and interpretation'. He suggests that, in opposition to the concentrated reader, it may be more useful to use Walter Benjamin and Siegfried Kracauer's conception of the distracted viewer to understand contemporary conditions of film reception that 'have changed so sig-nificantly that models of interpretative legibility, from newspapers to scholarly journals, seem to find themselves frequently befuddled' (p. 61). Corrigan extends this idea to formulate new reading strategies for cinema:

> At both the operatic spectacles of the theaters and the home spectacles of the VCRs, audiences now watch movies according to a *glance aesthetic* rather than a *gaze aesthetic*: movies and spectators are indeed 'closer' than ever before (in Benjamin's sense) but it is a closeness that encourages viewers to casually test and measure a film as part of a domestic or public environment rather than become part of a concentrated reading. [p. 62]

What writers since Corrigan have been describing and analysing as the textual and financial shape of 'New Hollywood' is intimately tied to large shifts in global capi-talism. For instance, Murray Smith observes areas that financial, technical, and aesthetic issues appear to both confirm and undo any deterministic reading of this beast called 'New Hollywood':[57]

Since the 1960s, there has been a proliferation of terms designating more-or-less fundamental shifts in the nature – and thus the appropriate periodization – of Hollywood cinema: the New Hollywood, the New New Hollywood, post-classicism, and more indirectly, post-Fordism and postmodernism. [p. 3]

Critics largely agree that, in the post-studio era, the American film industry is fuelled by finances from elsewhere; that the global spread of financing may lead to a similar multinational dispersal of post-production facilities so that an 'American' film product is no longer viable; and, finally, that the collapse of national-oligopoly studio structures appears to have inflected film narratives in such a way that we find, as Corrigan suggests, fragmented narratives where rules of continuity and closure are no longer dominant.

Corrigan's formulation ultimately remains absorbed with changes within Euro-American cinema. Similarly, critical work on early cinema and pre-classical spectatorship interrogates the dominance of psychoanalytical models based on narrative coherence and ideal spectatorship, yet scholars draw their examples largely from American cinema, a feature no doubt rising from a widely held assumption that various experiments with narrative structuring were fully worked out in Hollywood films. This unacknowledged focus on one national cinema has allowed critics either to assume an easy migration of theory across different national cinemas on the one hand or, in a gesture coloured by cultural relativism, to cast other national cinemas within a different sociological framework while preserving theoretical insights arising from textual operations as a prerogative of American cinema.

There has been little effort by critics to locate the extraordinary details of New Hollywood in relationship to other national cinemas, an effort that may have revealed that most national cinemas, particularly the Indian, have never had an elaborate studio system, but continue to operate in what Janet Staiger describes as the 'unit package system'.[58] From its inception, the economics of the Indian film industry never replicated the production conditions of the American movie industry, but instead relied on loan sharks, the personal capital of film-makers, and illicit or 'black' money.[59] Actually, the volatile conditions of the post-Vietnam American cinema cited by Corrigan have already been a feature of Indian cinema for over fifty years and have particular textual manifestations that are recognisable through various *interruptions*, as discussed above. The fragmentary narrative cited as a unique feature of New Hollywood has long been a cinematic style in Indian popular cinema, which invented the 'multi-starrer', a concept that Justin Wyatt identifies as the 'high concept' of the post-studio era in America.[60] What I am suggesting is that whereas the technical, economic, and aesthetic dominance of Hollywood is now common sense, its changing economic conditions and aesthetic styles may have more in common with less 'integrated' film industries elsewhere. In other words, in studying Indian popular cinema we are not simply looking for faithful or deviant versions of Hollywood as a nostalgic desire for a refurbished cinema emergent from a different spatial location; rather, we should see them as an opportunity to explore a global exchange of narrative styles. There is no doubt that the globalisation of capital throws up points of contact between different national cinemas that previously we would have found to be either unimaginable or only secured through a narrative of imperialism. These national manifestations of dominant genre principles call attention to postmodern or transnational aesthetics of disruptions and discontinuities in a master narrative. I have used the words global and local to describe the formation and reconfiguration of genre conventions in Indian cinema; however, in postmodern writings, the nation is often a receding figure overshadowed by a 'transnational imaginary' – a term coined by Rob Wilson and Wimal Dissanayake:[61]

> What we would variously track as the 'transnational imaginary' comprises the *as-yet-unfigured* horizon of contemporary cultural production by which national spaces/identities of political allegiance and economic regulation are being undone and imagined communities of modernity are being reshaped at the macropolitical (global) and micropolitical (cultural) levels of everyday existence. [p. 6]

Offering a more cynical reading of these new arrangements, Henry Jenkins and Dirk Eitzen argue that dominant sectors of global capitalism always refashion themselves to avert total collapse.[62] Considering these different positions, I would add that the movement of global capital does not erase local conventions even if at times it coalesces around the figure of the nation.

Interruptions and Action Genres

The selection of films in this book illustrates the links between local and global cinematic styles, a selection infused by cinephilia rather than by a hyperrational methodology of inclusion.[63] Not only are these films ideally suited to exploring the tension between local and global cinematic styles as a particular mode of double articulation, but they also demonstrate a confidence in film-making that is most visible in the strengthening of local conventions even as they overtly engage with the structuring of anticipation and pleasure found in genre films. Highlighting Indian cinema's indirectness, in-between-ness, its propensity for digression and interruptions, the book modulates reading strategies inflected by psychoanalysis and narratology, moulding them to sharpen our understanding of this cinema. Through close readings of films, each chapter of the book explores the ways in which interruptions are yoked to the structuring of global genres and how my own reading strategies inherited from film theory accommodate local difference.

Nowhere is the tussle between national desires and geopolitical aesthetics more apparent than in the chapter on the 'Avenging Women' genre, in which I argue that censorship regulations mould a globally available B film genre that is predicated on rape and revenge. Concentrating on *Insaaf Ka Tarazu/Scales of Justice* (1980), *Zakmi Aurat/Wounded Women* (1988), and *Pratighat/Retribution* (1987) as epitomising a trend that casts heroines as the main protagonists in a film, I explore a set of contradictory issues that shape the production and reception of these films.

The following chapter examines how Indian films appropriate masculine Hollywood genres by interrupting the linear narratives of action with local conventions, particularly the interval. Choosing J. P. Dutta's films *Ghulami*, *Batwara*, and *Hathyar*, I demonstrate how the interval shifts the structure of anticipation and pleasure in his reworking of Western and gangster films.

Looking at Mani Ratnam's *Nayakan*, the fourth chapter argues that this auteur's film reconfigures the gangster film by foregrounding the relationship between commodity fetishism and narrative verisimilitude. The chapter closes with an analysis of the song and dance sequences in his films as markers of Mani Ratnam's cinematic style. Chapter 5 discusses Vidhu Vinod Chopra's Hindi film *Parinda/Caged Bird* (1989) as another exemplary text that grafts interruptions with gangster film conventions through its innovative use of flashbacks. Speculating on the form of popular Indian film in the second century of cinema, the Conclusion chooses *Alaipayuthey/Waves* (2000) and *Hey! Ram* (1999) to explore the impact of digital technologies.

By choosing action genres, *Cinema of Interruptions* not only engages with the thematic preoccupations of violence in films, but also with how these films enunciate violence textually.[64] It celebrates various experiments in interruptions, directorial styles, and ongoing dialogue between different local cinemas. Hopefully, it will support the flourishing of different cinematic practices in India. My investigation interrogates the constituents of narrative cinema, which is far from settled. In doing so, I resuscitate André Bazin's query 'What is cinema?' and respond by saying that it is inextricably linked to our Utopian imaginings, it stages the most anxious impulses of our psychic and social life, and it gives us hope for a better world. At the same time, the book also supplants Bazin's paternal query by responding to a more prescient question posed by the opening credits of Sooraj Barjatya's film, 'Hum aapke hain koun?'/'Who am I to you?'

Notes

1. René Girard (1972), *Desire, Deceit, and the Novel: Self and Other in Literary Structure*, tr. Yvonne Freccero, Baltimore: Johns Hopkins University Press.
2. The artist M. F. Hussain saw the film over forty times just to see actress Madhuri Dixit perform the 'Devar ho to aaisa' dance number.
3. I wish to thank Ravi Vasudevan for drawing my attention to this meaning.

4. Pico Iyer (1988), *Video Nights in Kathmandu: Reports from the Not-So-Far East*, New York: Knopf.
5. Salman Rushdie (1988), *The Satanic Verses*, London and New York, Viking; Alan Sealy (1990), *Hero*, Delhi: Viking India Ltd; Farrukh Dhondy (1990), *Bombay Duck*, London: Cape.
6. Manjunath Pendakur (1985), 'Dynamics of Cultural Policy Making: The US Film Industry in India', *Journal of Communication*, Autumn, pp. 52–72; Manjunath Pendakur (1990), 'India', in John A. Lent (ed.), *The Asian Film Industry*, Austin: Texas University Press.
7. Personal conversation with P. C. Sriram, September 1995.
8. Manmohan Shetty (1994), 'Trends in Film Processing', *Lensight*, vol. III, no. 4, October.
9. Pendakur, 1985.
10. Film production in 1979: 113 in Hindi; 139 in Tamil; and 131 in Telugu. In 1995: 157 in Hindi; 165 in Tamil; and 168 in Telugu. Figures are from Ashish Rajadhyaksha and Paul Willemen (eds) (1999), *Encyclopaedia of Indian Cinema*, London: BFI (rev. edn).
11. Anupama Chopra (1997), 'Southern Invasion', *India Today*, 13 October, pp. 38–40.
12. For a comprehensive evaluation of alternative film-makers, see John W. Hood (2000), *The Essential Mystery*, New Delhi: Orient Longman.
13. On *Kaadalan*, see Vivek Dhareshwar and Tejaswini Niranjana (1996), '*Kaadalan* and the Politics of Resignification: Fashion, Violence, and the Body', *Journal of Arts and Ideas*, 29, January.
14. Conversation with O. P. Dutta, April 1999. Dutta tells of the 1950s and 1960s when the Soviets would purchase a number of films, but Indian film-makers never kept track of these exhibitions or purchases. On viewing Indian films in Nigeria, see Brian Larkin (1997), 'Indian Films and Nigerian Lovers: Media and the Creation of Parallel Modernities', *Africa*, vol. 67, no. 3, pp. 406–40.
15. *Newsweek International*, 10 May 1999. My thanks to Tejaswini Ganti for posting this article.
16. I wish to thank Haim Bresheeth for this wonderful example from Israeli cinema.
17. Stuart Hall (1996), 'When Was 'Post-Colonial'? Thinking at the Limit', in Iain Chambers and Lidia Curti (eds), *The Post-Colonial Question: Common Skies, Divided Horizons*, London: Routledge.
18. Achin Vanaik (1991), *The Painful Transition*, New York: Verso.
19. Veena Das (1992), 'Introduction', in Veena Das (ed.), *Mirrors of Violence: Communities and Survivors in South Asia*, Delhi: Oxford University Press.
20. Firoze Rangoonwala (1993), 'The Age of Violence', *Illustrated Weekly of India*, 4–10 September, pp. 27–9; Rashmi Doriaswamy (1995), 'Hindi Commercial Cinema: Changing Narrative Strategies', in Aruna Vasudev (ed.), *Frames of Mind: Reflections on Indian Cinema*, New Delhi: UBS.

21. Media Advocacy Group and National Commission for Women (n.d.), *People's Perception: Obscenity and Violence on the Screen*, New Delhi; The Media Advocacy Group and National Commission for Women (1993), *A Gender Perspective for the Electronic Media*, March, New Delhi. I wish to thank Roopal Oza for alerting me to these reports.

22. Ken Wlaschin (1976), 'Birth of the "Curry" Western: Bombay 1976', *Film and Filming*, April, vol. 22, no. 7, pp. 20–3. Touted as a 'curry Western' by film critic Ken Wlaschin, reviewing the Film Festival in 1976, Sippy's film fits quite easily into revisionist Westerns such as spaghetti Westerns.

23. Madan Gopal Singh (1983), 'Technique as an Ideological Weapon', in Aruna Vasudev and Phillipe Lenglet (eds), *Indian Cinema Superbazaar*, Delhi: Vikas.

24. Judith Mayne (1993), *Cinema and Spectatorship*, London: Routledge. Mayne provides a splendid and sympathetic critique of the ideal spectator in psychoanalysis.

25. Although Singh's formulation has critical value, I should like to question his reading of the song: a close analysis of the scene shows that the camera does not actively grope the dancer's body even though it fragments her body. Attributing movement to a phantom camera, Singh may be implicitly admitting to being taken in by the entertaining song and dance number!

26. Rashmi Doraiswamy and Aruna Vasudev – the author of the best book on Indian censorship – floated the film journal *Cinemaya* with the explicit intention of expanding interest in Asian cinema from an Asian location.

27. Interview with Naseeruddin Shah, *Filmfare*, May 1998.

28. *Sholay* emerges as the first important film in the life of several young stars in a survey conducted by *Filmfare*, June 1999.

29. Rosie Thomas (1985), 'Indian Cinema: Pleasures and Popularity', *Screen*, vol. 26, nos. 3/4, was one of the first to propose that the popular film industry be taken seriously, on its 'own terms'.

30. Colin McCabe (1986), 'Defining Popular Culture', in McCabe (ed.), *High Theory/Low Culture: Analyzing Popular Television and Film*, New York: St Martin's Press.

31. Paul Willemen (1994), 'Through the Glass Darkly: Cinephilia Reconsidered', in *Looks and Frictions: Essays in Cultural Studies and Film Theory*, Bloomington: Indiana University Press.

32. Susan Sontag (1996), 'The Decay of Cinema', *New York Times Magazine*, 25 February, pp. 60–1; *Vertigo*, no. 10 (1988); *Cahiers du cinéma*, no. 498 (1998), *Film Quarterly* Fall (1998). Peter Wollen (2001), 'An Alphabet of Cinema', *New Left Review* (Second Series), vol. 12, November/December, pp. 115–33 – part polemic, part eulogy, Wollen offers a delightful yet moving tribute to cinema in the form of first principles and cannot help proclaiming that the letter 'C' stands for cinephilia.

33. Christine Keathley (2000), 'The Cinephiliac Moment', *Framework Online*, no. 42.

34. Richard Dyer (1992), *Only Entertainment*, London and New York: Routledge.

35. Sharon Willis (1998), *High Contrast*, Durham, NC: Duke University Press.

36. Roger Cardinal (1986), 'Pausing over Peripheral Detail', *Framework*, nos. 30/31, pp. 112–30.

37. Naomi Schor (1987), *Reading in Detail: Aesthetics and the Feminine*, New York: Methuen.

38. Christian Metz (1982), *The Imaginary Signifier: Psychoanalysis and the Cinema*, tr. Celia Britton, Annwyl Williams, Ben Brewester, and Alfred Guzzetti, Bloomington: Indiana University Press.

39. Stephen Neale (1992), *Genre*, London: BFI (rev. edn); Stephen Neale (2000), *Genre and Hollywood*, London and New York: Routledge.

40. Rick Altman (1999), *Film/Genre*, London: BFI.

41. M. Madhava Prasad (1998), *Ideology of the Hindi Film: A Historical Construction*, Delhi: Oxford University Press.

42. Ravi S. Vasudevan (1995), 'Addressing the Spectator of a 'Third-World' National Cinema: The Bombay Social Film of the 1940s and 1950s', *Screen*, vol. 36, no. 4.

43. Erik Barnow and S. Krishnaswamy (1980), *Indian Film*, New York: Oxford University Press, p. 69.

44. Barnow and Krishnaswamy, p. 157.

45. American film producers have also started to see the commercial viability of soundtracks. Music stores now exclusively stack a separate section with movie soundtracks.

46. See Judith Mayne (1993), *Cinema and Spectatorship*, for a splendid exegesis on the cultural context of Hollywood production and its preferred spectator.

47. Peter Wollen uses 'multi-diegesis' to describe Jean-Luc Godard's film *Vent d'Est*, arguing that Godard is responding to both Hollywood and Mosfilm narratives, characterised by a single diegesis, by producing a film with multi-diegesis.

48. See Aruna Vasudev's (1978) ground-breaking book *Liberty and Licence in Indian Cinema*, Delhi: Vikas; Kobita Sarkar (1982), *You Can't Please Everyone: Film Censorship, the Inside Story*, Bombay: IBH; CLRI (1982), *The Indian Cinematograph Code*, Hyderabad, AP: Cinematograph Laws Research Institute.

49. Sergei M. Eisenstein, 'The Montage of Film Attractions', in Peter Lehman (ed.) (1997), *Defining Cinema*, New Brunswick: Rutgers University Press.

50. Peter Wollen (1982), 'Godard and Counter Cinema: *Vent d'est*', in *Readings and Writings: Semiotic Counter-Strategies*, London: Verso.

51. Tom Gunning (1990), ' "Primitive" Cinema: A Frame-Up? Or the Trick's on Us', in Thomas Elsaesser and Adam Barker (eds), *Early Cinema: Space, Frame, Narrative*, London: BFI, pp. 95–103; Tom Gunning (1990), 'Non-Continuity, Continuity, Discontinuity: A Theory of Genres in Early Films', in Elsaesser and Barker (eds), *Early Cinema*, pp. 86–94.

52. Miriam Hansen (1991), *Babel and Babylon: Spectatorship in American Silent Film*, Cambridge, Mass: Harvard University Press.

53. Christian Metz (1985), 'Story/Discourse: Notes on Two Kinds of Voyeurism', in Bill Nichols (ed.), *Movies and Methods*, Berkeley: University of California Press.

54. Laura Mulvey (1975), 'Visual Pleasure and Narrative Cinema', *Screen*, vol. 16, no. 3.

55. Timothy Corrigan (1991), *A Cinema without Walls: Movies and Culture after Vietnam*, New Brunswick: Rutgers University Press, p. 4.

56. Corrigan, p. 7.

57. Murray Smith (1997), 'Theses on the Philosophy of Hollywood History', in Steve Neale and Murray Smith (eds) *Contemporary Hollywood Cinema*, London: Routledge.

58. Janet Staiger (1985), 'The Hollywood Mode of Production', in David Bordwell, Janet Staiger, and Kristin Thompson, *Classical Hollywood Cinema: Film Style and Mode of Production to 1960*, New York: Columbia University Press.

59. M. A. Oomen and K. V. Joseph (1991), *Economics of Indian Cinema*, New Delhi: IBH.

60. Justin Wyatt (1994), *High Concept: Movies and Marketing in Hollywood*, Austin: University of Texas Press.

61. Rob Wilson and Wimal Dissanayake (1996), 'Introduction: Tracking the Global/Local', in Rob Wilson and Wimal Dissanayake (eds), *Global/Local: Cultural Production and the Transnational Imaginary*, Durham, NC: Duke University Press.

62. Henry Jenkins (1995), 'Historical Poetics,' in Joanne Hollows and Mark Janovich (eds), *Approaches to Popular Film*, Manchester: Manchester University Press, 1995; Dirk Eitzen (1991), 'Evolution, Functionalism, and the Study of American Cinema', *The Velvet Light Trap*, vol. 28, Fall, pp. 82–3.

63. I do want to add a note of caution that not all popular films in India contain articulations of local and global; several films made in Tamil, Telugu, and Hindi remain removed from global signifying systems.

64. Critical work on violence in South Asia by Veena Das and Valentine Daniel has been crucial to my understanding of the relationship between cinematic representations, narratives of violence, and the eruption of violence in the public sphere. See Veena Das (ed.) (1992), *Mirrors of Violence: Communities, Riots and Survivors in South Asia,* Delhi: Oxford University Press; Valentine Daniel (1998), *Charred Lullabies: Chapters in an Anthropography of Violence*, Berkeley: University of California Press.

2

Avenging Women in Indian Cinema

Violence and Films

That there has been an escalation of violence in contemporary Indian cinema is now a well-worn cliché. The *Illustrated Weekly of India* cashed in on this trend by publishing a round-table discussion among film-makers, critics, and stars in 1993 that explored the 'correlation between violence in films and violence in society and the various implications of the nexus'.[1] The discussion attentively dwelt on film as a mass cultural product, but failed to offer any specific link between a particular film or genre and its effects on society. What also remained unacknowledged in this discussion was how these films fed off the crisis of legitimacy of the Indian state, a crisis that unleashed an open display of the state's coercive powers and accelerated most visibly after the state of emergency between 1975 and 1977. Even if it is debatable that the state of emergency is the origin of the crisis of legitimacy of the Indian state, at the very least we can speculate that it did set into motion contestations between power *and* authority that have pressed upon a more thorough exploration of hegemony, citizenship, community, nationalism, and democracy in India.[2] In short, discussions of violence have to consider how films replete with avenging women, gangsters, a brutal police force, and vigilante closures stage some of the most volatile struggles over representations that shape our public and private fanstasies of national, communal, regional, and sexual identities.

With fewer programmatic overtones, but with a cinephile's nitpicking taste, Firoze Rangoonwala definitively names the years between 1981 and 1992 'The Age of Violence'.[3] Assembling Hindi films from both 'parallel' cinema – Govind Nihalani's *Ardh Satya/Half Truth* (1984) – and the commercial industry, he identifies a marked shift towards escalating violence in this period. Rangoonwala, however, does not comment on the social impact of these films as the round-table discussion tended to do, but directs his sharpest criticism towards popular cinema for having 'succumbed to a hackneyed formula'. Arguably, dismissing formula-ridden popular cinema, however hackneyed it may be, unwittingly grants it processes of standardisation of cinematic codes and narratives and, in turn, exorcises a widely held view that Indian cinema randomly picks up story lines only to finally deliver a 'masala' film.

M. Rahman offers a less disparaging report of the Indian film industry in the

1980s by spotting the workings and consolidation of a new 'formula' in Hindi cinema inaugurated by N. Chandra's film *Pratighat/Retribution* (1987) and soon followed by *Sherni*, *Khoon Bhari Mang*, *Khoon Bahaa Ganga Mein*, *Commando*, *Bhraschtachar*, and *Kali Ganga*. The common theme of these films, according to him, is their portrayal of women as 'hardened, cynical, vengeful creatures'.[4] Interviewing director N. Chandra and prominent actresses such as Hema Malini, Dimple, and Rekha, who have all played avenging women, Rahman provides us with alternative viewpoints from within the film industry. Whereas Chandra suggests that these violent films are generated in response to the voracious viewing habits of an audience that wishes to see something different from the stock male 'action' film, the actresses argue that screenplays with dominant and powerful women are a welcome break from stereotypical roles as submissive and dutiful mothers and wives.

Maithili Rao also identifies an emerging trend in the industry, set off once again by N. Chandra's *Pratighat*, a trend that she calls the 'lady avengers'.[5] Arguing that they 'reflect the cultural schizophrenia in our society', Rao reproaches these films for being 'hostile to female sexuality' and for passing themselves off as nothing more than 'victimisation masquerading as female power'. This feminist spectator's critique neither figures in Rahman's interviews with directors and actresses nor does it address the tremendous box-office success of these films, however perverse they may be.

This chapter assumes that these contradictory and diverse readings of 'aggressive women' films are provocative enough for us to take another look at their visual and narrative goriness; another reading of these configurations of femininity and violence staged in these films, I argue, will uncover the contours of their appeal. My reading strategies employed in this chapter are shaped by feminist film theory that argues for formal textual analysis as a means of grasping the articulation of sexual difference in cinema. Although it tends to focus heavily on Hollywood productions, feminist film theory remains useful for at least two reasons: first, deploying it for an analysis of Indian cinema interrogates a monolithic conception of 'national cinema' and opens the possibility of exploring points of contact with international film-making practices; secondly, its nuanced theorisation of scopophilia and spectatorship holds up extremely well for the films discussed here. Despite a general move to place this Indian cinema within international film-making practices, I do want to argue that any Indianness we attribute to this cycle of films lies in the various ways India's censorship laws shape and influence cinematic representations; in other words, we must acknowledge and theorise the presence of the state when discussing the relationship between films and spectators. Among the different kinds of interruptions unique to Indian popular cinema, these films are primarily organised around censorship regulations with both the interval and song and dance sequences playing a minor role in the structuring of the narrative.

Included in the critical reception of these films is the frequent use of the term 'formula', which is bandied about to belittle the structures of repetition between films and only tangentially accounts for the viewer's pleasure. This chapter explores how it may equally be possible that we are drawn not only to the visceral images in these films, but also the various circuits of intertextual relays between and among them. Redrawn in these terms, the theoretically more viable concept of 'genre' allows us to place both industry and spectator stereophonically: the industry's suggestion that these films are different from male action films juxtaposed alongside critical evaluation that may condemn these films for cunningly representing female victims as vigilantes. In other words, only genre simultaneously addresses the industry's investment in standardised narratives for commercial success and the spectator's pleasure in genre films with their stock narratives structured around repetition and difference.

Censorship and *Coitus Interruptus*

One of the most glaring textual manifestations of state intervention in film production is the Board of Censors' certificate that precedes each film. This inaugural moment of every film, whether imported or indigenous, that is publicly released in India informs the spectator that the film has been approved by the Board of Censors. The British colonial state introduced film censorship by passing the Cinematograph Act of 1918 for at least two reasons: first, to censor film footage that might incite anti-colonial riots and, secondly, to avoid (mis)representations of the West, particularly images of Western women for native audiences. These broad concerns targeted both Indian and imported films and set a pattern for post-Independence censorship practices, where the state perceives films as having a tremendous influence over its citizenry and thus directs its regulations towards the production and control of 'quality' films.[6] In the 1950s, there was a confluence between the film industry's national sentiments and the state's interests in good taste. In an address to the South India Film Chamber of Commerce in 1951, filmmaker Chandulal Shah declared:

> not only for the sake of safe censoring, but also as a duty of our own people we should try to produce and present clean pictures. Let it not be said that we could approach through the screen millions of eyes and ears, that we, for the sake of money, influenced young minds in such a fashion that they could say we were responsible for bringing down the moral calibre and behaviour of our own children.[7]

Shah's address offers the possibility of self-regulation within the industry, but various revisions and amendments to censorship practices since 1951 indicate that state censorship remains the dominant practice.

Commenting on the impact of censorship on film production, Aruna Vasudev offers a provocative insight into the dynamics of the relationship between the state and the film industry:

> It is clear that a strict interpretation of these rules would result in almost all films being banned. It is these sweeping restrictions which have provoked so much criticism of the censorship system by the industry as well as the press and public opinion. It has driven producers to resort to indirect, unrealistic, suggestive modes of expression which are often vulgar and unaesthetic and convey the precise impression that the authorities hoped to eradicate.

Although instructive, Vasudev's suggestion that there is a *direct* relationship between increased censorship and 'vulgar and unaesthetic' films is impossible to sustain scene by scene in every film. Instead of assigning a reactive response to the film industry, it may be more useful to reconsider the relationship between the state's interests in forming national subjects and their taste on the one hand, and the film industry's own interests in spectatorial pleasure and desire on the other, as a *productive tension* that marks the cinematic materiality of Indian films. In other words, the task here is to explore how Indian films address the disciplined and regulated national subject by playing on the latter's spectatorial pleasure and desire.

As I have suggested in the Introduction, the ongoing negotiations between the state's censorship regulations and film industry, particularly over the representation of the female body on screen, can be formulated as *coitus interruptus* – a cinematic technique that is most visible when the camera withdraws just before we see a sexually explicit scene.[8] In its most benign form the film replaces the 'lost scenes' with pastoral evocations of passions – waterfalls, rain, gardens and so on.

There are several manifestations of *coitus interruptus* that are instantly recognisable in various Indian film genres. A classic and familiar montage in a romantic song and dance sequence offers an overview of the landscape while the camera zooms in on the actors. Intercutting between close-ups of the lovers and a panoramic vision of a lush landscape, the alternating segment introduces us to a possible kiss before cutting away. Another convention is structured around inserting extra-diegetic scenes in a romantic sequence to indicate passion through representations of waterfalls, flowers, thunder, lightning, and tropical storms.[9] A more daring technique foregrounds the female body through extreme close-ups of the waist, breasts, and hips. A masterful employment of this technique is seen in Ramesh Sippy's *Sholay/Flames* (1975).[10] Madan Gopal Singh argues that this film's success is partly based on a crucial dance scene:

> What is unusual is the way the camera 'sights' her [the dancer] and, as a consequence,

reduces us into pitiable and unsuspecting voyeurs … . The final image that emerges on the screen is a rather bizarre close-up of the legs of the courtesan open wide apart (and we should not forget that she is all the time moving in a forward thrust) with our seeing reduced to an abject crawl on the floor.[11]

Proposing that *Sholay* opens up different voyeuristic positions for the spectator in this scene, Singh suggests that the spectator is drawn into a subjective position instead of being provided the more conventional objective point of view.

A variation of this technique recurs in Harmesh Malhotra's *Sherni/Lioness* (1988), a film that belongs within the emerging 'avenging women' genre and casts the popular film star, Sridevi, as its bandit heroine.[12] The film represents Sridevi's role as a powerful avenging woman by cloaking her in a full-bodied leather suit that occludes any close-ups of her body. Towards the end of the film, in a seduction scenario leading to the final act of vengeance, Sridevi exchanges her leather outfit for a courtesan's costume. The camera radically departs from the earlier guarded coding of her desexualised body and instead prowls and lingers over her breasts and hips, forcefully conventionalising her body as 'female'. *Sherni*'s box-office success can be attributed not only to its fit within a new genre, but also to its attempt to reconfigure the representation of the female body on screen by producing an oscillation between a sexually ambivalent body in full leather and a conventional sequence with close-ups of swaying hips and heaving breasts.

In Raj Kapoor's *Ram Teri Ganga Maili/The Holy Ganga Is Polluted* (1985), coitus is interrupted by scenes of violence and cinematically structured as an alternating sequence between scenes of murder and sex: disrobing the female body in the sex scene alternates with a chase sequence that ends in a violent murder, and the sequence closes with a top shot of the crisscrossed bodies of the couple.[13] Displacing the conventional code showing close-ups of breasts and hips, *Ram Teri Ganga Maili* draws the spectator into a heady scene alternating between murder and sex, refusing to allow the spectator to rest with any one scene of pleasure.

The Board of Censors subjects films in every language to a uniform set of rules and regulations, though over the years the Hindi film industry has frequently complained that, as their films are nationally distributed, they tend to be more severely censored. This complaint may be true, but in recent years some of the more defiant cinematic techniques and styles have emerged from regional film industries, especially Tamil films. For instance, the Tamil film *Varami Neram Sehapu/The Colour of Poverty Is Red* (1987) reconfigures a disrobing scene to present a radically different spectatorial position. In previously available filmic representations we would, as spectators, be positioned to watch the entire disrobing, structured through shot/reverse shots alternating between the villain and actress, punctuated with medium close-up shots of the scene. By contrast, this film offers us a frontal shot of

the villain facing the audience while removing the heroine's sari. Through this cinematic arrangement, the point of view of the camera equates the heroine with the
audience, suggesting that the subject of the disrobing is a condensed figure, incorporating the heroine, audience, and camera. The sequence strictly adheres to the
dictates of censorship by not showing us the disrobed female body, but it offers us
a new point of identification and pleasure by drawing us in to participate in *our own*
disrobing. This sequence keenly demonstrates the impasse produced by censorship
regulations in its insistence on 'clean images' that unwittingly disrupt the alignment
of national subject with film spectator.

These sequences from different film genres and regional films demonstrate the
recurrence of a cinematic device in Indian cinema: the camera withdraws and the
object in focus is a fragmented female body, especially breasts and hips. Kumar
Shahini aptly refers to the repeated focus on breasts as a symptomatic gesture that
produces 'sex objects as lactating machines'.[14] Shahini's cryptic suggestion enhances
the equivalence between *coitus interruptus* as cinematic technique and contraceptive
device, an equivalence that is delivered by tightly aligning the female body with
reproductive functions. In other words, as a cinematic technique and strategy, *coitus
interruptus* not only sexualises the female body through fragmentation, but also
chooses to fragment and sexualise those parts of the female body that are intimately
linked to reproductive functions.

The structuring of this forked cinematic device also inflects the tenuous connection between national subject and spectator by privileging and drawing the spectator
into a scene of masochistic pleasure. Part of the spectator's lure into this scene is
predicated on a guaranteed but paradoxical relationship to the law: it is precisely by
strict adherence to codes of censorship, or parody by oversubmission to these codes,
that *coitus interruptus* becomes a travesty of the law. Parveen Adams persuasively
makes a case for the masochist's relationship to the law:[15]

> What the masochist is doing, and it is quite contrary to Freud, is to defy castration
> and disavow sexual difference. And this of course is a complete travesty of the Law
> the Oedipus complex is supposed to institute. It is important to note that the
> masochist's disavowal does not make him psychotic; his perversion is a stable position
> grounded in his refusal of the symbolic father and in his contract with the phallic
> mother. The masochist can subvert the Law because he too knows the paradox of
> conscience that Freud had recognized, the paradox that the more strictly the Law is
> adhered to, the greater the guilt. And he submits to the Law all the better to make of
> it; for he takes his punishment first, in order to experience the forbidden pleasure.
> [pp. 24–5]

So for the spectator watching popular Indian cinema, the more complete is her/his submission to the spectre of the national subject, the less regulated are his/her viewing pleasures.

Such a close relationship to the law draws a proximate relationship between *coitus interruptus* and pornography. Quite commonly a pornographic scene is posited alongside and against a 'normal' love scene. Slavoj Žižek, for instance, writes:[16]

> In contrast to this limit of representability which defines the 'normal' love story or melodrama, pornography goes beyond, 'shows all'. The paradox is, however, that by trespassing the limit, it always already *goes too far*, i.e. it *misses* what remained concealed in the 'normal', non-pornographic love scene.

Žižek's formulation of a pornographic film scene is predicated on its marked difference from a 'normal' love scene, a difference that relies on a well-acknowledged limit of representability. In contrast, as a cinematic device, *coitus interruptus* undermines each of these assumptions by extensively focusing on mechanisms of withdrawal so as to render love scenes, cabaret dance sequences, or rape scenes precipitously pornographic by almost 'showing all'. Moreover, *coitus interruptus* exploits a close alignment between law and 'limit' by blurring or withdrawing from the site of sexual penetration and/or focusing on female breasts and hips at the very instance of submitting to censorship regulations. The continuing presence of censorship regulations shifts the onus of withdrawal from the film industry to the state or, in other words, the presence of a very obvious and distinct site of authority displaces the responsibility for cinematic fragmentation of the female body from the film industry to the state. Further, the varying configurations and recurrent use of *coitus interruptus* demonstrate the indispensability of censorship regulations on the current constitution of Indian cinematic materiality, for it is difficult to conceive that in their absence the film industry would be so preoccupied with the withdrawal-of-the-camera technique as a crucial source of surplus pleasure. It is this very indispensability of censorship regulations that belies the film industry's frequent laments about state intervention. It seems more likely that it waits with bated breath for the next censorship restriction.

Rape and Revenge Genre

After this detour on the mutually reinforcing relationship between censorship regulations and film narrative, I should like to return to the cycle of avenging women films. Pruning Rahman's loose cluster of films around the figure of the 'dominant woman' where *Sherni/The Lioness* (1988) – a film closer to the bandit genre – and *Zakmi Aurat/Wounded Women* (1988) – a film closer to the police genre – are grouped together, we can isolate a genre of films that I call, after Maithili Rao, 'avenging women'. A standard narrative obtains in the following manner. Films open around family settings that appear 'happy' and 'normal' according to Hindi film conventions, but with a difference: there is a marked absence of dominant paternal figures. The female protagonist is always a working woman with a strong presence on screen. These initial conditions are upset when the female protagonist is raped. The raped woman files charges against her assailant, who is easily identifiable. Courtrooms play a significant role in these films, if only to demonstrate the state's inability to convict the rapist on the one hand, and to precipitate a narrative crisis on the other. This miscarriage of justice constitutes a turning point in the film, allowing for the transformation of the protagonist from a sexual and judicial victim to an avenging woman.

The general features of this narrative and the production of horror in rape scenes point to the close similarity of this genre to rape–revenge narratives of Hollywood B films, especially horror films.[17] Critical writing on Hollywood rape–revenge films, particularly Carol Clover's work, suggests that the marginal status of these films, in contrast to mainstream Hollywood, permits them to address some of the unresolved and knotty problems on gender and spectatorship that are carefully regulated and managed by the mainstream. Clover turns to the sadistic and masochistic pleasures evoked by these horror films to suggest that B films are the 'return of the repressed' in mainstream Hollywood. Focusing on B horror films, where low production values couple with sex and violence, Clover argues that these films displace the woman as the sole site of scopophilic pleasure and open possibilities of cross-gender identification through the sadomasochistic pleasures encouraged by these films. The most compelling aspect of her work is the classification of these rape–revenge films within the larger rubric of *horror* films, a move that retains the sadistic and masochistic pleasures – prerequisites for watching a standard horror film – staged in these rape–revenge narratives. Clover concludes in the following fashion:

> I have argued that the center of gravity of these films lies more in the reaction (the revenge) than the act (the rape), but to the extent that the revenge fantasy derives its force from *some* degree of imaginary participation in the act itself, the victim position, these films are predicated on cross-gender identification of the most extreme, corporeal sort. [p. 154]

Instead of privileging the revenge narrative or the rape scenes as Rao does, it is more useful to explore how the narrative nuances of this genre are predicated on a cinematic logic that draws these two parts together. Rape scenes are not unusual in Indian cinema. They are, however, frequently subject to censorship rulings on grounds both of their irrelevance to the main narrative and the unseemly pleasure they evoke.[18] Yet rape scenes in avenging women films are indispensable to their narrative, repeatedly evoked as evidence in a courtroom sequence or repeated as a traumatic event experienced by the victim. In other words, the centrality of the rape scenes in the narrative heightens their intimate relationship to the subsequent revenge plot where once again there is a replay of negotiations between sex and violence.

Avenging Women

Although N. Chandra's *Pratighat* is frequently cited as an originating moment in the avenging women genre, the combination of rape and revenge was already secured in B. R. Chopra's *Insaaf Ka Tarazu/Scales of Justice*, produced in 1980.[19] The latter's initial box-office success can be partly attributed to the heroine of the film, Zeenat Aman. Rajadhyaksha and Willemen describe the conditions of reception that shaped this film:

> This notorious rape movie followed in the wake of growing feminist activism in India in the 70s after the Mathura and Maya Tyagi rape cases, the amendment to the Rape Law and the impact of, e.g., the Forum Against Rape which offered legal assistance to rape victims.[20]

References to the feminist movement are obviously one of the determining features structuring the reception of this film, but its notoriety points towards a different route of analysis where we have to consider how this film relies on our knowledge of these rape cases as a point of entry into fantastical stagings of our anxieties about women, sexuality, and law, anxieties that in turn are set into motion, but not resolved, by anti-rape campaigns.[21] Re-evaluated through generic details identifiable in later avenging women genre films, *Insaaf Ka Tarazu* unquestionably stands out as one of the early experiments in rape–revenge narratives.

Insaaf Ka Tarazu opens with a rape scene. A colour sequence showing us a medium shot of a screaming woman in a sari rapidly changes into a black-and-white shadow play. The silhouette of a man first chases, then disrobes the woman. Another male figure enters the scene, and a fight begins between them. The film returns to full colour when the potential rapist is fatally stabbed. The following credit sequence is a montage of stills from various religious and tourist sites in India with the soundtrack playing the title song of the film. These two sequences juxtapose rape against representations of India, and this association with India is further played out in the film by naming the female protagonist Bharati – the feminine name in Hindi for India. These first scenes suggest the consideration of female rape as an allegory of a beleaguered nation state, a suggestion that is not, however, developed further in the film.

The second rape sequence in the film is distinguished from the opening sequence by the continued use of colour footage and the absence of a male saviour. Using a

Wall poster for *Insaaf Ka Tarazu*
(courtesy of the National Film
Archive, Pune)

calendar art print of a woman in bondage in the victim's (Arti's) bedroom as a reference point, the sequence provides glimpses of a rape scene that includes both coercion and bondage. Furthermore, the scene offers us another point of identification through the victim's younger sister, Nita, who accidentally walks into Arti's bedroom during the rape. Arti files charges against the rapist, Gupta. A number of social encounters between Gupta and Arti preceding the rape, combined with Nita's confused eyewitness testimony, are employed in the courtroom to suggest that Arti was not raped, but consented to have sex with Gupta. The court finds Gupta not guilty.

The court's verdict in Arti's rape case comes as no surprise to the spectators, for the film mobilises this doubt throughout the scene. For instance, Nita's testimony is crucial to her sister's case, but the defence lawyer convincingly argues her inability to tell the difference between coerced and consenting sexual relationships. The film frames Nita very much in the position of a horrified voyeur witnessing a primal scene, thus infusing the scene with both fear and pleasure of sexual knowledge, instead of recognising it as sexual violation pure and simple. The sado-voyeuristic pleasure also pointedly surfaces here through the poster on the bedroom wall. The viewer might expect the poster's subject to be identified with the aggressor, a traditional strategy. Instead, the poster shores up a confusion between representations of rape and rape itself – thus eroticising the scene of violation and escalating our masochistic identification with it. Privileging Nita's relationship to the scene, the film also exposes and depends on our inability as spectators to tell the cinematic difference between a scene of sexual consent and rape.

Notwithstanding the relationship between Nita's credibility as a witness and the court's verdict, Nita's ambivalence presses upon another aspect of the film's narrative – the unfolding of the revenge plot. Keeping pace with the ambivalence around the charge of rape in Arti's case, the film delays and reserves the revenge scenario until it can represent an unambiguous rape scene. It is only after Gupta proceeds to rape the virginal Nita in his office that Arti's revenge is allowed to unfold. In the film's climax, Arti shoots Gupta, circumventing a judicial verdict on Nita's case. The film closes with another court scene where this time the judge resigns office for failing to deliver justice in earlier rape cases. Closing the rape–revenge narratives around a court scene or a figure of the state is now a standard feature of this genre and stands in sharp contrast to the male vigilante genre where the figure of the state is repeatedly undermined, for example in *Nayakan/Don* (1987). Although *Insaaf Ka Tarazu* had no imitators for another seven years, the film established some of the basic conventions that squarely locate it as the inaugural moment in the avenging women genre.

N. Chandra's film *Pratighat* (1987) is a classic of this genre because of the manner in which it consolidates some basic strains of the rape–revenge narrative.[22] The film revolves around corrupt politicians and a continuing crisis over law and order in a small town. The female protagonist is a college teacher, Lakshmi, who lives with her lawyer husband and his parents. The film opens with several scenes of hooliganism orchestrated by Kali, a *lumpen* youth leader, in Lakshmi's town. These scenes are also strung together to lead us through Lakshmi's conversion from an ordinary, disinterested citizen to an active interventionist against Kali's reign of terror. Her complete conversion to an avenging woman hinges on a crucial scene when she openly confronts Kali by filing a criminal suit against him and refuses to withdraw it even when he threatens to harm her. As the stakes continue to rise in their confrontation, Kali finally resorts to a gendered resolution: he disrobes Lakshmi on the street in front of her house, with all her neighbors and family watching fearfully. This violation establishes the primary conditions for Lakshmi's revenge against Kali and his gang and at the same time seals her estrangement from her husband. Lakshmi is rescued from this scene of public humiliation by Durga, whose own life has been scarred by Kali's violence – she was gang-raped by Kali's men and her husband tortured to death – but who nevertheless continues to galvanise support against Kali. Lakshmi moves into Durga's home, recovers, and receives support for her own revenge plan.

Pratighat displaces the conventional representation of rape by reconfiguring the rape scene as a disrobing sequence at both the visual and narrative registers. Ironically, while Kali declares that disrobing is part of a Hindu tradition, evoking the

Mahabharata, cinematically the film disengages with all the conventional representations of rape. The entire disrobing scene is spliced as a medium long shot, and in the final moment of complete nudity the film converts to colour negative, conveying the full extent of this violation in Indian cinema. Moving away from the standard representations of rape scenes, *Pratighat* draws our attention to the visual proximity between scenes of rape and disrobing in Hindi cinema, and interrogates the ethics of a 'full view' circumscribing such scenes.

The scene of revenge where Lakshmi confronts Kali is also framed with narrative references to Hindu mythology and filmic gestures suggesting crossovers with mythology films and the *Ramayana* and *Mahabharata* television serials.[23] Clad in a red sari, Lakshmi garlands and anoints Kali at a public meeting, then repeatedly strikes him with an axe originally intended as a gift to him. The final killing scene is edited by juxtaposing shots of Kali's larger-than-life cardboard cut-out against the onstage altercation between Lakshmi and Kali, fight scenes between Kali's men and Lakshmi's students, and colour-negative stills from the original disrobing scene. The cardboard cut-out evokes an intertextual relay from the poster in *Insaaf Ka Tarazu*, playing on the unrepresentativeness of rape in the former and suggesting that Lakshmi's aggressive attack in *Pratighat* is equally horrific. Moving the narrative focus away from a single killing scene to a general murderous chaos replays the film's own pet themes where rape is located alongside other social crimes such as hooliganism and corruption.

Two contradictions must be noted. Even as the film is critical of rape, rape scenes figure periodically in the narrative, signalling in each instance the consolidation of criminality and vigilantism with an increasing displacement of the state's law and order role. Similarly, criminalising rape, the conceit employed in this film, appears to identify with a progressive legal position, but we find it cannot respond to the sado-voyeuristic pleasure prompted in the cinematic representations of rape. Kali's death may bear a formal resemblance to the disrobing scene, but is not subject to the same censorship regulations that underscore sexual representations in Indian cinema. *Pratighat* nevertheless irks us with the limits and possibilities of equating rape and revenge scenes, and thus persuades us to reconsider the masochistic underpinnings of the rape scenes in this genre. Although the film relies on our masochistic identification in the rape scene to fully play out its horrifying potential, the sadistic dimensions of this very scene propel the revenge plot and remind us retrospectively that the ensemble of elements in the rape scene is always a volatile marriage between sex *and* violence.

The (Anti)Climax: *Zakmi Aurat*

There are several reasons for *Pratighat*'s success, but its ability to summon horror in the revenge sequences is one that, in turn, opened the gates for other permutations and combinations of rape and revenge. The full import of prompting horror in revenge scenes is further developed in Avatar Bhogal's *Zakmi Aurat/Wounded Women*, released in 1988.[24] Retaining the rule of targeting 'modern' women as victims – a fashion model in *Insaaf Ka Tarazu* and a college teacher in *Pratighat* – *Zakmi Aurat* picks a policewoman as its protagonist. With the rape scene occurring early in the narrative, the pivotal turning point emerges when the judicial system refuses to convict the rapists, in spite of policewoman Kiran Dutt's own testimony. Abandoning legal recourse, Kiran Dutt now joins forces with other rape victims in the city. Together, the women come up with a fitting revenge plan: to snare the rapists and castrate them.

Kiran's gang rape is edited as a fight sequence that closes around a conventional representation of rape. The rape scene returns to the bedroom familiar from *Insaaf Ka Tarazu*, but with a twist. Refusing to linger on Inspector Kiran Dutt's body as the rapists strip her, the film instead focuses on the rapists as they tear down her jeans and fling them on the ceiling fan. The unrepresentativeness of the sexual act in this rape scene climaxes through a series of shot/reverse shots of fetishised objects – the ceiling fan and a medium close-up shot of Kiran's screaming face.

The shot sequence employed in the gang rape of the female police officer creates the basic template for the castration revenge scenes. Again, details on the edge, such as the doctor's operating gown, her mask, and the overhead lamp, are excessively in focus and fetishised. The camera cuts off the entire abdominal region of the man, refusing to zoom in on a cloaked genital area. Rapid freeze shots of men's faces and ninety-degree shots of the overhead lamp in the operating theatre signal the continuing process of castration. This equivalence between the gang rape and castration scenes, spliced by repeating shot/reverse shots of a face and an overhead object cinematically, attempts to balance rape and revenge.

Critics have lambasted this film for offering an improbable resolution to rape; however, such a reading assumes that films have an indexical signification to political reality instead of examining how their narratives repeatedly stage various fantastical possibilities of these very same realities for the spectator.[25] One of the crucial constitutive features of this genre is its vociferous stagings of 'reality' through familiar references: shots of real newspapers, photographs of Gandhi on courtroom walls, footage of the Indian flag, and so on. *Zakmi Aurat* relies more extensively on these elements than other films: the opening sequence shows us actual newspaper reports of rape cases in India, and the film draws an obvious link between the Kiran Dutt character and Kiran Bedi, a well-known female police officer in Delhi. Inhabiting the *mise en scène*, these authenticating details appear to be strategically placed to heighten our viewing pleasure of the unravelling horror plot, reeling the spectator into scenes of escalating horror that culminate precisely at the very juncture when the film plays on an uncanny resemblance to extra-cinematic icons and events. These narratives in general may not

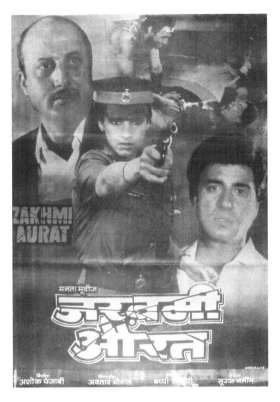

Wall poster for *Zakmi Aurat*
(courtesy of the Andy Muisili
Art Gallery)

directly respond to or satisfy demands of justice in particular rape cases, but they do
unleash scenes of resolution that both extend beyond the law of the state and expose
the spectator's complicity in the terrifying rape sequences.

Defending the spectatorial pleasures ensuing from *I Spit on Your Grave* (Meir
Zarchi, 1977) – a film that bears an intimate relationship to *Zakmi Aurat* – Carol
Clover writes in *Men, Women and Chain Saws*: 'what disturbs about *I Spit on Your
Grave* is its perverse simplicity, the way it closes all the intellectual doors and windows and leaves us staring at the *lex talionis* unadorned' (p. 151). Clover's comment
is aimed at up-market films such as *The Accused* (Jonathan Kaplan, 1988) where the
legal process takes over the narrative, leaving little space for the rape victim to articulate her torment, and substantially closes off the possibility of direct vigilante
action. Her defence bears on my reading of *Zakmi Aurat*, where, despite the film's
narrative simplicity, it significantly precipitates the problems attending the visual representation of revenge in these films. As we have seen, films in this genre rely on
convincingly meting out vigilante revenge that must equal, or even surpass, the horror of rape. Although this equation produces continual narrative tensions, visual
representations of rape in Indian cinema also remind us of the authority of censorship regulations and suggest the possibility of sadomasochistic pleasures structuring
these rape scenes.

As I argued in a previous section, the Indian film industry, despite overt protests over film censorship, is crucially dependent on the presence of the state at the register of cinematic materiality for generating sadomasochistic pleasure. The female body is always the object in focus and is repeatedly subject to a withdrawing camera that banks on an intimate relationship between the law ruling taboos and the state overseeing censorship. The rape scenes in the avenging women genre are not far from this formulation, where the narrative informs us that the horror of rape is in part motivated by the absence of the state, but attention to cinematic materiality suggests that the state, as censorship authority, is very much present as one of the crucial negotiating sites. Until the arrival of the revenge plot in these movies, rape scenes appear to be mere substitutes for sex, relentlessly eroticising violence. It comes as no surprise that the criticism levelled against these films is sparked by a suspicion that violent sex is being flaunted as rape, a suspicion that also guides censorship regulations.

To mitigate and ward off such criticism, revenge scenes in these films have to be equally horrific in order to allow us to read the scenes of violent sex as rape *retrospectively*. The narrative and visual machinations of this genre thus revolve around the problem of balancing rape and revenge: *Pratighat* settles rape by evoking figures of Hindu Shakti goddesses and killing the rapist, whereas *Zakmi Aurat* resorts to an anatomical equation by suggesting castration as an act of revenge and escalates the horror of rape by visually locating the castrated male body in an analogous position to the raped female body. Settling rape through castration resonates with a feminist Utopia, where, at least momentarily, the easy economic equation between the penis and phallus resolves the differences between gender and power that are constantly complicated by and subjected to the symbolic *difference* between the penis and phallus. The question is, while revenge narratives in this genre seek continuously to 'match' the horror of the rape, can they ever succeed?

Zakmi Aurat brings to a head the entire problem of visually and narratively matching rape with revenge through its absurd logic of five rapes to fifteen castrations, a logic that heralds a moratorium on this genre in its current configuration. At the same time, *Zakmi Aurat* spawned films such as *Aaj Ki Aurat/Today's Woman* and *Damini*, where the narratives not only stress the difference between the raped woman and avenger, but also return to exhaust the possibilities of pleasure in violent rape scenes.[26] Even though revenge narratives, as Rahman informs us, provide female stars with more dominant roles, because women's access to avenging power in these films is intimately predicated on rape as a violent litmus test of gender identity, rape scenes are never so neatly cordoned off from Indian cinema's extensive use of the woman's body as a stand-in for sex, as a crucial site of scopophilic pleasure. Faced with these contradictory demands, the avenging women genre surfaces as a giddy masculine concoction: the rape scenes provide the narrative ruse for the revenge plan while also providing the spectator with a conventional regime of scopophilic pleasure. Revenge allows female stars to dominate the screen, but the genre demands that a violent assertion of masculine power in the form of rape is the price that has to be exacted for such power. Clearly, at the periphery of this genre where the interlocking narratives of rape and revenge are less than minimally finessed, gratuitously deploying rape does not sufficiently dislodge or displace conventional representations of women in Indian cinema or appease Rao's suspicions.

Avenging Women and Sadomasochism

Located within the larger rubric of other violent action films produced in the same period, the more taunting feminist aspects of the rape–revenge films are most apparent in their narrative closures. Here the avenging woman's unhindered access to power is always limited by the arrival of the police; this finale differs markedly from the more assertive vigilante resolutions of masculine genres such as gangster and bandit films. Coupled with the prolonged judicial sequences revolving around rape cases, the appeal of these rape–revenge narratives arguably rests on their ability to stage all the anxious points that attend the relationship between patriarchy and the state. If the social imaginary promotes a unity between symbolic law and the state, rape cases inject a dissonance between these sites of authority to remind us that 'issues' of honour and shame are only provisionally resolved through legal proceedings. For the victim, the state's betrayal in rape cases is equally accompanied by patriarchal abandonment, and together they consolidate as the precipitating moment in the narrative that allows it to shift towards the revenge narrative. Faced with an orderless universe, the avenging women narrative proceeds on a transgressive vigilante path, incites masculine anxiety about the phallic female, and opens the representational circuit for women on the Indian screen. However, this unfettered power is undercut by finally reeling in the authority of the state and revealing the avenging woman's own overwhelming investment in the restoration of the social imaginary. Casting women as embodying and sustaining tradition recycles an old stereotype from Indian films; however, the forced closure in this genre only provisionally irons out the anxieties between patriarchy and the state.

Although both the narrative closure accompanied by the very conventional reintegration of the woman into the social order and the precarious necessity of rape in these films weigh down the radical potential of the revenge narrative, they cannot completely regulate the series of unstable desires and identities set in motion through the continuing dynamics between rape and revenge. Finding anything subversive about rape–revenge narratives at both the register of the cinematic form and the spectator's pleasure leads us to some tangled issues plaguing feminist film theory. Laura Mulvey's classic essay 'Visual Pleasure and Narrative Cinema' argues that 'Hollywood style at its best (and of all the cinema which fell within its sphere of influence)' offers pleasure by enacting a conventional heterosexual division of labour in its narrative structure between active/male and passive/female for the masculine spectator.[27] Because narrative cinema is loosely linked to and depends on scopophilic pleasure, this erotic investment in the image of the woman also evokes a castration anxiety for the spectator. Warding off this anxiety, Hollywood offers two avenues of protection: voyeurism, particularly with a sadistic investment in narrative, and fetishism, where the threatening figure of the woman is converted into a reassuring object. Identifying the contradictory paths of desire in Hollywood films, Mulvey's essay draws heavily on Freud's essay 'Fetishism' and reproduces some of the heterosexual assumptions of the original essay.[28]

Subsequent feminist revisions continue to challenge Mulvey's essay on two fronts: the first challenge is that of feminist interests in psychoanalysis that have moved the debate from Freud's essay 'Fetishism' to 'A Child is Being Beaten', readings that have frequently been motivated by interests in the genealogy of masochism.[29] Among the feminist writing on the subversive potential of masochism, Parveen Adams's essay 'Per Os(cillation)' is exemplary because she argues that 'it is not possible to determine sexual position through identification'.[30] Returning to Freud's beating scenario in his 'A Child is Being Beaten', Adams provokes us to consider a constant bisexual oscillation between activity and passivity, masculinity and femininity, at the psychical register, and cautions us that psychical reality inflects but does not simply match gender differences in social reality. The second challenge to Mulvey's essay has been mounted by feminist theorists as they move into other genres of Hollywood – Mulvey's own interest in melodrama figures centrally in a later revision of her initial formulation – particularly to B films that include horror, slasher, and pornographic elements.[31] Focusing on the less-than-best cinematic styles of B films that are directed at, and have, a loyal female audience and incorporate a heady combination of sex and violence, feminist film theory – Carol Clover's work on slasher films and Linda Williams's on pornographic films – has been forced to a reconsider the dynamics between identification and pleasure, particularly sadomasoschistic pleasure.[32] Arguing for the presence of *sadomasochistic* pleasure in violent pornographic films, Williams writes:

> it seems to me preferable to employ the term *sadomasochistic* when describing the perverse fantasies that inform these films. While still problematic, the term at least keeps in play the oscillation between active and passive and male and female subject positions, rather than fixing one pole or the other as the essence of the viewer's experience. At the same time, it does not allow us to forget, as some celebrations of masochisms (e.g. Studlar or Samois) do forget, where ultimate power lies. [p. 217]

It appears that the rape–revenge scenes in the avenging women genre similarly rely on the generation of sadomasochistic pleasure, a pleasure that unwittingly challenges, however provisionally, the straightforward sadistic impulses of rape in Indian cinema. Because rape scenes are inextricably meshed with the revenge plot in this genre, the masochistic dimensions of the rape scenes far outweigh their conventional sadistic associations, while at the same time the unfolding revenge plot leans on provoking the spectator's sadistic investments in revenge and punishment. Interweaving sadism and masochism through different filmic moments, this genre upsets the normalising fetishistic economy with the fragmented woman's body as the central object, but complicating these generic pleasures is the continuing tussle between every Indian film-maker and the state over censorship. As a result it is precisely through overt submission to censorship regulations that the commercial film industry parodies the authority of the state, a relationship that is not unlike the masochist's relationship to patriarchal law; therefore, we may have to consider the possibility of the rape–revenge device as yet another ruse to circumvent censorship, resorting once again to the woman's body.

At the same time, tightening the rape–revenge equation unwittingly opens possibilities for cross-gender identifications. Not resolving the gender imbalance prevalent in social power relations, the contradictory forces of Indian commercial cinema beg for a reconsideration of the other identifications available in this heady combination of sex and violence. Responding in part to the debates on violence in Indian cinema that cast these representations solely in terms of their regressive effects on society, I suggest instead that violent scenes circumscribed by intersecting genre features and social pressures can in surprising ways challenge patriarchy's normalising overtones on the issue of gender and constitute one of the crucial axes of spectator interests in these films.

Arguably, rape–revenge narratives are not available as positive models for feminist Utopias, but they do stage the aggressive and contradictory contours of sexual identity and pleasure that in turn throw up aggressive strands of feminism. I am not redeeming the film industry's regressive casting of female roles, but I do want to suggest that crosscutting pressures from both the female star system and the feminist movement have colluded to stage some of our unacknowledged aggressiveness, both public and private, which also underscores our understanding and articulations of sexual identities.

Double or Nothing: Vijayshanti

Before we commit ourselves to the idea that all roads to female aggression inevitably lead us to rape scenes in Indian cinema, it is worth remembering that this tight relationship between rape and revenge is a recurrent feature of Hindi cinema. Whatever peculiar production rationale helps to strengthen this link, the yoking of rape with revenge cannot be disconnected from the modes of address structuring Hindi cinema; a national audience is always already its imagined addressee. In other words, its desire to command a national audience severely reduces Hindi cinema's ability to stray from a successful yet conventional paradigm.

However, an appraisal of other regional cinemas, particularly Telugu films with the actress Vijayshanti in the lead, demonstrates that there are other contours to aggression, without the routine rape scene. Dispensing with rape scenes, these films allow aggression to shadow desire. On another register, these films lend themselves to a rich reading of regional and global cinematic issues. For instance, as Telugu films, they are in constant dialogue with political dramas – a *forte* of the Telugu film industry – challenging the masculine rule of this genre. As female-centred action films, they recall Nadia's stunt films from 1930s to the 1950s, and the agility they portray reminds us of a large number of films and television shows from *Suzie Wong* to *Charlie's Angels*. In addition, as films initially made in Telugu and subsequently dubbed in Hindi and Tamil, they raise interesting issues about the new economics of dubbing that has gained a national market for regional cinemas.

Rumours and reports from the industry claim that Vijayshanti is one of India's highest-paid female stars whose cachet at the box office is greater than most of her male counterparts. However, she, too, has had her share of rape–revenge narratives – N. Chandra's *Pratighat*, for instance, is a remake of a Telugu film, *Pratighatana* (1985, dir. T. Krishna), that has Vijayshanti cast as the avenging woman – and is not altogether protected from playing the submissive wife in *Eashwar* (1992); nevertheless, she manages to corner some of the most spectacularly aggressive roles in Indian cinema. Vijayshanti's self-representation does not rest on emulating other heroines, but as she puts it, 'I always have to kick and pound the villains to pulp. That's why I'm called the Amitabh Bachchan of Andhra Pradesh.'[33]

When examining rape–revenge narrative, I steered away from considering the influence of the female star economy, choosing instead to focus on textual analysis. But when faced with Vijayshanti's films – for example, *Tejaswini* (1991), *AutoRani* (1992), *Rowdy Inspector* (1991), *Streetfighter* (1994), and *Superlady* (1991) – despite their different directors, they hold together as if to constitute a genre and challenge my own marginalisation of the female star economy in previous readings of the avenging women films. Each of her films overturns several conventional associations between femininity and aggression, but all too often their narratives tend to characterise female aggressiveness as a feature belonging exclusively to the pre-Oedipal phase. Kodi Ramakrishnan's *Police Lock-up* (1992), however, refuses any narrow casting of female aggressiveness and, in turn, allows for an intriguing relationship between law and desire.[34]

The narrative takes the following route: Vijaya (Vijayshanti) is an upright police officer who arrives in town (Vishakpatnam) to investigate a political assassination. She has to contend with corrupt policemen and a conniving and ambitious chief minister (Panjaraja), whom we know is responsible for the assassination. Panjaraja accuses her of being a terrorist, and Vijaya is thrown into jail. A second storyline now unravels: Shanti – Vijayshanti's double role – is the wife of a zealous police inspector (Ashok) who is frequently transferred because of his honesty. Shanti is obviously cast as Vijaya's alter ego: meek, clad in a sari, devoted to her husband, and pining for a child. It is precisely this guilelessness that lands her in jail one curfew night. The police throw her into Vijaya's cell, and the two see each other for the first time. Unlike stories of lost sisters and brothers that recur in Indian films, this scene does not drag in mothers and fathers to claim kinship between the two women.[35] Instead, it moves quickly through the respective events that brought the two women to jail. The crucial detail that lends credibility to Vijaya's story of her capture is Shanti's encounter with a dying journalist who, mistaking Shanti for Vijaya, passes on details of yet another assassination scheme. Shanti suggests that they switch places so that Vijaya can complete her investigation and arrest the corrupt chief minister. Vijaya reluctantly agrees, and the following morning leaves with Ashok, now passing as his meek wife. The film now gallops along, plotting Vijaya's pursuit of the chief minister. We see her move effortlessly from sari to jeans, from submissive daughter-in-law to strong and masterful police official. Through various twists and turns that include the notorious international assassin John, the film ends in a temple courtyard where Vijaya and Ashok annihilate the villains. The wily politician is the last to go; Vijaya blows him up with his own bomb, strapped in a belt, reminding viewers of the way Rajiv Gandhi was killed. The film closes with Vijaya and Shanti embracing.

Departing radically from both the rape–revenge narratives and male action films, *Police Lock-up* reconfigures the relationship between power, authority, and gender, opening up a wide range of fantastical possibilities for feminist identifications. Many obvious scenes of positive identification are secured in the film. For instance, the film introduces Vijaya as a police officer driving her jeep through a series of slow-motion shots, thus breaking away from the routine logic of passage from victim to avenger in the rape–revenge genre. The film ungrudgingly celebrates her ability and success as a police officer by showing us elaborate details of her work: there are several fight scenes where both guns and kung-fu fighting styles are exhibited; her acumen and confidence with technology occur more than once. My favourite is when Vijaya, dressed as Shanti, uses a video camera to shoot an exchange among Panjaraja's hoodlums. She then replays this scene in slow motion and decodes their conversation through lip-reading in order to discover where a kidnap victim is hidden. These scenes suggest the presence, possibility, and intervention of female control over modern sites of technology that are all too frequently represented as male prerogatives. Collectively, these details easily constitute the bedrock of any feminist primer on positive identifications, but they fit too neatly and are too far from the messy economies of identification and desire that cinematic spectatorship thrives on. What we do see in *Police Lock-up* is a woman's excessive investment in the law, a law that we often mistrust for the ways in which it gives feminism short shrift.

The cornerstone of this film's innovativeness, however, is its deployment of the double role. Indian cinema has long been fascinated with double and triple roles, and utilises them both to recognise and bank on a star's popularity. When female double roles surface – for example, in Ramesh Sippy's *Sita aur Gita/Sita and Gita* (1972) – the narrative revolves around the separate lives and identities of twins, and conventionally closes on family romance: lost siblings, cast as opposites, find each other, find their parents, etc. In sharp contrast, *Police Lock-up* refuses to recuperate the family: Vijaya and Shanti are not lost-and-found twins, and their resemblance is never resolved narratively in the film. Demonstrating that the two women effectively and easily pass for the other – Vijaya as the submissive wife and Shanti as an aggressive officer – the film mobilises change in each woman and closes around a less polarised distinction between the two. Obviously, the blurred distinction between them draws this film dangerously close to the horror film genre on twins.[36]

Rejecting a narrative closure around biological kinship, this film wrings out the full effects of masquerade. Vijaya's competency is asserted through her ability to masquerade not only as Shanti, but also a telephone-line repair man and the killer John at various points in the film. Masquerade controls and mobilises this film's narrative.

Masquerade and Its Possibilities

Masquerade as a theoretical concept in feminist film theory arrives through Joan Riviere.[37] The oft-quoted passage from her essay reads as follows:

> Womanliness therefore could be assumed and worn as a mask, both to hide the possession of masculinity and to avert the reprisals expected if she was found to possess it – much as a thief will turn out his pockets and ask to be searched to prove that he has not the stolen goods. The reader may now ask how I define womanliness or where I draw the line between genuine womanliness and the 'masquerade'. My suggestion is not, however, that there is any such difference; whether radical or superficial, they are the same thing. [p. 38]

Mary Ann Doane initially employed this concept to theorise cross-gender identifications that attend the female spectator when viewing a masculine-ordered universe in Hollywood cinema.[38] Doane argues that while watching films that direct themselves to a masculine subject, where a female figure is repeatedly fetishised, female spectators masquerade as masculine subjects thus generating a viewing pleasure that evokes sadomasochism. In a revised version of this essay, Doane picks on the racial and class fantasies that are embedded in Riviere's theorisation of the masquerading intellectual woman.[39] Both versions, nevertheless, are limited by an exclusive focus on the viewing subject's heterosexual desiring economy that tends to occlude other possible subject positions. John Fletcher's reworking of Riviere's masquerade not only presses on a more radical reading of the essay, but also returns to the signifying form of the film to elaborate on masquerade.[40] Fletcher writes:

> Riviere's distinction comes down to one between the mask of femininity as
> reaction–formation, renouncing and reversing wishes, and the mask of femininity
> covering the refusal to renounce them … The importance of Riviere's conception of the
> masquerade is that it constitutes a transgressive doubleness, an inscription of alternative
> wishes. The potential for a critical distance from the mythemes of femininity (passivity,
> responsiveness, deference, flattery, etc.) is lodged already within it and the narratives it
> might generate. [p. 55]

Turning to Riviere's formula of masquerade as theft, Fletcher suggests, in a Lacanian twist, that this fantasy is a theft of the paternal phallus. Desiring the phallus inaugurates the subject into the economy of desire and simultaneously into the linguistic universe and, in turn, this desiring and speaking subject recognises both the lack and plenitude encompassing the phallus. This Lacanian inflection on Riviere dislodges the possession of the phallus from a simple anatomical assignment of gender for the speaking and desiring subject. In other words, masquerade can be extended to both masculine and feminine subjects when there is an attempt to cover their refusal to be compliant. Fletcher deftly uses this reworking to undermine previous readings of *The Locket* (1946) and *Marnie* (1964), films that have been read exclusively as attempting to hold up a fetishised female figure for a masculine viewing subject. His analysis closes on an extremely instructive note:

> In these films Riviere's scenario of the masquerade generates narratives of the woman
> as an intransigently desiring and active subject, within the heterosexual economy of the
> phallus, whose key signifier she re-signifies and re-routes in her relay of alternative
> wishes and demands. [p. 70]

Reconsidered for the film under consideration, it can be said that masquerade functions at different levels in *Police Lock-up*. The film is clearly located within the male action film genre where restoration of law and order dominates the narrative and films always close on a conventional rearrangement of law and order. Usurping the standard male hero's role, that is, masquerading as a police officer, Vijayashanti plays this role to the full. The film supports this masculinisation completely, for instance, by holding off song and dance sequences exclusively around her. Reeling Shanti into the narrative as an upright inspector's wife is a perfect foil for providing a feminine domestic space that both cushions and counterpoises Vijaya's aggressive public self, and together the two roles demonstrate Vijayshanti's ability to perform across different and competing terrains. Doubleness is further supported by naming the characters by splitting parts of the star's full name, thus 'assuring' the masculine subject, as proposed by Riviere, that behind the mask lies this powerful phallic figure that unites both halves of polar screen personalities.

The double role in this film also actuates a different fantastical staging of desire. The lack of parental origin as a reason for their resemblance unhinges the film from closing around a cosy sibling unity, while simultaneously unleashing a desire for the other. For instance, when Shanti suggests they switch places, the scope of this offer clearly extends to her spouse – we see Vijaya effortlessly passing for Shanti in her home, even masquerading her love for Ashok. It is only later in the film that Ashok reveals that he suspected Vijaya was not Shanti when she rejected his sexual demands. Of course, the film suspends all knowledge of the exact moment of his discovery, leaving open the possibility of a sexual interaction between Ashok and Vijaya. The switch thus opens the possibility of Ashok being exchanged as a sexual object between them.

We have seen the male version of this arrangement first proposed by Lévi-Strauss and then ingeniously resurrected by Lacan and revised by feminists.[41] Eve Sedgwick's reformulation in *Between Men* shifts the exchange of women between men from a heterosexual to homosexual matrix.[42] Sedgwick proposes that women are exchanged between men to avert, ward off, and occlude the articulation of homosexual desire for each other while simultaneously oppressing women and producing homophobia. These terms seem uncannily reversed in *Police Lock-up*, raising the possibility that Vijaya and Shanti's full-scale switching is driven by a desire for the other, however narcissistic it may appear. This reading is further endorsed by the final moment of the film where we see them embracing, a closure that displaces and postpones heterosexual resolutions.

Although Vijaya has been the focus of most of the dramatic moments in the film, Shanti, too, provides enough dissonance in the plot, despite her conventional representation of passive femininity: she not only initiates the idea of the switch, but also remains extremely loyal to her role as Vijaya in spite of arduous conditions in the jail. But it is in a more eccentric detail that her location in the plot allows for displacements. The film elaborately informs us that Shanti's anxiety about having children has absurd effects on her behaviour: she daydreams about phantom children, upsets her husband's work routine by demanding his presence at various fertility rituals, and, above all, she has a pathological attachment to a dog that she treats as her child.

I am reminded here of Edmund Leach's stimulating essay 'Animal Classification and Verbal Abuse', where he argues for an intimate relationship among human classification of animals, verbal abuse, and incest taboos.[43] There is an unrelated, yet similar, take on domestic pets by Avital Ronell in an interview where she expounds on the Bush family and pets after Millie's 'autobiography' was published.[44] She comments: 'I remember telling people, "Watch their rapport to the dog, because here is where they articulate things that are taboo, that are unconscious"' [p. 142].

Shanti's attachment to Caesar, her attempts to anthropomorphise, casts aspersions on the fertility of this heterosexual unit, particularly on her husband and his ability to reproduce. Furthermore, her incapacity to differentiate between dog and child in many scenes, a difference that conventionally marks so many sexual, dietary, and verbal taboos, throws asunder all normative images of a reproducing human family and even anticipates the remarkable switch suggested and promoted by her. The film encourages her attempts to humanise Caesar by giving the dog, on more than one occasion, subjective point-of-view shots. Notably, Caesar supports her switching places with Vijaya without a bark of protest, and, unlike Ashok, he can spot the difference between the two women. These exchanges, and the circulation of fetishised objects like dogs between them, allows us to read these movements as circuits of desire between Vijaya and Shanti, thwarting our expectations of a normative heterosexual closure to most tales about twins. Curiously, this intimate bond between Vijaya and Shanti permits representations of other kinds of transgressions: Ashok's uncle is indisputably cast as a stereotypical homosexual and surfaces as a symptom of the film's nascent homophobia; and Panjaraja, the chief minister, schemes to have his daughter kidnapped to gain political ground, a motive that violates most conventions of paternal affection.

The film galvanises one of the most common signs of love we can find in Indian cinema to stage desire – a song and dance sequence spliced together as a dream sequence from Shanti's point of view. Triggered by Vijaya's visit and finding herself pregnant, Shanti longs to go home, but instead lulls herself to sleep by singing a song. This sequence is set around a pregnancy ritual, and she begins a duet with her husband; however, she soon substitutes him with Vijaya, and the song closes around their embrace. Like the final embrace of the film, here, too, the heterosexual convention of these songs in Indian films is subverted. In the absence of any clear performative declaration of a lesbian identity in the film that may allow for a straightforward reading of a lesbian desire plot, *Police Lock-up* approximates a female buddy film genre that allows and encourages a staging of lesbian fantasies.[45] As a police narrative, the film shadows and masquerades the male action genre to the hilt while surreptitiously displacing conventional expectations and resolutions attending its masculine counterpart.

In sharp contrast to the avenging women genre, where the inept law and order system allows for the avenging plot to unfold with a closure that reintegrates the woman into the social and civic order, *Police Lock-up* and other Vijayshanti films harbour a less antagonistic relationship to the law. Located directly within the law, most prominently played out in *Police Lock-up*, the female protagonist is constantly settling law and order problems produced by corrupt politicians and policemen, a relationship with the state that is unabashedly accommodational. Nevertheless, Vijayshanti films raise some of the most knotty and unresolved problems attending representational struggles around femininity, violence, and the state.

Conclusion

Assertive through the early 1990s, the production of avenging women films in Hindi cinema has since subsided. The small, steady output of films with titles such as *Putlibai* (1999), *Mere Aagosh Me* (2000), *Daku Ramkali/Dacoit Ramkali* (2000), *Basanti* (2000), and *Heerabai* (2000) lingers on, with the trade papers forecasting their success in 'small centres' and 'interiors', a venue that these films have long enjoyed before up-market versions were spotted on the film critics' radar. Instead of being women-centred narratives for the reigning women stars, these small-budget films seem ideally suited for second-rung actresses who have been relegated to dacoit and sex films. The ebb in the cycle of films in the mainstream genre can be attributed to a number of reasons: other genres such as the love story and nationalist dramas resurface; female stars retire or shift to playing minor roles; and the peculiar shift in the popular representations of the female body propelled by the rash of beauty pageants and crowning of several Indian women as Miss World and Miss Universe and so on.[46] These different social and cultural phenomena index changes in the representation of the Indian woman, changes that also normalise the presence of powerful women on screen such as Madhuri Dixit in *Mrityudand/Death Sentence* (Prakash Jha, 1997), Shabana Azmi in *Godmother* (Vinay Shukla, 1999), and Kajol in *Dushman/Enemy* (Tanuja Chandra, 1998) without magnifying sexually violent scenes.

However, the intimate relationship between censorship and the female body on screen that inflects the production and reception of this particular genre in Indian cinema has also faced challenges from offshore productions. While we struggle for the right nomenclature that will describe the transnational financing, multinational cast of actors, and international address of the films, several of the films borrow conventions from Indian and international cinema to successfully push the limits of national cinema. For example, Shekhar Kapur's *Bandit Queen* (1994), produced by the UK's Channel Four, with an Indian crew and post-production work in London, highlights the limits of an 'Indian' film.[47] Yet the film extensively borrows the codes and conventions of the avenging women genre – with one exception: the film eschews the censorship regulations of the Indian state. Its release in India was stymied on several fronts: the Board of Censors recommended a number of cuts; the late Phoolan Devi, a Member of Parliament until her murder in July 2001, lobbied against its release on the grounds that the film did not faithfully represent sections of her life as it proclaimed to do; and feminists were annoyed by its ampli-fied representation of sex and violence.[48] The film was finally released without cuts, and in several cities movie theatres had separate showings for women. Having cir-cumvented censorship regulations during the production process, Kapur's film did not engage with the interruptions that we associate with Indian cinema, such as the interval and song and dance sequences, and in effect unleashed uncut scenes into the film that included elaborate rape sequences and frontal nudity. This disengage-ment from the state confirms the weight of censorship regulations in shaping the narrative parameters of this genre as well as guiding our viewing pleasure. The post facto censorship recommendations may have sounded a death knell for this genre as we recognise it in Indian cinema.[49] As an unhindered and uninhibited manifes-tation of the genre, Kapur's film shores up the limits of available representations of the female body on screen under the watchful eye of the Indian state, limits that are continually challenged and undone by other, similar productions – Meera Nair's *Kama Sutra* (1996) and Deepa Mehta's *Fire* (1996) – that have undone the alchemy of sex and violence by infusing their narratives with a range of desires. All these films point to an impasse in a privileging of the state as a crucial coordinate in feminist imaginings and politics, as well as in policing the narrative contours of film narra-tives, while simultaneously nudging us to acknowledge that our viewing pleasures are predicated equally on the presence of state censorship.

Notes

1. 'Imaging You', *Illustrated Weekly of India,* 29 May–4 June 1993, pp. 24–37. The participants included N. Chandra, Prakash Jha, Javed Akhtar, Meenakshi Seshadri, and Maithili Rao.
2. See Itty Abraham (1998), *The Making of the Indian Atomic Bomb: Science and Secrecy,* London: Zed Books.
3. Firoze Rangoonwala (1993), 'The Age of Violence', *Illustrated Weekly of India*, 4–10 September, pp. 27–9.
4. M. Rahman (1998), 'Women Strike Back', *India Today,* 15 July, pp. 80–2.
5. Maithili Rao (1988), 'Victims in Vigilante Clothing', *Cinema in India*, October–December, pp. 24–6.
6. See Aruna Vasudev's (1978) ground-breaking book *Liberty and Licence in Indian Cinema*, Delhi: Vikas; Kobita Sarkar (1982), *You Can't Please Everyone: Film Censorship, the Inside Story*, Bombay: IBH; CLRI (1982), *The Indian Cinematograph Code*, Hyderabad, AP: Cinematograph Laws Research Institute; C. K. Razdan (ed.) (1975), *Bare Breasts and Bare Bottoms*, Bombay: Jaico.
7. Quoted in Aruna Vasudev, *Liberty and Licence in Indian Cinema*, p. 96.
8. See P. K. Wattal (1958), *Population Problem in India: A Census Study*, Delhi: Minerva Bookshop.

9. This technique is practically non-existent in Hindi cinema, but continues to flourish in regional cinemas.

10. *Sholay*, dir. Ramesh Sippy, with Dharmendra, Amitabh Bachchan, Hema Malini, and Jaya Bhaduri; G. P. Sippy Productions, 1975.

11. Madan Gopal Singh (1983), 'Technique as an Ideological Weapon', in Aruna Vasudev and Phillipe Lenglet (eds), *Indian Cinema Superbazaar*, Delhi: Vikas, pp. 119–25.

12. *Sherni*, dir. Harmesh Malhotra, with Sridevi, Pran, Kader Khan; Ranjeet Productions, 1988.

13. *Ram Teri Ganga Maili*, dir. Raj Kapoor, with Rajeev Kapoor, Mandakini, Raza Muradd, Saeed Jaffrey; Raj Kapoor Productions, 1985.

14. Kumar Shahini (1986), 'Myths for Sale', *Framework*, 30/31, pp. 71–8.

15. Parveen Adams (1988), 'Per Os(cillation)', *Camera Obscura*, May, pp. 7–29.

16. Slavoj Žižek (1989), 'Looking Awry', *October*, 50, pp. 31–55.

17. See Carol J. Clover (1992), *Men, Women, and Chain Saws: Gender in the Modern Horror Film*, Princeton: Princeton University Press; Peter Lehman (1993), ' "Don't blame this on a girl": Female Rape–Revenge Films', in Steven Cohan and Ina Rae Hark (eds), *Screening the Male: Exploring Masculinities in Hollywood Cinema*, New York: Routledge. This explicit resemblance to Hollywood B movies throws up a set of new issues: it draws limits to 'national' styles of cinema, forcing us to consider the exchange and appropriation of cinematic styles across national boundaries. Every 'national' cinema has, of course, to contend with Hollywood hegemony, but if the points of contact between Indian and Hollywood film are the much maligned yet often experimental B films, it raises a host of fascinating questions relating to taste and the distribution networks of B films in the developing world.

18. See Aruna Vasudev, *Liberty and Licence in Indian Cinema*.

19. *Insaaf Ka Tarazu*, dir. B. R. Chopra, with Zeenat Aman, Padmini Kolhapure, Raj Babbar, Deepak Parashar; B. R. Films, 1980.

20. Ashish Rajadhyaksha and Paul Willemen (eds) (1995), *Encyclopaedia of Indian Cinema*, London: BFI, p. 416.

21. For a useful discussion on the public discussion of rape and the women's movement, see Ammu Joseph and Kalpana Sharma (1994), 'Rape: A Campaign Is Born', in Ammu Joseph and Kalpana Sharma (eds), *Whose News?: The Media and Women's Issues*, New Delhi: Sage, pp. 43–50.

22. *Pratighat*, dir. N. Chandra, with Sujata Mehta, Arvind Kumar, Charan Raj, Rohini Hattangady; Usha Kiron Movies, 1987.

23. On the ethnography of television, see Purnima Mankekar (1999), *Screening Culture, Viewing Politics: An Ethnography of Television, Womanhood, and Nation in Postcolonial India*, Durham, NC: Duke University Press. For her discussion on disrobing, see her chapter entitled 'Television Tales, National Narratives, and a Woman's Rage: Multiple Interpretations of Draupadi's "Disrobing" '.

24. *Zakmi Aurat*, dir. Avatar Bhogal, with Dimple Kapadia, 1988.

25. Farhad Malik (1981), 'Fact and Fiction', *Cinema in India*, August, pp. 5–8; Shoma A. Chatterji (1998), 'From Hunterwali to Bandit Queen: Women in Male Masquerade', in *Subject Cinema, Object Women: A Study of the Portrayal of Women in Indian Cinema*, Calcutta: Parumita, pp. 222–59.

26. Other film productions include the Tamil *Serai*, the Telugu *Prema Pasa*, and the Hindi *Khoon Bhari Mang*.

27. Laura Mulvey (1998), 'Visual Pleasure and Narrative Cinema', in Constance Penley (ed.), *Feminism and Film Theory*, New York: Routledge, pp. 57–68.

28. Sigmund Freud (1919), 'Fetishism', in James Strachey (tr. and ed., 1987), *On Sexuality*, New York: Viking Penguin, pp. 345–57.

29. Sigmund Freud (1919), '"A Child is Being Beaten" (A Contribution to the Study of the Origin of Sexual Perversions)', in James Strachey (tr. and ed., 1987), *On Psychopathology*, New York: Viking Penguin, pp. 159–193.

30. Parveen Adams (1998), 'Per Os(cillation)', *Camera Obscura*, 17, pp. 7–30.

31. Laura Mulvey (1981), 'Afterthoughts on "Visual Pleasure and Narrative Cinema" Inspired by King Vidor's *Duel in the Sun* (1946)', in *Visual and Other Pleasures*, Bloomington: Indiana University Press.

32. Linda Williams (1989), *Hard Core: Power, Pleasure, and the 'Frenzy of the Visible'*, Berkeley: University of California Press.

33. Interview with Vijayshanti, *Filmfare*, July 1993.

34. *Police Lock-up*, dir. Kodi Ramakrishnan, with Vijayshanti; Kumar Films, 1992

35. See Jyotika Virdi's essay (1998) on *Sita aur Gita/Sita and Gita*, published in *Visual Anthropology*, 11, pp. 355–72.

36. Horror films on twins similarly do not possess the cushion of a family romance and play on all the horrific aspects of twin identities and the twinning reproductive process itself. The most competent film in this genre is David Cronenberg's *Dead Ringers*, which takes on both Peter Greenaway's avant-garde film *Zed and Two Noughts* and Bette Davis's *Dead Ringer* to render a techno-horror film that borders on incest.

37. Joan Riviere (1986), 'Womanliness as a Masquerade', in Victor Burgin, James Donald, and Cora Kaplan (eds), *Formations of Fantasy*, London: Methuen, p. 35.

38. Mary Ann Doane (1991), 'Film and Masquerade: Theorizing the Female Spectator', in *Femmes Fatales*, New York: Routledge, p. 17.

39. Mary Ann Doane (1991), 'Masquerade Reconsidered: Further Thoughts on the Female Spectator', *Femmes Fatales*, p. 33.

40. John Fletcher (1988), 'Versions of Masquerade', *Screen*, vol. 29, no. 3, pp. 43–70.

41. Claude Lévi-Strauss (1969), *The Elementary Structures of Kinship*, tr. James Harle Bell, John Richard con Sturner, and Rodney Needham, Boston: Beacon. For a pithy elaboration of Lévi-Strauss and Lacan, see Jane Gallop (1982), *The Daughter's Seduction: Feminism and Psychoanalysis*, London: Macmillan.

42. Eve Kosofsky Sedgwick (1985), *Between Men: English Literature and Male Homosocial Desire*, New York: Columbia Unversity Press.

43. Edmund Leach, 'Anthropological Aspects of Language: Animal Classification and Verbal Abuse', in Eric H. Lenneberg (ed.), *New Directions in the Study of Language*, Cambridge: MIT Press, p. 23.

44. Avital Ronell, interview, *Re/Search*, no. 13, San Francisco: Re/Search Publications, p. 127.

45. On lesbian desire, see Lynda Hart (1994), *Fatal Women: Lesbian Sexuality and Mark of Aggression*, Princeton, Princeton University Press. On aggressive women, see Sharon Willis (1997), 'Combative Femininity: *Thelma and Louise* and *Terminator 2*', in *Race and Gender in Contemporary Hollywood Film*, Durham, NC: Duke University Press.

46. See Inderpal Grewal (1999), 'Traveling Barbie: Indian Transnationalities and the Global Consumer', *Positions*, vol. 7, no. 3, Winter.

47. After the release of his film *Elizabeth*, Kapur claimed that his film on a British monarch was structured very much like an Indian popular film. What a fabulous story on the reversal of the East–West opposition!

48. See Shohini Ghosh (1996), 'Deviant Pleasures and Disorderly Women', in Ratna Kapur (ed.), *Feminist Terrains and Legal Domains: Interdisciplinary Essays on Women and Law in India*, New Delhi: Kali for Women; Priyamvada Gopal, 'Of Victims and Vigilantes: the *Bandit Queen* Controversy', *Thamyris*, vol. 4, no. 1, pp. 73–102.

49. See Kamal Haasan's reading of *Bandit Queen* at the Toronto Festival in 1994. He writes: 'Shekar Kapur made the film for Britain's Channel 4. So, he had more freedom than an Indian film-maker. Since nudity and expletives are forbidden by censors, our scenes begin where the scenes in western films end … . The entire outlook is something else, thereby making *Bandit Queen* so different from the same director's *Masoom* and *Mr India*.' Kamal Haasan (1994), 'Our World, Their World', *Sunday Times of India*, 2 October.

3

Masculinity at the Interval in J. P. Dutta's Films

In the middle of Anand Patwardhan's documentary film *Father, Son, and Holy War* (1995), the camera pans from one billboard to another in Mumbai while the voice-over proclaims that commercial Hindi cinema has imperceptibly influenced male behaviour in the public sphere, particularly the crude display of muscle power. I want to freeze one moment when Patwardhan's camera lingers on a hoarding of J. P. Dutta's film *Hathyar/Weapon* (1989) as an emblematic instance of militant masculinity in Hindi commercial cinema. Given its title, Dutta's film lends itself easily to representations of masculine aggressiveness, but we have also learned from the theorisations on masculinity to be more suspicious about a deterministic relationship between aggression and masculinity. Building on Eve Sedgwick's formulation on the inextricable tie between homosocial relationships and homoeroticism, cultural critics argue that aggressive representations of masculinity masks, or even regulates, eroticism in a homosocial universe.[1] In a similar vein, we could argue that Patwardhan's fine layering of the representation and performance of masculinity in the public sphere should include a consideration of desire that may undercut the naturalised continuum from men to violence. However, I did not evoke the pan in Patwardhan's film for this reason, but rather to question its rhetorical move that posits a homogenous terrain of masculinity in commercial films, conflating Dutta's films alongside other, run-of-the-mill narratives.

In sharp contrast, this chapter argues that Dutta's films undercut popular representations of masculinity by strengthening and subtending conventions in Hindi films. The move to discussions of auteurism and representations of masculinity in this chapter clearly shifts the argument from the relationship between censorship regulations and representations of avenging women in the previous chapter to masculine action genres. In equal measure, the shift in focus also opens consideration of the interval as an interruption structuring the narrative movement of these films.

J. P. Dutta belongs to the cohort of film-makers that includes Rahul Rawail, Mukul Anand, Subash Ghai, and Rajkumar Santoshi, Young Turks inspired by Ramesh Sippy's *Sholay* (1975), as well as by Manmohan Desai's star-focused spectacles starring Amitabh Bachchan in the lead. In one way or another, they had all accepted the dominance of the star system and were either exploiting it or curtailing its influence by reworking Hollywood-inspired genre films. Although most of these film-makers did succeed, I would place them within the *Cahiers du cinéma* category of *metteurs en scène*, a term that recognises their well-crafted films, but fails to identify a discernible individual style.[2] J. P. Dutta on the other hand, I argue, not only commands the *mise en scène* of his films, but also stamps his films with his unique signature, exemplifying his status as an auteur. Although such an assertion clearly smacks of a cinephiliac's partiality, this chapter will demonstrate his particular style through close analysis of some of his films. Evoking auteurism may seem like an archaic idea in film studies reeking of cinephilia, but there is no doubt that there is a resurgence of auteur-based critical works: Tom Gunning on Fritz Lang, Judith Mayne on Dorothy Arzner, Lesley Stern on Martin Scorsese, and so on.[3] In each case the writers seem well aware of Roland Barthes's scandalous obituary for the author, but nevertheless see fit to group the study of films under the banner of the director. Undoubtedly they carefully plot thematic continuities, formal preoccupations, and market considerations to support their classification, but ironically, in film production and distribution, the idea of a director as a marketable commodity has been thriving, paying no heed to the critical rumble on his or her death. The director/auteur in Hindi cinema is no exception, emerging from a dense intersection of various signifying chains. For instance, distributors may publicise a film as a director's rather than a star's film; fans notice recurrent thematic and cinematographic styles; and critical reception identifies the director as the central producer of meaning. These different chains of signification mesh in myriad ways to exploit the director's name for profit at the box office, providing the viewers with a peep into product differentiation that works against conceptions of a homogeneous terrain. Dutta's films are primarily publicised as his vehicles, even though he has not been consistently rewarded with box-office success.

Acclaim for Dutta's status as a director with a distinct stamp on his films has been slowly filtering in from both within and outside the industry. Trade reviews of his films, especially after *Batwara/Partition* (1989), identify him with a distinct cinematic style. For instance, *Trade Guide* reviewing *Batwara* praises him: 'Technically marvellous with the typical J. P. touch, which is indisputably the best we have'; on *Yateem*: 'J. P. Dutta – just the mention of this name raises expectations. Hopes multiply tenfold and one eagerly awaits to witness the master touch of the young director.'[4] Cinematographer Peter Pereira sees J. P. Dutta's films as the first elegant employment of the wide-screen format.[5] Critical reviews of his films include Iqbal Masud's congratulatory note in his book *Dream Merchants, Politicians and Partition*: 'A director, who is a class apart, J. P. Dutta is one of those whose works can be enlisted both under art and commercial cinema. He has a peculiar haunted way of presentation which puts his films *Ghulami* (1985), *Yateem* (1989), and *Hathyar* (1989) and his other films in a category by themselves.'[6] Arguing for a 'conglomerate narrative' in *Deep Focus*, one of the magazine's editors, M. K. Raghavendra, places J. P. Dutta 'as the only auteur in popular Hindi cinema'.[7] Additionally, responding to *Sight and Sound*'s annual listing of 'Best Films', *Deep Focus* proposed its own list and remarks how 'a maverick like J. P. Dutta finds his way into a list of ten best Indian films'.[8] Assessing the place of directorial style in Hindi cinema for *Filmfare*, Anil Ranvir Khanna gushes: 'For sheer look and design the films of J. P. Dutta – shot in the great outdoors with the kind of sweep associated with Hollywood masters like William Wyler and John Ford – are incomparable.'[9] After the commercial success of *Border*, Subash Jha describes Dutta's work in the following manner: 'Right from the late 70s, J. P. Dutta has always given us films that have broken the barriers between the classes and masses, besides redefining pop aesthetics and relocating audience perceptions.'[10]

Elements from Dutta's films have reappeared in other Hindi films – Shekhar Kapur's *Bandit Queen* (1994), for example, reuses locales from *Yateem*. Although Vidhu Vinod Chopra's *Parinda* (1989) was released in the same year as Dutta's *Hathyar*, there is enough evidence from studio assistants to suggest that the *mise en scène* in the former's film was inspired by Dutta's film. Most recently, Ram Gopal Varma's *Satya* (1998) quotes at substantial length from *Border* (1997). The protagonist Satya and his girlfriend, Vidya, go to see Dutta's film. During the actual interval in *Border*, the film within the film, Satya is spotted by a man whose face he had slashed earlier in the film, who now rushes off to the police. Hoping to snare Satya as he leaves the theatre, the police cordon off the exits, urging the audience to exit through one door. In a calculated manner, Satya fires his gun, thus causing a stampede and making it possible for him to escape undetected. Although *Satya* uses *Border* as the preferred date film, the scene is a dense quote from Dutta's *Hathyar*, where the protagonist is similarly spotted by a rival gang member. Besides these homages, *Satya* also reminds us of the fire incident at Uphaar theatre in New Delhi during a screening of *Border* where a number of moviegoers died in a stampede. Transforming the fire incident into a gang member's wily getaway plan, the film rewrites several discrete events that occurred around *Border*'s release – music director Gulshan Kumar's assassination, the fire in the movie theatre, and so on. For my purposes here, I want to point out that, unlike the swipes at Spielberg's *Jurassic Park* in *Satya*, these dense quotes from Dutta's films attest to his currency as a director with a distinct style among his peers.

Dutta's career within the industry began as an assistant director to Randhir Kapoor in *Dharam Karam* (1975). He subsequently graduated to direct seven films: *Ghulami/Slavery* (1985), *Yateem/Orphan* (1989), *Hathyar/Weapon* (1989), *Batwara/Partition* (1989), *Kshatriya/Warrior* (1992), *Border* (1997), and *Refugee* (2000). Dutta's own evaluation of the film industry, published in *Trade Guide*, is heavily influenced by the power of the director. He laments:

Anything can click. Comedy can click, action can click. There is no hard and fast rule these days. There are no directors left. There are only money-makers around. Indian cinema is going through a complete degeneration right now and the current-day directors are only helping that degeneration to take place.[11]

In other interviews, Dutta's admiration for Stanley Kubrick and David Lean reveals his partiality for directors who have swum against the tide within what may be described as mainstream cinema or studio dictates.[12]

Each of his films draws on the violence structuring the bonds between men, a thematic concern that obtains in Hollywood genres such as the Western, gangster, and war films and now available in global popular cinema. Although his films draw on thematic and stylistic elements from international genres, Dutta equally appropriates cinematic conventions developed within Hindi cinema, such as the multi-star cast, multiple narrative strands, and song and dance sequences, that result in a nexus of international and local (that is, Hindi) conventions. The conventions of Indian commercial cinema are not consolidated a priori, rather it is an auteur's work that these conventions are more fully accounted for and, at times, even parodied. For instance, Dutta's films gather a posse of well-known stars to produce what the trade papers call 'a multi-starrer film', a ploy that enhances their appeal at the box office, but simultaneously mocks this convention by overloading his film with stars even for minor roles.

This chapter considers Dutta's individual approach within a global system of cinematic styles so as to better grasp his penchant for reworking well-known Hollywood genres such as the Western and gangster films within the rubric of Indian cinematic conventions. Giving shape to these popular masculine genres in which male protagonists repeatedly brush against the law, Dutta's films recast these universal figurations of masculinity to include Indian peculiarities of caste, class, and region while engaging with the rhythm of anticipation and expectations. Simultaneously, his films ingest conventions peculiar to Indian cinema into these global circulating genres and, in effect, force us to consider the place of local cinematic styles when reading films in these genres. Paul Smith's work on Clint Eastwood's career in Sergio Leone's films shows how junior or forgotten branches of a genre can often mobilise change in a fossilised genre, a reminder that guides my reading of Dutta's films as a riposte to Hollywood.[13] At the same time, unlike the 'conglomerate' or 'disaggregate' descriptions of Indian commercial cinema, we can recognise the different ways in which Dutta's films adopt the structuring of genre films to streamline the multi-plot narrative of Indian films.

How does Dutta transform a ninety-minute Hollywood film into a two-and-a-half-hour Hindi screening? Among all the conventions and codes in Hindi cinema with which Dutta engages, and at times subverts, his location of the interval emerges as the most important marker in his films foregrounding the different ways in which they accommodate global and local conventions. By noting the location of the interval in Dutta's films, we fully comprehend his interventions that engage with both local and global conventions of reading films.

To effectively plot the moves of a protracted Hindi film that interweaves both local and global conventions, certain propositions offered by narratology provide reading strategies that fully address temporality in a narrative.[14] Since the location of the interval is crucial to my reading, I offer a linear unravelling of both *Ghulami* and *Batwara*, films that rewrite the Western. In contrast, my reading of *Hathyar* departs from a minute segmental reading and instead meditates on the recurrent motif of the train in Dutta's films, allowing us to read the different genre alignments in this film. These readings refer to other of Dutta's films – *Ghulami, Yateem, Kshatriya,* and *Border* – but will not dwell on the peculiarities of their narrative structure, even though they may exemplify the visual skills of this director. One of the reasons for their marginal status here is because these films tend to absorb the interval mechanically to narrate the male protagonist's distance from both psychic law and social authority in the second half, a choice that, to be honest, simply bifurcates the narrative with little innovation. This chapter is equally concerned with Dutta's forays into both Hollywood and Indian commercial conventions, as well as the ways in which the interval directs the flow of desire and weight of the law. Together, these shape the articulation of masculinity that underpins these genres.[15]

The Interval

Among the various reading strategies we customarily resort to, the opening segments of films have a place of honour because they allegedly compress certain critical features that successively unfold in a work.[16] Even as there has been a move towards a less systematic unravelling of the whole film, a cursory perusal of film journals will bear testimony to their efficacy as a methodological tool for analysing Hollywood films.[17] The most persuasive defence of this line of enquiry obtains in Thierry Kuntzel's classic essay 'Film Work, 2', which exhaustively untangles the credit and opening sequences of Ernest B. Schoedsack and Irving Pichel's *The Most Dangerous Game* (1932), where a structuring of repetition and difference are set in motion.[18] Picking up this studio product, Kuntzel proposes:

> the analysis will deal with the *beginning* – the credits and opening sequence – considered as endowed with a certain structural autonomy (the sequence) and as a privileged link in the chain that constitutes the film: a segment where the entire film may be read, *differently*. [p. 1]

Stephen Heath's masterful reading of *Touch of Evil* (1958) extends both Kuntzel's reading of the opening sequences and Roland Barthes's meticulous reading of

Balzac's novella *Sarrasine* by suggesting that an opening could well extend halfway into Welles's film before the play on repetition and difference commences.[19]

In contrast, Richard Neupert's book *The End* challenges this dominant reading strategy by arguing that closing moments of films not only remain central to our retroactive comprehension of the narrative, but also shape our pleasures of *closures* and *ends*.[20] Isolating the different discursive strategies employed by films, Neupert suggests that these ultimate moments are decisive in the ways in which we understand closure in genre films and, at the same time, signal their difference from avant-garde and experimental films, where endings are usually more open-ended. Neupert is suggesting that, just like opening segments, film endings equally condense some of our expectations from the narrative that are mobilised earlier and hence are good indicators of genre structuring.

We can transport these reading strategies to Indian commercial films, where opening segments initiate a structuring repetition and difference on the one hand, while closing sequences suggest Utopian possibilities that lie outside the film's signifying system. Yet they do not take into account all the various structures of narrative expectation, development, and closure that coalesce around a narrative device unique to Indian commercial cinema – the interval. Signalled either by an intertitle declaring 'Intermission' or by simply having the words run across the last frozen shot, Indian films come to a decisive halt for ten minutes. A vivid reference to this momentary arrest in the narrative surfaces in Ram Gopal Varma's *Rangeela/Colourful* (1995): Muna, the movie-ticket tout protagonist, assures his anxious date who desperately wants to reach the theatre on time that films are stacked with songs before the interval, songs that she can always see on Zee TV, thus implying that the story qua story only begins after the interval.

According to Theodore Baskaran, a historian of Tamil cinema, intervals have existed since the early 1930s, when the feature film as a genre took root.[21] Arising, in part, from the constraints of working with a single projector in the early years of film exhibition, the projectionist would stop the film more than once, in effect producing two or three intervals. Besides the whims of the projectionist, he notes that the films themselves referred overtly to this break in the narrative: in *Apoorva Sagodrigal/Strange Friends* (1949), a song and dance sequence set in a garden ends with the word 'Edivali' ('Interval' in Tamil) strung together by flowers dropping from the trees; and in *Velaikkari/Servant* (1949), Mani, one of the protagonists, devises a plan that, he gestures, will take place later – after the interval. Baskaran speculates that intervals probably persisted in order to pace the narrative, which could be laden with at least a dozen songs, a feature that he thinks has retained this cinema in a primitive stage of film-making reliant on attractions.

Castigating the intermission for impeding the growth of Indian film narrative, Baskaran implicitly refers to classical Hollywood narrative, whereas I am more interested in the constancy of the interval that points to its indispensability to both film-makers and viewers. Moreover, research on early cinema by Tom Gunning and Miriam Hansen throws a cautionary net over the natural place of classical Hollywood narrative in our viewing histories, as well as our speculations on spectatorship.[22] By evoking early cinema, their work demonstrates that myriad ways of viewing films were available before the move towards narrative cinema in the studio era, where we witness a propensity for seamless editing. According to Gunning, early cinema or pre-classical cinema frequently relied on sequences of attractions to stimulate interest in its audience; actors often directly addressed the audience, thus breaking the two-dimensionality of film screen images. Regulated and suppressed by the move towards classical narrative, Gunning suggests that we may catch glimpses of this 'cinema of attractions' in underground and avant-garde films that are, at times, in direct opposition to Hollywood codes and conventions. By calling attention to a range of exhibition and production practices in pre-classical cinema, historians have helped circumscribe classical Hollywood as one among many cinemas, a move that has far-reaching implications, beyond the confines of American cinema for film theory's speculations on spectatorship. Their work has helped us see how certain assumptions of the ideal spectator in perfect viewing conditions are specific to Hollywood and has persuaded us to temper the use of this model as the desired template for the study of non-Hollywood cinemas.

Although the interval is a focal point of making meaning in Indian cinema, there is no doubt that a number of other non-Hollywood cinemas also resort to this break for various reasons. For instance, the interval figures as a crucial ingredient of the narrative alchemy in Sri Lankan commercial cinema. Laleen Jaymanne quotes B. A. W. Jaymanne, who offers the following structure of the formula film:

> the duration of the film has to be two and a half hours. One hour of this had to be given to scenes with dialogue, half an hour to songs (about ten songs), another half-hour to silent background scene, with an interval of fifteen minutes.[23]

There is additional evidence from Dimitris Eleftheriotis and Geoffrey Nowell-Smith on film-going experiences in both Greece and Italy, where intervals are habitually included.[24] In India, this break in film viewing extends to all imported films as well: the projectionist arbitrarily stops at the end of a certain number of reels (twelve in most cases), allowing members of the audience to discuss the film or buy snacks, activities that enhance the relationship between films and adjacent consumer economies, even at the cost of breaking the spell of the narrative. Additionally, the main feature commences after a series of shorts that include film and slide advertisements, trailers of coming attractions, and occasionally documentary films. Although these breaks may be contrary to the norm of film-viewing habits moulded and dictated by Hollywood, they do beg us to consider the dominance of continuity in our analysis of film texts. Discussing the concept of the 'flow' in television programmes, Mimi White similarly argues that the commercial breaks frequenting network programmes are not entirely independent of the main programmes themselves; they also upset notions of continuity that are exclusively the purview of commercial cinemas and cannot be simply be imported into television studies.[25] There is no doubt that the interval resembles the four to five breaks that structure American television programmes – the cliffhangers and pauses in narrative – and have etched their influence on our video-watching habits as well.[26]

The interval in Indian cinema is an antecedent to both American television programming and video watching, even if in more recent years some film-makers have calibrated the pacing of the interval in the manner of television. As if to challenge Varma's protagonist in *Rangeela*, S. Shankar's Tamil films *Gentleman* (1993), *Indian* (1996), and *Jeans* (1998) use the interval to construct a distinctly separate storyline whose connections to the first half are only established at the end. The interval in these films functions as a partitioning device that breaks the narrative into two distinct sections; the second half relies on an Oedipal narrative that explains the peculiar actions of the protagonist. More recently, Rakesh Roshan's *Kaho Na Pyar Hae/Tell Me You Love Me* (2000) exploits the interval to build a double role for his star son's Hrithik Roshan's first film. In short, these films insist that, if you miss the first half, you have missed the entire story. By contrast, in Ramesh Sippy's *magnum opus*, *Sholay*, the interval provides closure to one of the enigmas of the film: why the elderly *thakur* can no longer provide safety for his subjects from dacoit invasions. The film stops after the *thakur* explains his predicament to the two bounty hunters through a flashback and walks away from the village square, towards his home on the hill. The film zooms out from the word 'Intermission', which runs across the frame, and holds it for a few seconds to the accompaniment of music reaching a crescendo. The interval in *Sholay* bolsters a narrative firmly structured around a bracketing device of arriving and departing trains by revealing one of the riddles of the narrative: why a police officer needs two hoodlums to settle scores for him.

There is no doubt that the location of the interval is crucial to Indian film-makers as an indispensable device to organise the narrative structure. For instance, when asked, 'Do you write a screenplay, like a play, in three acts?' scriptwriter Salim Khan responds:

> I need a simple, nice plot in which I must have a definite beginning, a middle, and a crucial end. The end must be clear in my mind and then I start working on the subplots and the characters. I go on developing material, then I arrange it till the interval point, and then further the progress of the story.[27]

Sagar Sarhadi, another scriptwriter, answers similarly: 'No. Normally I have two. There are two dramatic movements – the interval and the end. The screenplay is written to heighten these dramatic movements' [p. 158].[28]

The nomenclature of this break in the narrative recalls Dziga Vertov's theorisation of montage in *Manifesto WE* launched in 1919.[29] Elegantly synthesising 'Theory of Intervals', Annette Michelson explains how 'Vertov takes into account relations of movements within the frame of each piece, relations of light and shade, and relations of speeds of recording.'[30] Vertov's radical employment of the disjunction between two shots undergoes transformation in Indian films where thematic breaks in the narrative supersede the formal differences between the two parts, thus assuaging the shock effects associated with the cinematic cut.

Far from being an arbitrary break in the narrative instituted at the time of projection, the interval lies at the bedrock of our comprehension of the structuring of narrative expectation, development, and closure in Indian cinemas, at times exceeding the intentions of the film-makers whose rational choice of the interval may be one among several ways to read the film. If we gloss over the particular location of the interval in Indian cinema, we do run the risk of assuming, as is all too often done, that Indian films are too long and unwieldy. In a round-table discussion entitled 'Towards a National Cinema', Satish Bahadur complains that the plot construction in most commercial films (he calls them entertainment films) is composed of so many diverse elements that this 'mixing of objectives [between serious and entertainment films] doesn't work'.[31] This complaint has reached clichéd proportions due to the lack of attention to discursive conditions within the industry, where evaluation of a film includes the structuring of the interval. The trade papers, on the other hand, reveal how the relationship between the first and second halves remains an integral part of film review. As an obvious code, the interval deserves an intimate defamiliarising of its functions so as to come to terms with the place of ideology in popular cinema.

Unlike an arbitrary break at a halfway point, Indian films often use the intermission as a definitive break linking it to the opening and closing segments. This distinct punctuation not only emerges as a unique marker of 'Indian' cinematic style, but also locates the place of innovation and authorial style. Reconsidered in these terms, the interval stands out as an obvious strategy to pace the narrative and, instead of rationalising it as a moment of relief from the tedium of a long film, this unique form of cinematic punctuation is the cornerstone of inventiveness in Indian cinema, a structuring device that inflects our reading of this cinema. Since it falls in between two moments in a film, I suggest that we can explore the ways in which it steals the closing strategies usually anticipated later in the film and, at the same time, permits narrative strands to bloom in the second half. Rearranging narrative expectations instructs us to reconsider the charge of derivativeness aimed at Indian commercial cinema, a charge that overlooks the different ways in which a film accommodates Hollywood genre features within the constellation of interruptions. Alternatively, the 'interval' seems to have seeped into films produced outside India: Stanley Kubrick's *Full Metal Jacket* (1987), Quentin Tarantino's *Pulp Fiction* (1994), Wong Kar-Wai's *Chunking Express* (1994), Milcho Manchevski's *Before the Rain* (1994), Alejandro Gonzalez Inarritu's *Amores Perros/Love's a Bitch* (2001), Marzeih Meshkini's *Roozi Khe Zan Shodam/The Day I Became a Woman* (2001), and Jeremy Podeswa's *Five Senses* (2000) appear to have hijacked the interval to heighten their narratives of disjunctions and dispersal.

Although the interval belongs to the realm of resistant practices that certain national cinemas have to adopt when faced with Hollywood dominance, a word of caution may be useful on the extent of its radicalness. In India, commercial cinema particularly is not shy of aggressively deploying every tactic to snare its spectators as consumers, and this may be evident not just in the *mise en scène*, on which I have written elsewhere.[32] An array of non-stop entertainment, including song and dance sequences, comes at us with none of the pauses that one usually associates with commercial cinema. Frequently, the first fade-out is the interval that halts the narrative, allowing the viewer to break out of the spell that has been cast for the past eighty to ninety minutes, a halt that encourages us to see how Indian commercial cinema solicits its viewer in multiple ways, consumerism being one among many. Each film stages the battle between these different addresses to complicate the outcome in the hope of increasing the equation between pleasure and profit.

Dutta's films have a paradoxical relationship to the interval. Repeatedly, his films gloss over the interval by resorting to an intertitle frame instead of the common practice of a flourish across the last frame. In my interviews with him, Dutta was reluctant to accord any significant weight to the interval and implied, as he did in another interview, 'I like full attention for my films.' Nevertheless, a close textual analysis of his films suggests that the interval weighs in as a crucial punctuation in the narrative structure and shifts the terms of expectation in such a manner as to strengthen his riposte to Hollywood genres such as Western, gangster, and war films. Bearing in mind that the opening and closing sequences are indispensable to Dutta's films, the interval emerges through a double movement. First, it recalls the overarching bracketing devices in his films, yet punctures the narrative flow in ways that remind us that the particular logic of action in his films amalgamate both Hollywood and Indian cinematic conventions. Secondly, as a narrative juncture in the masculine genres, the interval allows us to read how the films modulate a conventional feature of these genres – the relationship between desire and law of the male protagonists. Arguably, by damming the flow of the narrative, the interval effects both primary and secondary identification for the spectator as conceived in psychoanalytical film theory. The pause bursts the hermetic world of the narrative and reminds the spectator of the workings of the cinematic apparatus; a secondary identification leads the spectator to the homosocial world of Dutta's films where the plight of the male protagonist is carefully staged to suggest that the circuits of law and desire are less than satisfactorily mapped for the male subject. However, recent work on masculinity in queer theory cautions us that the travails of male protagonists soliciting a masculinisation of the spectator are far from being settled in film theory.[33]

Whereas the second half of Dutta's films allow us to plot his overt engagements with Hollywood genres, the connections between the first and second half of his films – the entire viewing experience – allow us to consider the status of the spectator in Hindi commercial cinema. The bifurcated narrative initiated by the interval hints at the ways in which commercial cinema accounts for our viewing pleasures by relying on our utter familiarity with the structuring of repetition and difference, predicated on our film-going experience. Genre films exploit this paradox: the more extensive our film-going experience, the greater the pleasure in recognising familiar themes and the greater the demand for innovation. In short, genre films assume that we are already seasoned film-goers.

If this is true, a reading of the first half of Indian popular films suggests that its protracted narrative, which functions as a primary condition for every film, assumes that the intended viewer has had no prior film-going experience. The sequences in the first half extensively explain and offer rationales for various moves in the narrative and, in effect, guide us towards the first principles of watching a film. The pedagogical implications of the first half coincide with the interests of the post-colonial Indian state, where films are still seen as an important vehicle of modernisation, especially in their ability to construct national taste. Conversely, the second half assumes our familiarity with visual and narrative clues generated by global and local cinemas, which then permits the film to make certain leaps in the conventions of verisimilitude particular to each genre. This dyadic or bifurcated address of Indian commercial cinema smooths the different histories of viewing experience in its imagined constituency, but does not completely assuage its megalomaniac desire to touch everybody. Alternatively, these twin attempts to solicit viewers infuse new ways of thinking about narrative structure and its attendant pleasure in commercial films and simultaneously impress upon us that a national audience always already exists at the interstices of local and global cinematic practices.

Dutta's Westerns

Since the 1970s, Indian film-makers have been drawn to revisionist Westerns, particularly Sergio Leone's spaghetti Westerns, Japanese Samurai films, and Sam Peckinpah's 'blood ballets' such as *The Wild Bunch* (1969), films that have had a profound impact with their experiments with frontier landscapes, cinematic representation of violence, and articulation of masculinity. For instance, *Khote Sikkey/Bad Penny* (1974), *Kala Sona/Black Gold* (1975), *Wanted* (1983), and *Sholay* pay extensive homage to Leone by borrowing from the soundtrack and *mise en scène* of his films, as well as the rapid zoom-ins and swish pans.[34] Most recently, Rajkumar Santoshi's *China Gate* (1999) returns to the structure of Akira Kurosawa's *Shichi-nin no Samurai/Seven Samurai* (1954) to explore the plight of a group of retired army officers in the rural frontiers. At times, by narrating social antagonisms set in frontier landscapes, these films recall early sub-genres such as frontier dramas, which precede the Western as well the Japanese samurai film.[35] More often than not, the Indian version retains iconographic details from revisionist Western fused with the indigenous '*daku*' or dacoit films whose point of view is usually the landed upper caste. In the final version, the narrative criminalises the dacoit succeeding in perpetrating his crimes from a long history of feudal oppression. Although these films paradoxically spurred the growth of the dacoit as star–villain, the narrative revives the landlord's point of view, drawing these films closer to Ford's early Westerns, which sympathised with white settlers who ostensibly had to defend themselves against savage Indians.[36] This peculiar rehabilitation of Ford's Westerns dressed up as the upper caste's point of view cautions us from overemphasising their revisionist impulse or classifying them within the 'subaltern genre', a term coined by Paul Smith for Leone's films. Rather, their narrative of accommodation blunts the radical politics of the revisionist Western, framing these films within Madhava Prasad's formulation of Indian popular films as 'super genre' that periodically annexes reformist tendencies.[37] In other words, by poaching from the classic Hollywood Western, the revisionist, and the '*daku*' film, these films manage to accommodate several points of view.

The most obvious and successful synthesis of Western and '*daku*' films is Ramesh Sippy's *Sholay/Flames*, where the narrative rests on an antagonistic relationship between the *thakur* – an upper-caste landlord – who once served as a conscientious police officer, and the villainous outlaw Gabbar Singh. The *thakur* hires two ex-convicts as bounty hunters to capture Gabbar Singh. The film's superb cinematography, astute handling of several narrative strands, impeccable song and dance sequences, and an extremely well-developed antagonistic plot at the centre of the narrative deservedly crown it as a classic.[38] Notwithstanding its canonical status, I want to propose that by privileging the *thakur*'s point of view, the film reinforces the upper caste and class's natural right to govern. Cinematically, this is conveyed when we first enter the village: a high-angle shot captures an idyllic picture of the quotidian routine of the village. We see ironsmiths hammering, cotton weavers beating bales of cotton, and women washing and drawing water. Steadily, this high-angle shot is associated from the point of the *thakur*'s residence up on the hill (a point of view that is at one moment even occupied by his widowed daughter-in-law in the Holi dance sequence). The narrative rests on re-establishing the idyllic order of the village that has been disturbed by Gabbar Singh's invasions. However, this order is established without even explaining how the villain became an outlaw, a lack that asserts that his propensity for violence arises from intrinsic evil.

Dutta's films *Ghulami* and *Batwara* challenge *Sholay*'s premise by inverting the conditions structuring the *'daku'* or dacoit genres found in Hindi cinema, an inversion that rehabilitates an engagement with revisionist Westerns. *Ghulami* takes on caste antagonisms in remote regions of Rajasthan, where lower-caste sharecroppers fight upper-caste dominance. Ranjit Singh Choudhury leads the farmers' rebellion. The film ends with the rebels successfully burning the *thakur*'s account books, which meticulously recorded every loan that held generations of lower-caste sharecroppers in subjugation. As a straightforward tale of rebellion, the film focuses on the alliances forged by the rebellious Ranjit Singh with his comrades Gopi and Jawar, who are similarly humiliated by the upper-caste *thakurs*. *Ghulami*'s reception in Rajasthan ignited caste riots, provoked especially by the scene in which the *thakur* orders Ranjit's mother to place her shoes on her head.[39] Dutta confirms that the *thakurs* tried to stop its projection in a theatre in Jodhpur.[40] While these reception conditions suggest how a narrative of caste/class antagonisms can have volatile consequences, they also indicate how far this film diverges from *Sholay*'s pro-*thakur* narrative. Nevertheless, the figuration of masculinity in Dutta's film falls within a conventional rubric of a masculine universe where we witness homosocial bonds overtaking caste and class rebellion up to a certain point, eventually superseded by heterosexual romance.

Men and Action in *Ghulami*

Unpacking the rebellion within a homosocial universe, *Ghulami* relies on several formal and narrative strategies to stave off desire between men, an angle more elaborately developed in *Batwara*. The film opens and closes with a voice-over that prepares the viewer for the narrative of caste rebellion led by Ranjit Singh, which is temporally located in the transition from colonialism to independence in Rajasthan. The film closes with the promise of a future free from caste oppression. This bracketing device emerges in Dutta's films as a means to hold on to a singular linear narrative, which I offer as a particular symptom of a heterosexual masculine narrative in genre films. Although not wanting to labour its linearity and its links to a tightly ordered proairetic system, the convention of a calling or mission that sets a masculine narrative into action is often a powerful foil held up against the more fraught relationship between law and desire.

In the first half of *Ghulami*, the film depicts the humiliations from the protagonist Ranjit Singh's point of view, beginning as a teenager in a village school in colonial India. Rather than a simple story of caste and class antagonisms, the film

J. P. Dutta directing Smita Patil and Reena Roy in *Ghulami* (courtesy of J. P. Dutta)

dwells on Ranjit's friendship with Sumitra, the landlord's daughter. Among several scenes of discrimination between the lower and upper castes, one crucial montage conveys the difference between the castes through juxtaposition: Himmat Singh (Sumitra's future husband) guillotines a calf's head as a ritual sacrifice, and the film cuts to the village where the schoolmaster chokes to death after drinking poisoned water. We then quickly cut to a pond where a number of village cattle have succumbed. Using a cow as a graphic match, the film conveys the difference between upper-class ritual excess and lower-class subsistence. Ranjit Singh leads the villagers to the *thakur*'s well. Socially prohibited from using the upper-caste well, the procession of farmers is scared off by the nephews who shoot into the crowd. Arming himself, Ranjit Singh faces the *thakur*'s gang. He fortuitously receives support from a travelling soldier, Jawar, who hears the gunshots. This arbitrary inclusion of a new character into the close village community opens the antagonisms between the farmers led by Ranjit Singh and the landed *thakurs*. Within the film's diegesis, the space beyond its parameters has always signalled change: Ranjit leaves the village as a teenager to returned armed with education and a copy of Gorky's *The Mother* to upset the trenchant caste and class oppression of his community; trains cut through the landscape indicating change and associated with Moira's long wait for Ranjit; and finally, when Ranjit negotiates with the *thakurs* not to evict the schoolteacher Sukiya, he rides into the scene to the accompaniment of the theme music from David Lean's *Lawrence of Arabia*, an audio detail that allows us to consider Lean's films as a revisionist Western or, better still, a frontier genre. Together, these details frame the diegetic universe in ways that alert us that a resolution of caste and class antagonisms cannot be obtained without breaking out of the hermetic universe of the village and calling on the nation state.

The film does not shy away from detailing the *thakurs'* authority over the local police. In a trumped-up charge, Ranjit is imprisoned for his alleged ties with the dacoit Suraj Bhan Singh. Scenes of torture heighten the tale of oppression. When he finally escapes from the prison hospital into the open desert, he joins Gopi, a the local police officer from a lower caste, who has also had a run-in with both the police and the *thakurs*. His crime was to appropriate the upper-caste custom of the bride-groom riding on a horse through the village. In this moment of complete distance from the law and order economy of the village, the film stops for an interval at the moment when police paste 'Wanted' posters of Ranjit and Gopi for five thousand rupees all over the village. Enumerating the oppression suffered by the lower caste, the first half provides a rationale for Ranjit and Gopi's emergence as outlaws (*bhagi*) and not dacoits (*daku*), a conceptual difference ordered by the colonial state that criminalises the dacoit. The narrative mode employed in the first half is recognisably within the neo-realist conventions found in Hindi cinema of the 1960s and 1970s, a cinematic style that attempted to minimise the spatial disruptions mobilised by song and dance sequences.

After the interval, the film orchestrates a grafting between a realist narrative of caste oppression in Indian 'middle cinema' and a melodramatic mode more typical of the revisionist Westerns. It resumes with a romantic scene between Jawar and the schoolteacher's daughter Tulsi, set in a space distant from the village community. Beginning with Jawar, the narrative intimates his central role in the second half, especially as a supplier of arms to Ranjit and Gopi, without which their incursions against the landed castes would be impossible. Elaborating on Jawar's role touches on another convention heightened in Dutta's work – the multi-starrer film, where the second half acknowledges the influence of the movie-star economy at the box office, as well as its ability to exert a separate yet intersecting chain of signifiers in our reading of films. Jawar's inclusion and dominance in the second half of the film are indispensable to its narrative logic, which has fully exhausted the various options available within the current system of redress and justice, and prompts us to imagine an option from without. However, the weight of the opening voice-over in Dutta's films allows Ranjit to re-enter the narrative: Gopi and Ranjit rescue Jawar from police imprisonment, and they band together to overthrow both upper-caste and upper-class dominance. As the three men ally themselves in the second half, their homosocial desire is regulated not only by their incursions against the police and the landlords, but also by women.

Iconographic details resembling the Western surface in the second half when Jawar herds his cattle after they have been scattered by the *thakur*'s men. The high-

Herding cattle: Western genre imagery
from *Ghulami*

angle shot of fleeing cattle is reminiscent of Hollywood Westerns where poaching another man's herd often starts a shoot-out. The second half also mobilises a familiar trope of the Western – the indispensability of women.[41] Although Jawar provides guns and ammunition for Ranjit and Gopi, it is only after Tulsi dies while running away from sexually aggressive *thakur* men that he fully throws his lot in with them. Not only does Tulsi augment the proprietorial battles of the lower-caste men that have so far focused exclusively on land ownership and the indignities of daily life, but also her death introduces a revenge strand that ends with Jawar killing the *thakur*'s nephews. In the first half, by contrast, women have a marginal role in the narrative, and in general economic and political interests take precedence over romantic coupling. For example, Ranjit and Sumitra's friendship is always interrupted by caste difference, and once, when there is a romantic possibility in a night scene at the temple, bandits corner them. On the other hand, Ranjit and Moira's relationship acquires the durability of a marriage from the very beginning and is not threatened by either caste or class rebellion.

Besides engaging the revisionist Western, the interval differentiates the diverse ways in which the film regulates homoeroticism in this homosocial network. In the first half, positing caste antagonisms as the primary source of male bonding, the film chooses a narrative of overcoming humiliation rather than articulating desire between men. As the interval allows a definitive break with the existing social system by casting off the men into the desert, the second half uses Tulsi to stymie the possibility of homosocial desire among Ranjit, Gopi, and Jawar. For instance, on the eve of Jawar's wedding, the three men celebrate with alcohol and sing 'Pi le, pi le/'Drink up', a scene that restricts homoeroticism through reminders of the heterosexual union elsewhere in the form of insertions of scenes with Tulsi dancing. Employing three men as protagonists, in addition, obstructs binary coupling, yet reminds us of René Girard's classic formulation that the preferred structuring of desire is always triangular.[42] Unlike *Sholay*, *Ghulami* engages pugnacious caste politics within the framework of the revisionist Western after the interval while retaining conventions of social realism in the first half. Dividing the narrative into two different cinematic styles, *Ghulami* allows us to plot the overlaps between the social realism perfected in Indian popular cinema and the revisionist Westerns. The interval also punctuates the homosocial narrative by directing it towards the heterosexual paradigm favoured by these genres, thus heightening our understanding of compulsory heterosexuality dominating the revisionist Western that otherwise undercuts many of the presuppositions of the classic Western, including race and class.[43] However, in Dutta's next film, *Batwara*, the interval modulates this formulation for a different end.

Batwara and Masculine Romance

Batwara rewrites *Ghulami* as straightforward narrative of caste and class antagonisms by accounting for desire in a homosocial universe. It also returns to Rajasthan during the transitional period from colonialism to independence to narrate a tale of friendship between Vikram Singh, or Vicky, an upper-caste *thakur*, and Sumer Singh Choudhury, a lower-caste police officer. Political shifts affect land relationships in this region, but Vikram's father and his brother Devan are reluctant to accede to the new democratic order. Attempting to exercise the traditional rule of the *thakurs*, Devan confronts the rebellious farmers who, instead of cowering to his dictates, beat him to death. Vicky avenges his brother's death by killing a number of villagers, including the brother of Jinna (Sumer's girlfriend). This violent act alienates him from both his other brother Rajendra Singh (also called Rajan in the film), a conscientious police officer who sees this as vigilante action, and Sumer, who reads it as caste violence and breaks off his friendship. However, Sumer's alleged closeness to Vicky costs him his job and soon both men are at large, wanted by the police. Rajan's sense of the law is constantly contaminated by his assistant Hanumant Singh, who works to retain the power of the *thakurs*. Rajan's wife, Priya, Vicky's wife, Roop, and Sumer's partner, Jinna, move in and out of this tale of male friendship. Refusing to give in to the police, the two men, now reunited, ride into a hail of bullets at the end of the film.

The first half of the film, right up to the interval, can be partitioned into three narrative strands: the primary conditions, *thakurs* and police, and the farmers' revolt. The film opens with Amitabh Bachchan's voice-over narrating how winds of freedom changed many traditional relationships – those who were most apprehensive about such changes were the powerful and landed who resorted to either despair or anger. Bachchan continues that, for the poor peasant, these winds of change were distant hopes that could finally grant them freedom. What did they want? A piece of land that they could call their own. In the midst of these changes, the voice-over adds, is the undying friendship of *thakur* Vikram Singh and Sumer Singh Choudhury.[44] The voice-over matches a desert landscape where a cart drawn by a lone horse rides towards the camera. As soon as the voice-over ends, Lakhiya, the headman riding the cart, runs into a farmer's caravan. We gather that the farmer is sneaking some of his harvest to the open market instead of handing it over to his feudal chief, Vicky's father, who is variously referred to as the Raja Sahib (king) or the *thakur*. The headman threatens to tell the Raja Sahib, but is bought off by a sack of grain. As the headman rides away, we see a car coming along the desert road. The farmer hides among the sand dunes and spots the young prince, Devan, in the back seat. The voice-over resumes, and we are told that Devan has exercised undue control over his subjects. The films cuts to the palace courtyard, where the car rolls in.

This short opening segment establishes some of the antagonisms that are developed further in the film. We understand the unfair relationship between sharecropper and feudal chief, which is further complicated by a collaborationist relationship between the headman and landlord. Although this economic and caste relationship serves as the backbone of the narrative, their recalcitrance is heightened by contrasting it against cross-caste friendship and conflicting loyalties within the *thakur*'s household. The film prioritises some of these relationships in the opening segment. Instead of juxtaposing these contrasting social relationships, which appear to be harmonious despite the unequal economic and power relationship, the triangular relationship among farmers, headman, and *thakur, and* between Sumer and Vicky, works as the primary conditions against which the film's narrative unfolds. In other words, evoking Sumer and Vicky's friendship on the soundtrack, with matching images of the headman and farmers, suggests the circulation of distinct and separate economies of friendship and caste/class antagonisms that the film will progressively dismantle and finally bring about a disengagement between the concerns of the soundtrack and the images.

In the first half, the film maintains a strict separation between Sumer and Vicky's friendship, the caste and class antagonisms that were more fully attended to in *Ghulami*. Nowhere is the independence of these two narrative strands more apparent than when the film cuts from Devan's petulant comments to his wife about his negligent older brother, to Vicky and Sumer pig-sticking with an entourage of beaters. The film suggests that as long as Vicky is estranged from his family and Sumer from caste consciousness their friendship can survive. The film slowly muddies the distinct narrative strands to shore up some of the tensions attending to this inter-caste friendship. For instance, one afternoon, the farmers arguing over land ownership in the village square inadvertently wake Vicky from his afternoon nap. Vicky throws a fit and is quieted by Sumer. Refusing to call on Vicky's temper, which is a characteristic display of his upper-caste and upper-class position, Sumer complies with *thakur* dominance.

Their friendship does not remain unremarked by the other characters in the film: Jinna rejects Sumer's romantic advances, complaining that he loves the *thakurs*. Similarly, Vicky's brother Devan rashly suggests that Vicky loves Sumer more than his brothers. Vicky slaps Devan for his impudence and is as surprised as his brothers at his own rashness and apologises by hugging them. This outburst may help to explain his violent actions in a future scene that is excessively imbued with a discourse of fraternal vengeance.

Besides the changing land relationships between the *thakurs* and farmers, the police complicate the status of the state in this remote outpost. Vicky's brother Rajan firmly believes in the letter of the law, while his assistant Hanumant Singh seeks to protect the rule of the *thakurs* and uses his power as a police officer to harass the villagers. Sumer, who is lower in the police hierarchy, obeys orders with little resistance. But when Sumer's loyalties to Vicky take precedence over his obligations as an officer of the law, Rajan dismisses him from the force in the second half of the film.

The precipitating events in the first half bring to a head various economic and social tensions. It all begins when Devan commands the villagers to falsify their rights to land ownership in order to subvert land reforms in post-colonial India. The farmers collectively rise against him, chase him through the village lanes, and finally beat him to death. News of Devan's death shatters Vicky, who charges off, dressed in black and armed with a rifle, to avenge his killing. Vicky kills a number of men from the village, including Jinna's brother. The scene ends with a long view of the burning village from Vicky's point of view. The first half closes by showing us reactions to Vicky's actions: at the palace, Rajan protests over Vicky's lawless reaction to Devan's death, a point of view that will estrange him from his father, who approves of Vicky's response. At the village, Sumer finds out about Vicky's violent actions from Jinna and Lakhiya. The film closes with Sumer consoling Jinna, thus reserving the confrontation between the friends for the section after the interval.

The interval in *Batwara* brings to a head a narrative that teeters between homosocial alliance and homoeroticism as a means of articulating a relationship between these two men in a remote region that is undergoing rapid social and economic change. Unlike the obsession with law that inflects *Ghulami* and separates it from desire, *Batwara* relies on intertwining law and desire in a homosocial economy in such a way as to inflect the timing of the interval. Instead of a symmetrical division between inside and outside the law, here we close at a volatile moment that will prospectively affect both Sumer and Vicky's friendship and swing the film towards a masculine melodrama that frequents Hollywood Westerns. The interval ends a number of minor narratives that help both bolster and repress the friendship. For instance, the dynamics between women in the *thakur*'s household are simply brought to an end. Rajan and his wife leave the palace after the interval, but the film does not care to develop this further. Similarly, the other theme – the farmers and their demands for land reform – expires, and we are no longer privy to these transactions. The interval also permits us to examine many intertextual relays between Dutta's films, where we may find a resolution to a number of premature endings: *Batwara* returns to the *mise en scène* of feudal antagonisms in *Ghulami*, but it also anticipates *Kshatriya*, which deals with intra-caste tensions among the upper-caste landed *thakurs*. The interval also reminds us of the opening sequence, and the sections after the break will return exclusively to Sumer and Vicky's friendship.

Dutta's most direct engagement with Westerns commences after the interval, when the film resumes the iconography we associate with Westerns. Vicky rides into the desert to the sound of howling winds on the soundtrack. He stops at a well and is served by the owner, who initially fails to recognise the *thakur*. Soon thereafter, Vicky establishes alliances with Shakti Singh's gang, declaring that hereafter outlaws will rule the region. Sumer is suspended from the police force, but the confrontation with Vicky converts him politically. He mobilises the farmers in the village and consolidates their opposition to the *thakur*'s rule. Tracking Sumer and Vicky's estrangement through alternating sequences, the film hints at other developments – Hanumant Singh's brutal authority as a police officer and his ability to preserve upper-caste dominance by rigging Rajan's transfer to another post. As in the first half, women surface to regulate the homosocial bond, even though it appears to be estranged at this moment. For instance, in the second half, the film employs the song 'Jo me aisa janathi/'If I knew ...' lip-synced by Roop and Jinna as they leave their respective spouses' hideout to emphasise the divergent yet similar paths of rebellion undertaken by the two men. The film describes their tattered friendship through a series of attacks and counterattacks. Vicky's gang kills a number of farmers who are ostensibly smuggling grain across the border; Sumer in response joins forces with Kala Daku – another dacoit gang – and raids the *thakur*'s palace. Vicky, in turn, attacks the village. Unable to endure yet another battle between Vicky and Sumer, Roop intervenes in an armed combat between the two men to reveal various double-crossings and new alliances that have been struck to undermine their friendship – Shakti Singh and Kala have joined forces with Lakhiya to kill Vicky and Sumer, and Hanumant Singh plots to kill Rajan. These revelations jolt the two men out their estrangement and into seeing their future once again as friends battling a common enemy.

The last sequence reiterates their friendship and foregrounds the homosocial desire of the narrative. Surrounded by a cordon of police, the two men ponder how to skewer Hanumant Singh in a manner similar to their hunting of the wild pig seen earlier in the film. As a reassuring gesture, Sumer recalls a childhood moment when they both danced naked in a hailstorm, hardly feeling the impact of the ice pellets,

a memory of an event that, he suggests, will be similar to the rain of police bullets.[45] Not unlike the last scene in *Butch Cassidy and the Sundance Kid* (1969), they ride into a volley of police bullets and proceed to skewer Hanumant Singh. The film closes with a freeze shot of Vicky and Sumer holding hands and, unlike the voice-over in *Ghulami*, we have a song celebrating their friendship on the sound-

Vicky and Sumer ride into a hail of bullets at the conclusion of *Batwara*

track. The dual focus on the separate yet parallel lives of the two friends in the second half and their final death is very much in the convention of the star-crossed love stories circulating in Hindi cinema. Surfacing in a 'Western', it allows us to consider the melodramatic aspects of the genre, which are routinely displaced on to violent action.

Hathyar and Gangster Films

Of all Dutta's films, the trade papers were most critical of *Hathyar/Weapon*. *Trade Guide* berated the film for some of the following reasons: 'Alas, *Hathyar* is everything – everything minus life … J. P. gets a raw deal in fight composer Ram Shetty! To say the fights lack punch would be an understatement! … On the whole, *Hathyar* is a letdown.'[46]

In sharp contrast to the vitriolic reviews of the film and its unsuccessful run at the box office, *Hathyar* has received substantial critical acclaim from cinephiliacs: *Deep Focus* lists the film as one of the best ten Hindi films, and Ajit Duara sees it as Dutta's finest work.[47] Dutta himself believes that *Hathyar* is his best film, but is unable to explain its disaster at the box office; perhaps he should have had a different title, he muses.[48] Notwithstanding the film's box-office failure, *Hathyar* is one of Dutta's best works, where his response to genre classifications is keenest, and visual and thematic concerns are worthy enough to be emulated in *Parinda* and *Satya*. It is not simply his deftness at combining two genres – Western and gangster – that makes this film interesting, rather it is the way it addresses the film's spectator's histories of viewing and foregrounds the cinematic conventions of Indian cinema. Unlike the clear-cut engagements with the Western in both *Ghulami* and *Batwara*, *Hathyar* straddles both gangster and Western genres to expose the limits of each when we face a male protagonist's troubled relationship with the law in contemporary India. Retaining his theme of masculinity on the frontier, Dutta bridges the feudal province of Rajasthan and the underworld of Mumbai (Bombay) through his usual preoccupations with landscapes. The film unravels the protagonist, Avinash (Avi), campaigning against social authority by shuttling him between these two different spaces, imbuing his Oedipal struggles with nostalgia for a world arrested at unchallenged narcissism. The interval organises the grafting of genres as it continues to emphasise the male protagonist's increasing isolation from law and order, a recurring theme in Dutta's films. But *Hathyar*'s critical point, I argue, lies in the ways in which it attempts to tie our cinephilia with these genres.

Opening Segment and Primary Conditions

Hathyar's opening captures its relationship to the Western and the viewer's location vis-à-vis the camera. It opens with a statement disclaiming any resemblance between fictional characters and the extra-cinematic universe, a recurring feature of Dutta's films with the exception of *Border*. The narrative proper begins with a father singing to his young son about a king's son who rides a flying horse and in his long flight around the world solves various problems. The mother enters and gently chides her husband, insisting that her son will never leave home. An uncle arrives with a gift for the young boy – a toy gun. The father, Ajay Singh, reprimands his brother for bringing such violent toys from the city, but his son, Avi, insists on playing with it.

The film cuts from an extreme close-up of the toy trigger to one of a real rifle – a graphic match signals the passage of time – with the credits rolling against the image. After the title card naming the producer, the credits roll against close-up shots of a hand loading a rifle; the film moves to a frontal medium close-up shot of a young man aiming at the camera, and through reverse shot we realise he is aiming at a deer. As he steadies his gun, the film cuts to an extreme close-up shot of his eyes. Cutting to an establishing long shot of a landscape, the camera aggressively zooms in on him and through a series of shot/reverse shots we see the deer again. At this point J. P. Dutta's name scrolls on the screen crediting him for screenplay, story, and direction. The title cards are in the playbill type style associated with the Western.[49] As the credits end, the film cuts to a point-of-view shot of the hunter: the camera and the gun are fused into a single object – both, after all, employ the bull's-eye principle to zone in on their subject. Just as we get ready to shoot the deer, a woman's voice from an off-screen space interrupts the hunt. The deer skips away, and a woman's body moves in to serve as target.

The pre-credit sequence sets the basic narrative conditions. The differing views on guns and pacifism, on urban toys, and father–son Oedipal crisis are fleshed out later. Avi's love for guns and his father's distaste for violence will form one element of the narrative. However, the father's song of a travelling prince on a flying horse takes a macabre turn with Avi constantly bouncing back and forth between different spaces as his restlessness suffuses the Oedipal narrative. The rule of the father is challenged initially by his wife, who typically wants her son close to home. Yet the film trivialises her interventions to make room for an aggressive male narrative. More than any other object, it is the uncle's gift – the gun – that holds the story of destruction in the narrative: it indicates a space outside rural feudal bloodbaths, yet fails to deliver peace to Avi's family. Guns also break down the difference between rural and urban spaces – flaunted as a sign of legitimate authority in the former, but relegated to the underworld in Mumbai.

The credit sequence shifts between Avi the hunter and Avi being pursued by the camera. For a brief moment his hunt is confused with Suman, his child bride. This alternating segment between hunting and romance decisively moves towards the hunt when Avi rushes after the deer right after Suman confesses that she loves him. As the camera tracks Avi hunting from left to right, the film replays the rhythm on an empty landscape, but from right to left, and swerves jerkily to the left to show us a group of men riding together. The film intercuts Avi's chase with another scene: the horsemen and a jeep ride into the village. They shoot into the air and, as women shriek, the scene conveys the tension of a marauding group. Avi's uncle is singled out and dragged behind the jeep through the streets. Cutting to Avi and Suman walking together after their successful hunt, we see from Avi's point of view the men riding out of the village leaving behind his battered uncle.

Dropping his kill, Avi rushes to his uncle's side, who at this moment is being helped by Avi's father. Enraged, Avi insists on avenging the attack on his uncle by Suman's relatives. His father urges him towards pacifism; Avi refuses to take any notice, but finally relents when his mother threatens to kill herself if he chooses a vengeful response. Having appeased Avi, she asks Suman to return home immediately before her father and relatives begin harassing her.

The pre-credit, the credit, and the post-credit segments present the moral economy of the film, which decries violence, and is repeated at the end: the bracketing device reminds us of the futility of violent retaliation. However, the section between the bookend sequences of the film narrates Avi's quick temper, his inclination to settle scores through fights, and his love for guns, all of which are indicated in the graphic match of guns in the opening segment. Just as the camera hunts him down, the rest of the film dwells on Avi's conversion from an angry youth to a mercenary in the Mumbai underworld, or, as the film's title declares, a '*hathyar*' or weapon, who moves between one boss and another.[50]

Train Tracks in Dutta's Films

Hathyar rehearses a number of thematic concerns that recur in Dutta's films, especially the relationship of the male protagonist with the law in a homosocial universe. However, grafting two masculine genres – Western and gangster – throws up a different visual terrain. We have seen how Dutta employs Rajasthan landscapes to locate men in a transitional phase from feudalism to a post-colonial regime in *Ghulami* and *Batwara*. When we subject these films to a close reading of its iconography, we realise that trains also emerge as an important visual motif, rupturing the hermetic universe of homosocial worlds and attenuating the impression of reality in his films. Sightings of trains in Dutta's films confirm Lynne Kirby's argument in her book *Parallel Tracks* that trains were used to indicate progress and modernity in early narrative cinema, supplanting their sensational role in early thrill films.[51]

Trains make a recurrent appearance in Indian films. In Satyajit Ray's art-house productions trains signal modernity: in *Pather Panchali/Song of the Road* (1955), we initially hear trains on the soundtrack and are subsequently rewarded with a stunning scene of Durga and Apu waiting among reeds for the passing train; in *Nayak/The Hero* (1966), a 24-hour train journey between Calcutta and Delhi unfolds. Popular cinema has extensively used trains to amplify movement within the film. *Sholay* opens with a top shot of an arriving train, emphasising Ramnagar's remote location from legitimate law; *Virasaat*, too, uses trains to accentuate distance from the urban world. An armed train carrying freshly minted currency is hijacked in *Thiruda Thiruda/Thief! Thief!* (1993). In a modern interpretation of the *Mahabharata*, a young mother abandons her newly born infant on a moving train in *Thalapathy* (1991). Elaborately choreographed fight sequences between train coaches and on the top of moving trains add to the spectacle in *Sholay*; at the end of *Yaadon ki Bharat/A Procession of Memories* (1973), railway tracks snare the villain, making him a deadly target for the oncoming train. Ghostly stations haunt Avtar Kaul's tightly wrought *27 Down* (1973). In a homage to 1970s-style disaster films, Ravi Chopra's *Burning Train* (1980) exploits the dangers of train travel. The railway station appears as the ideal setting for various social antagonisms in *The Railway Platform* (1955), and later in a more calculated fashion in *Coolie/Porter* (1983). Films on the partition of 1947 portray trains carrying corpses to convey the horrors of the events on the border between the newly independent countries. Perhaps their most endearing presence on the Indian screen occurs in the song and dance sequences: in *Aradhana* (1969), Shakti Samant choreographed the number 'Mere sapno ki rani/ The queen of my dreams' between a moving train and a jeep; in *Jab Pyar Kisise Hota Hai/When You Fall in Love* (1961), its title song and dance are set in a moving train; Dharmendra eulogises the train in *Dost/Friend* (1974) in the song 'Ghadi bula rahi hai'/'The train beckons me'; and a train provides the ideal vehicle for philosophising in the song 'Zindagi ki safar me'/'In life's journey'. In all these instances, railway tracks and moving trains emerge as indelible parts of the post-colonial fabric where movement through landscape promises change and progress.[52]

In Dutta's films, trains are not an accidental choice in the *mise en scène*, but are carefully planted to stimulate movement and heighten spectacle. Dutta admits to his long affair between film-making and trains by flatly stating: 'I love trains.'[53] Both *Ghulami* and *Batwara* employ moving trains in the *mise en scène* to suggest that the feudal rural areas are not self-contained universes that lie outside the post-colonial state; rather, they display a tenuous relationship with the state, whose promises of democracy and freedom for all its citizens are far from complete. *Ghulami* is vehement in maintaining that trains deliver change in the static hierarchical world: Ranjit escapes the caste-driven world by boarding a train and returns years later by train. The film suggests that, as long as trains cut across the landscape, the male protagonist believes in negotiating a justice within the existing regime of authority. It is after the interval, when both Ranjit and Gopi are wanted by the police, that the train almost exits from the *mise en scène*, appearing only once in Moira's reverie. The absence of the train moves the narrative towards a more revolutionary resolution of antagonisms.

There is no doubt that trains are closely associated with female characters in Dutta's films, suggesting a link between civilising and feminising impulses that prototypically recurs in Westerns. In *Batwara*, where, as I have suggested, the friendship between two men bears an ambivalent relationship to the official histories of frontier dramas, the association between civilisation, trains, and women is asserted when the two women spot each other in a train compartment on their way out of the wilderness. In *Kshatriya*, Dutta uses London tube trains and trains in Rajasthan to convey the proximity of industrial modes of living to the feudal outpost where hoary traditions are evoked in the name of masculine honour. In *Yateem*, Gowri watches a train curving through the landscape after bidding goodbye to her boyfriend, Krishna. Similarly, in *Border*, Bhario Singh's new bride watches trains moving across the Rajasthan landscape immediately after her husband leaves for the war after their wedding night.

In *Hathyar*, however, trains are wrenched from this positive association with progress and instead expose another side of modernity. As a vital *attribute* in the narrative, Dutta's film recalls a moment from Jean Eustache's *The Mother and the Whore* (1973) when Jean-Pierre Léaud comments to his girlfriend, as they sit in a restaurant at a railway station, that their own location between the train and the city mirrors Murnau's films, in which a constant movement between two points – rural/urban, city/country – structures them.[54] Trains constantly move across the frame in *Hathyar*, and their presence on the soundtrack reverberates on to the peripatetic dimensions of the narrative, where its protagonists move between rural and urban spaces. This effect replays the film's shuttle between two commercial genres – gangster and Western – and its reluctance to be contained within the narrative expectations of either. The hither-thither movement between two spaces and, by extension, between two genres, figures the male protagonist's anxious relationship with the law. Dutta manages to bridge the gap between the two genres by playing on the idea of the frontier in two distinct landscapes, a feudal province in Rajasthan and the underworld in Mumbai. Trains signal the move from primordial rural alliances to anonymous urban space. Evoking George Miller Beard's diagnosis of 'neurasthenia' as the American disease arising out of overwork, Kirby isolates the train in King Vidor's *The Crowd* (1928) for exacerbating this stress associated with urban living. In similar ways, *Hathyar*, too, employs images and sounds of moving trains to amplify urban despair, poverty, and the alienation of its protagonists. Ajay Singh's hope that the city is more civilised is undercut by the film, which encourages us to see a continuum between the rural bloodbaths he was escaping and anonymous urban violence. More than any other element in the *mise en scène*, the cacophony of moving trains is an integral part of the verisimilitude of urban life whose association with despair and death steadily increases in the first half.

We first see trains in a high-angle shot indicating the arrival of the protagonists –

Thakur Ajay Singh, his wife, and son Avi – from their rural home to urban Mumbai. We know that Ajay Singh decided to leave his vengeance-obsessed brothers behind when they were planning to avenge their brutalised brother. The camera pans right to an establishing shot of a sprawling multi-family dwelling that later becomes their home in the city. Sounds of running trains smoothly segue to the screeching noise of an approaching taxi now in medium long shot. Before they can even alight from the vehicle, a young man picks a fight with the driver for splashing his clothes. The taxi driver responds with equal aggression, and this exchange quickly escalates, with the young man brandishing a knife. Avi intercedes, but his parents plead with him to withdraw. As he moves towards the tracks in the background, we see a train passing, and on the soundtrack we once again hear the sound of running trains. The fight dissipates when Samir arrives. We later find out that Samir's brother is the powerful underworld don Kushal Khan, who emerges as an alternative figure of law in the film.

This first train scene establishes the spatial proximity of Avi's Mumbai home to the railway tracks, a location that conveys his family's precarious economic standing in the city. The closing moments of this scene overtly link Avi with the sound of moving trains, an association that will steadily increase in the film to variously convey his urban angst and his tenuous relationship both to his father's pacifism and to social authority. As the family approaches their first-floor apartment, the sounds of moving trains resume once again. The mother notices a dead body on the tracks, and their host, Mishra, says that it is a normal part of urban life in Mumbai, a rationale that is registered as fear by the mother. Once they all move into their new home, the train sounds disappear and only resurface briefly when we see Avi staring out of the window.

All the scenes shot in their first Mumbai home consistently have trains on the soundtrack or we see their movement in the background, conveying on each occasion the despondency and grind of urban life. For instance, we see and hear moving trains when Ajay Singh returns home after a long working day at the toy shop trying in vain to sell his handmade mud toys to children hungry for modern toy guns and tanks. Dutta also uses trains to signify the empty time in urban life caused by unemployment: we hear them running when Mishra visits Ajay Singh after he has lost his job, and later, after Ajay dies, Avi and his mother note the passing hours by the sound of moving trains. Their absence, for instance, during Ajay Singh's visit to Kushal Khan's bungalow suggests that economic prosperity can extinguish them from the *mise en scène*. In contrast, when Kushal Khan visits Ajay Singh to finally settle the latter's run-in with muggers, we hear the trains passing by at least five times on the soundtrack.

Trains lend narrative verisimilitude to memory. In a reflective mood one night, Samir confides to Ajay Singh his estranged relationship with his brother Kushal Khan. In his flashback, the brothers go their separate ways with trains running in the background, sounds that enhance the pain of their parting. A top shot of trains seals that scene through a graphic match of moving trains at night. Returning to Samir and Ajay Singh, the film assuages the temporal disjunction by placing moving trains in the background.

Trains also witness crimes. Muggers rob and beat Ajay on his way home, and we see a train passing behind the fence separating his road from the tracks. Later, the film will invert this association of trains with crime when Avi chases a pickpocket and finally corners him on a railway track. Catching up with Avi on the railway tracks, the owner generously rewards him.

If trains signal urban despair, their shadowy links to death seen in the first scene assert themselves when Ajay Singh dies crossing the tracks. The scene of the actual death is not filmed, but we visit the scene with Avi and Samir. A low-angle shot of trains passing on two tracks sandwiches Samir and Avi into a frontal shot; moving from bottom to top, the camera provisionally cushions us from a vulnerable position found in the disaster films of early cinema cited by Kirby, where trains assault their viewers through frontal shots. Nevertheless, their ability to kill within the diegetic space of a film is unequivocally conveyed to us through Ajay's death. The trains do not stop moving until Avi finally realises that the unrecognisable corpse on the tracks is his father.

However, trains disappear from both the soundtrack and the screen after the interval. We see and hear them only once after the interval, when they appear in a transition shot indicating Avi's return to the city with his wife and mother, a shot that repeats the family's first move from the village to the city, but with a difference. Earlier, a similar shot signalled the family's – father, mother, and son – flight to Mumbai, escaping the blood feuds of the village. Repeated again as a transition shot, the reconstituted family, now headed by Avi, returns to the city to escape the consequences of yet another blood feud. We realise that, as moving trains trail out the film, they diminish Avi's rapprochement with social authority and mobilise a narrative akin to the gangster genre. This lurch towards the gangster genre depends on us recalling the association of trains with progress in Dutta's films, an association that allows us to understand the intimations of a different set of conventions after the interval. Far from rehearsing his usual concerns of male protagonists and their fractured relationship with the law, Dutta marshals the gangster genre to tell us how an agonised male protagonist's inability to succumb to both psychic and social authority finally drives him towards death.

The film's innovativeness lies in the ways in which it uses the bookends to present its overarching interests in the dilemma of the masculine subject's tortured relationship with the law articulated in two genres. The opening segments shot in the rural countryside raise the possibility of a narrative closer to the Western. The first half closes on a convention closer to the narrative economy of the gangster genre when Kushal Khan instructs Avi to return to the village after the latter has committed the most heinous crime in the underworld – killing a police officer. Finally, it is moving trains that influence our reading of a cross-genre structuring in this film and inflect the location of the interval, which also responds to this agitated narrative.

The film resumes with a close-up shot of Suman's grandmother. Ruling her fiefdom as she does, she goads her sons to confrontations and forbids her granddaughter to see Avi, her husband. Her authoritarian reign outside the realm of the state's law and order economy is very much within the conventions of frontier dramas in Indian cinema. However, the film quickly extinguishes its partiality for this narrative path: Avi's skirmishes with Suman's family leave him extremely vulnerable to yet another blood feud. Apparently, the only resolution is to leave this frontier landscape. His final departure from the village (and, by extension, the Western genre) with his wife and mother exacerbates his fraught relationship with the law.[55]

Instead of seeing the film's promiscuous relationship with both genres as a symptom of Hindi cinema's disaggregate narrative, as Ravi Vasudevan theorises, or as a sign of a conglomerate, as Raghavendra suggests, the bridging of two genres is viewed as a means to undermining our anticipation of a narrative built around intervals. Contrary to a clichéd partitioning of one where the first half unfolds as a Western and a gangster narrative commences after the interval, this film complicates our anticipation as viewers of genre films. By accentuating the presence and absence of trains at the visual register, and articulating a masculinity with a strained relationship to the law, the film encourages us to identify crossovers in narrative structures between the two genres. Finally, one cannot help thinking that, by amalgamating two genres, Dutta's films shore up the temporal limits of a Hollywood genre when he weds it to Indian cinematic conventions; his film addresses, in a film distributor's parlance, both urban and 'interior' audiences.

Gangsters and Cinema

Unlike his floundering, alienated character in the first half, Avi rises in the ranks of the underworld in the second half. Working for Kushal Khan, he quickly earns his trust and becomes his lieutenant. The film reminds us that criminals also have codes governing behaviour – loyalty between them is mandatory, and the most sacred of them all is the fraternal bond, a convention that recurs in Hindi commercial cinema. This feature is set in motion when a gang war flares up because of brotherly love. Kushal Khan's rival, Anna, seeks to strike a bargain on behalf of his brother who we know is wanted by the police for a kidnapping incident that Samir witnesses. Anna coaxes Kushal Khan to help him, or else, he threatens, Kushal Khan's brother Samir will also become vulnerable.

Their negotiations come unstuck when Samir volunteers to help the police.

Homosocial alliances in Khan's gang break down through betrayals and counter-threats: Afzal, a long-standing member of the gang, and Avi fall out when the former in a drunken, belligerent mood kills Anna's brother despite Khan's warning to bring him in alive. Avi transgresses the most sacred of all taboos, beating Khan's brother Samir when the latter asks him to think about his mother who can smell the stink of each of his murders. Avi's friend in the city, Pakiya, the youth who wielded the knife in the first scene in Mumbai, telephones Khan to report this beating. Betrayed by his friend, Avi beats up Pakiya, but subsequently makes amends, albeit for a short time. As the two men share a drink at a local restaurant, Afzal arrives flanked by his gang and shoots at Avi. In a final show of friendship, Pakiya takes the shot, saving Avi. Fleeing Afzal, Avi is rescued by Anna, who offers to protect him from Khan's wrath. Anna's oft-used phrase '*ulata, palata*', which translates as 'topsy-turvy', offers us a metaphor to understand the rapidly shifting loyalties of the underworld. Hired as Anna's mercenary (*hathyar*), Avi colludes with him to kidnap Samir's son from the marketplace; Khan retaliates by sending Afzal to kidnap Suman. Unfortunately for Khan, Samir intervenes, threatening to kill himself at the cost of losing his child.

Towards the end of the film, Avi switches sides again during the final shoot-out, which takes place in a nightclub where Anna waits for Kushal Khan with Samir's child. Intertwining a nightclub scene with kidnapping, Dutta undercuts the blatant exhibitionism of this kind of song and dance sequence in Hindi cinema. The striptease cabaret act appears to resonate into the exchange between the two underworld dons as Anna strips Khan of his power by seeking territorial rights over his domain in exchange for Samir's child. Khan accedes, but Afzal protests and threatens to kill Khan for being magnanimous; in a sudden move, Avi switches camps again by first shooting Afzal and then helping Kushal Khan to escape with the baby.

The scene ends with Avi driving his car into the nightclub. In a violent confrontation, Khan shoots Anna and his lawyers. Khan, Avi, and the child escape, leaving behind a club erupting in flames. Once they are out on the road, Avi distracts the police (who have obviously been tipped off by Samir), who thus turn their attention on him. The police chase him towards a toy shop. Hiding inside, Avi shoots at the police, who have not only surrounded the place, but also use his mother and wife to force him to surrender. In a parallel scene, the police corner Khan, who hands over the child to Samir as he promised to do, then walks towards the police barricade shooting his machine gun. In slow-motion shots, both Khan and Avi face a volley of bullets. Samir tries to wrest the machine gun away from his dead brother, but the corpse holds it fast. Meanwhile, Avi is hallucinating in the toy shop where his father's voice delivers a moral line for the film. As Suman and his mother walk into the bullet-strewn and shattered shop, the first song replays again. This bracketing device is clearly the film's anti-violent message, where Avi's reluctant passage into his father's universe is only through death.

Spiralling violence at the film's end recalls a number of conventions of this genre that obtain both locally and globally. Organising taboos in the homosocial world around fraternal bonds is another way to regulate homoeroticism in a circuit that links men and violence in an arbitrary fashion. Surfacing regularly in narratives of urban dystopia in Hindi films, brotherly love rationalises the escalating violence in these films and emerges as a convention in the gangster dramas of Hindi cinema.[56] *Hathyar* not only exploits this convention, but also encourages us to reconsider the incest taboo beyond the heterosexual matrix on which it is usually mapped, so opening the possibility of fraternal love as a particular figuration of homosocial bonds regulating homoeroticism.

Although *Hathyar* participates in the conventions of Hindi cinema, its ingenuity lies in those moments when it self-consciously reflects on filmmaking and film-going experiences. Dutta confessed his discomfort with song and dance sequences by once saying that 'I just can't have actors bursting into songs.'[57] The first song and dance sequence, although signifying love, is carefully edited so as to rationalise the spatial and temporal disjunctions. Samir falls in love with Julie when they are both at a film song recording session; he plays for the orchestra and she is part of the chorus that is led by real playback singers Anuradha Paudal and Pankaj Udhas. The film uses the recording session to narrate their love through spatial disruptions: it cuts to beaches in Goa and Islamic monuments to underscore the interreligious romance, but studiously returns to the recording session.

The more pointed engagement with cinema and urban life occurs when Avi's mother encourages him to see a film after he is generously rewarded for rescuing a stranger's purse from a pickpocket. We see Avi watching Rakesh Kumar's *Yarana/Friendship* (1981) at a drive-in theatre. To those familiar with the narrative, it is the last sequence in the film that we see, when close friends Amitabh and Amjad Khan destroy their enemies who have tried to separate them. The entire film, as the title suggests, deals with the durability of male friendship against all odds. In my interview, Dutta said he chose this film because it was a Nadidawala film, the producer who used to finance Dutta's films. Notwithstanding the weight of copyright law or the rationale of convenience, Dutta's quotation from this film points to the hysterical extent of male friendship that is appropriated by commercial cinema as entertainment. Dutta splices the last sequence of *Yarana* into two and introduces both parts, including an interval, into the diegesis of his own film. During the interval, Avi goes to the men's room and is spotted by the pickpocket. Unaware of being seen, Avi returns for the second half and the 'second half' of *Yarana*. Distracted by activity in an off-screen space, Avi turns away from the film and sees the pickpocket, who has returned armed with men and weapons. He tries to slip out, but is caught in a vicious fight with several men, including his friend Pakhiya. Dutta's arbitrary rewriting of *Yarana* reveals his disparaging view of run-of-the-mill films, where it appears sequences can be randomly reordered without altering narrative unity. However, by linking us to hoodlums and masculine bodies on the edge, Dutta's provides insights into an imagined audience of his own films, not those watching *Yarana*, yet very much identified with those watching *Hathyar*.

If quoting *Yarana* contributes to urban despair and violence, then this line of enquiry allies itself closely with Kirby's suggestion that early moving images were very much tied to urban displacement, and the temporal disparities of cinematic images fed into the construction of cinematic spectatorship. In his seminal formulation of cinema and urban experience, Kracauer argues that: 'Berlin theatres were "palaces of distraction"' where its audience saw itself reflected in the pure externality and fragmentation of surface glamor. The entire cinemagoing experience, including the film, either reflected the film viewer's fragmented existence and reminded them of their alienated labor or the films had the reactionary power in them to smoothen the fragmented parts through distractions like multiple visual effects which make distractions an end in themselves.[58]

In a not so dissimilar manner, as a commercial film *Hathyar* naturalises the fragmentary aspects of urban life by equating the sounds of moving trains to sounds of moving images, an audio match that the film supplies when Avi moves from home to the movie theatre. The film maintains a continuum of violence in the theatre by choosing it as the locale for a fight between Avi and the local hoodlums, a choice that suggests that the absence of trains does not lighten our association between neurasthenia and urban life.

Deserted Masculinity

As he subverts and encourages the formation of conventions both locally and globally, Dutta's films suggest that they are also available for diverse readings of cinematic spectatorship. His obsession with outdoor shooting and wide-screen formats allows us to see the various intersections between cinematic spectatorship and tourism. His strong preference for masculine genres – Western, gangster, and war – provokes us to reconsider the figure of masculinity in genre films, particularly the way in which it responds to and is shaped by the interval.

Abducting theories of masculinity developed from readings of Hollywood films, I would now like to consider how Dutta uses the interval to rework certain masculine action genres available internationally, though long associated with Hollywood. Although there is a burgeoning industry on representation in film and cultural studies, I want to return to Steve Neale's classic essay 'Masculinity as Spectacle', which initiated discussion on images of heterosexual masculinity in Hollywood cinema as a way to respond to Mulvey's formulation that the gaze in classical cinema is always from the point of view of a masculine subject.[59]

In her original argument, Mulvey pinpoints a particular circuit of looks: looking is aligned closely with activity and, by extension, to the masculine spectator, and the object to passivity and femininity. Mulvey turns our attention to shot/reverse-shot editing as a mechanism that encourages the spectator to identify alternatively with the camera and male protagonist. Neale revisits the heart of Mulvey's thesis and wonders how mainstream films avert eroticising masculine images on screen, a question that we can surmise addresses the question of making the male body the fetishised object. Mulvey herself remarks on this possibility:

> A male movie star's glamorous characteristics are thus not those of the erotic object of his gaze, but those of the more perfect, more complete, more powerful ideal ego conceived in the original moment of recognition in front of the mirror. (Mulvey 1975:12)

Turning to questions of identification, Neale evokes John Ellis's thesis that cinematic identification involves two different tendencies: first, of dreaming and fantasy, and secondly, narcissistic identification. As much as identifications are shifting and mobile, Neale suggests they equally involve 'constant work to channel and regulate identification in relation to sexual division, in relation to the orders of gender, sexuality, and social identity and authority marking patriarchal society' (p. 11). Circumscribing his enquiry to narcissistic identification, Neale proffers:

> Inasmuch as films *do* involve gender identifications, and inasmuch as current ideologies of masculinity involve so centrally notions and attitudes to do with aggression, power, and control, it seems that narcissism and narcissistic identification may be especially signification … . Narcissism and narcissistic identification both involve fantasies of power, omnipotence, mastery, and control. [p. 11]

Neale suggests that this formulation of identification holds for films where the male heroes have omnipotent, god-like powers. He develops this idea by suggesting that, in part, the power of the male protagonists is 'marked not only by emotional reticence, but also by silence, a reticence with language' (p. 12). It is here that Neale propounds his central argument on the spectator's identification with masculine ideals:

> Language is a process (or set of processes) involving absence and lack, and these are what threaten any image of the self as totally enclosed, self-sufficient, omnipotent. The

construction of an ideal ego, meanwhile, is a process involving contradictions. While the ideal ego may be a 'model' with which the subject identifies and to which it aspires, it may also be a source of further images and feelings of castration, inasmuch as that ideal is something to which the subject is never adequate. [pp. 12–13]

Obviously, this inadequacy ruptures any stable identification with the image of the ideal ego, and Neale suggests that such identifications 'can entail a concomitant masochism' (p. 13). He concurs with David Rodowick's suggestion that 'there is always a constant oscillation between that image as a source of identification, and as an other, a source of contemplation. The image is a source both of narcissistic processes and drives, and inasmuch as it is other, of object-oriented processes and drives' (p. 13).

Neale continues by considering an important contradiction in the type of masculinity found in Anthony Mann's films initially proposed by Paul Willemen: 'It is the contradiction between narcissism and the law, between an image of *narcissistic* authority on the one hand and image of *social* authority on the other' (p. 14). This obviously touches on Mulvey's own observation on two diverging images of masculinity commonly at play in the Western: symbolic and nostalgic narcissism. Neale suggests that we 'could go on to discuss a number of nostalgic Westerns in these terms, in terms of the theme of lost or doomed male narcissism' (p. 15). Extending Willemen's observation about the sadomasochistic scenes in Mann's films, Neale suggests that, as most action genres are populated with reticent, omnipotent heroes, we should look for sadomasochism in the spectacular action sequences: 'both forms of voyeuristic looking, intra- and extra-diegetic, are especially evident in those moments of contest and combat referred to above, in those moments at which narrative outcome is determined through a fight or gun battle, at which male struggle becomes pure spectacle' (pp. 16–18).

What Neale's astute reformulation of Willemen's argument suggests is that in mainstream cinema spectacles of action lift male images from an erotic circuit, a device that may account for the way in which it systematically both denies eroticism of the male body and regulates homoeroticism. Neale turns to the Oedipal scene to tease out how masculinity is tied to desire and law, and 'the moral of the Oedipal drama is the need to *know* and *accept* one's place under the law – or face devastating consequences' (p. 76).

Neale's compelling engagement with Mulvey and Willemen, however, does not make enough of the relationship between psychic law and social authority, a link developed by Frank Krutnik in his book *In a Lonely Street*.[60] Krutnik begins his chapter entitled 'Masculinity and Its Discontents' at a point of surfeit in psychoanalysis, especially from the font of speculation on these matters, Freud. Summarising Freud's varied position on the male child's place under patriarchy, Krutnik delineates how the child initially 'develops a relation to two sexual objects – the mother and *itself* (this latter mode of object cathexis designated by Freud as "primary narcissism")' (p. 77). At this early stage of development, the child's relationship to the mother involves the bonding of sexual drives to ego drives (this process is described by Freud as 'auto-eroticism') (p. 77).

Krutnik makes a great deal of the pre-Oedipal condition, which he reads as being infused with an overvaluation of the mother with an attendant bisexual subjectivity. Although there is an overemphasis on the wholesomeness of the pre-Oedipal scene, Krutnik's most provocative point appears when he tries to establish links between the Freudian scene and the male protagonists of film noir. Isolating male masochisms as an effective way of understanding the predicament of these tough noir heroes, he offers:

> male masochism can be seen as manifesting a desire to escape from the regimentation of masculine (cultural) identity effected through the Oedipus complex. The masochist seeks to overthrow the authority of the paternal law and the determinacy of castration … .
> Indeed, the 'tough' thrillers continually institute a discrepancy between, on the one hand, the licit possibilities of masculine identity and desire required by the patriarchal cultural order, and on the other hand, the psychosexual make-up of the male subject-hero. Of course, this dramatic is articulated, elaborated and resolved in various ways, but these are all unified by what can be seen as an obsession with the non-correspondence between the desires of the individual male subject and the cultural regime of 'masculine identification.' [p. 85]

Krutnik's elaboration of pathologies afflicting male heroes is alas relegated to a footnote:

> Masochism, paranoia, psychosis, homosexuality, various forms of 'corruptive' sexuality, etc.: these are some of the principal ways in which this crisis of confidence in the possibilities of masculine identity is articulated within the *noir* 'tough' thrillers. Of course, though the films may often seek to convince otherwise, such a large-scale investment in scenarios of male psychological and sexual instability cannot be easily be ascribed to instances of purely internal breakdown, for what is at stake are the culturally conventionalised modes and parameters of masculine identity in relation to individual desire. [p. 242]

Although these different formulations on viewing and reading articulations of masculinity refer exclusively to Euro-American films, their insights will guide my reading of Dutta's Hindi films.[61] His films oscillate between these two points of narcissism, but always with the suggestion that social authority is infected and needs to broach the post-colonial ideal that is never expressed. Since the films doubt the existing pattern of patriarchal feudal authority, the various battles in the narrative also cast doubts on established conventions of narcissistic authority by underlining a nexus of class and caste interests: in *Ghulami* the protagonists' desire to overthrow upper-caste hegemony resembles Krutnik's mapping of the Oedipal complex; in *Batwara* homoeroticism gingerly locates itself within 'highly ritualised' scenes of violence and combat akin to sadism formulated by both Willemen and Neale; *Yateem* returns us to the Oedipal scene where the seducing mother rushes the masculine subject into the patriarchal order of honour; in *Kshatriya* the 'anxious aspects' of looking at male bodies is muted through evocations of tradition and patriarchy; *Hathyar* openly flirts with masochism, where its protagonist seeks to overthrow the authority of the paternal law and the determinacy of castration; in *Border* male masochism, expressed as patriotism, services the call to fight for the motherland.

I am being cryptic only to suggest that psychoanalytical scenarios map with sufficient facility in Dutta's films, but I am less interested in the durability of these theoretical positions than in the ability to incorporate local manifestations of masculinity. By this I do not mean a representation of an authentic Indian masculinity, but rather how narrative structures in Dutta's Hindi films mould representations of masculinity. Instead of focusing on an elaboration of secondary identification while assuming that primary identification is universally similar, identification with the camera exceeds identification with characters, even in feature films.[62] It is here that returning to Mulvey, Neale, and Willemen instructs us to attend carefully to formal mechanisms and primary identifications that precede secondary identifications and thematic concerns. What Krutnik's analysis ignores are the links between cinema and modernity that shape notions of history through temporal unfolding or consumerism through *mise en scène*. After all, cinema's location within debates on modernity exceeds an exclusively psychoanalytical reading.

Mindful that the interval, for instance, in Dutta's films heightens our understanding of his engagements with Hollywood genres, it equally influences the tenuous links between homosociality and homoeroticism in these genres. Yet the interval also opens up ways in which commercial or popular cinema in non-Hollywood sectors offer different ways of storytelling, a notion that could be named post-colonial modernity.[63] Similarly, we can identify other features in Dutta's films that call on particular motifs of Indianness even as narrative structures locate his films within international genres. Here, I am referring to the *mise en scène* in his films where he habitually sets his narratives against desert landscapes of Rajasthan or the urban underworld, spaces that have a fraught relationship with the official histories of post-colonial modernity. Consideration of the weight of *mise en scène* in Dutta's film returns us to theories of masculinity, where the overwhelming presence of psychoanalytical theories has tended to sideline questions such as how frontier spaces bolster the masculine subject's tortured relationship to the law. Neale refers to spectacles of action sequences in action genres as a way to manage homoeroticism set into motion in these homosocial narratives. His line of enquiry begs us to consider how spectacles of particular landscapes such as frontier landscapes naturally lend themselves to tales of masculine bravery, loss, and love.

Attending to the *mise en scène* accounts for viewing pleasures beyond the oscillations of sadomasochistic pleasures, to include consumer desire, nationalistic sentiments, or nostalgia for a different political order, none of which can be reduced simply to the vagaries of the Oedipal scenario. Far from being amorphous rural landscapes in popular films as some of its critics have asserted, specific spaces in films carry enough ideological charge to inflect and colour our understanding of the narrative.[64] In these terms, Dutta's return to Rajasthan or other regions of the northern plains paves the way to our understanding of how these spaces lend themselves to representations of frontier lands in the imagined cartography of the post-colonial nation state. Dutta himself remarked on his predilection for these wide, open spaces when asked why he chooses Rajasthan:[65]

> In fact, *Yateem* was not shot in Rajasthan, but in Gwalior and Agra. The same with *Hathyar*. Two of my films were not shot there at all. Yes, you must have thought so because the terrain looks similar. The northen part of India looks the same. Not desertified, but rugged. So the feeling of the desert is there. The common factor in all my films is ruggedness. The place is rugged and the men are very macho. I had a caption made for *Border* which I will not be using. It said, '*Border*, where men are men.' I like my heroes to be macho, rugged people who make a woman feel secure in their arms.

In addition to an imagined machismo flourishing in these spaces, they allow Dutta's films to play on the limits of the post-colonial authority of the state and its impact on masculinity. In addition, evoking Rajasthan or spaces akin to it mobilises a battery of association that circulates in our popular conceptions of history and taste.

Historian Barbara Ramusack suggests that photographs and accounts of Rajasthan kingdoms replete with palaces, princes, and flamboyantly attired Rajputs have well served British orientalist imaginings of despotic grandeur, decadence, and prowess. In post-colonial India, she continues, the same representations smoothly slide into nation-state tourism aimed at the rising global middle class, which has been amply aided by the development of both railways to make these visits possible and photography to prepare, plan, and record these encounters.[66] From the point of view of national tourism in India, we can speculate that Rajasthan continues to hold sway over our imagination through its oppositions – princely grandeur coexists with pastoralism of nomads; it throws up a temporal space that seemingly either exists before or is independent of colonialism.

Dutta's camera depends on our understanding of this conflicted relationship to colonialism and post-colonialism articulated through representations of this space, but instead of affirming the coexistence of different economies, his films lay bare caste oppressions and class inequalities that underscore this *mise en scène* where extreme antagonisms hold sway. Whereas the striking landscapes, through his deft use of wide-screen format, assuage the hoarier aspects of his narrative, their intimate relationship to tourism evokes consumerism as a vital address of commercial cinema that tends to be submerged in classical narrative. If we retain Dutta's films – *Batwara, Ghulami, Yateem,* and *Kshatriya* – within the 'Western' genre, representations of Rajasthan offer a complicated alignment between men and history in this space. According to Laura Mulvey, a hallmark of Westerns (she generalises this point to the entire genre, but I shall circumscribe her reading of *The Man Who Shot Liberty Valance* as a particular illustration of the Fordian universe) is the unfolding of narrative structure in the following manner:

> The tension between two points of attraction, the symbolic (social integration and marriage) and nostalgic narcissism, generates a common splitting of the Western hero into two, something unknown in the Proppian tale. Here two functions emerge, one celebrating integration into society through marriage, the other celebrating resistance to social demands and responsibilities, above all those of marriage and the family, the sphere represented by woman … . The narrative structure is based on an opposition between two irreconcilables. The two paths cannot cross. On one side there is an encapsulation of power, and phallic attributes, in an individual who has to bow himself out of the way of history; on the other, an individual impotence rewarded by political and financial power, which, *in the long run*, in fact becomes history. [p. 34][67]

Mulvey's tight formulation of masculinity in the Western fits nicely into the Fordian universe, which, we know from other commentaries, lends itself into a neat unfolding of narrative mobilised through oppositions. But revisions of this master narrative have called on an elision of histories of conquest and subjugation, citing specifically the myth promoted in these films – Monument Valley as a savage territory that begs to be civilised. Responding to the Fordian universe, Peckinpah's Westerns scar the *mise en scène* with histories that do not afford a path towards nostalgic narcissism.[68]

Similarly, Dutta's films rewrite this master narrative by iconically signifying Rajasthan as a site already marked with histories of caste and class oppression, and thwart an unqualified abstraction of heroic justice in an empty space waiting to he historicised. This highly stripped-down version of this narrative obtains in *Ghulami*, a film that sustains its antagonisms by only allowing for three songs and killing its heroes.[69] His other films repeatedly complicate this narrative of oppression with crosscutting desires that impact the articulation of masculinity and, by extension, are more conciliatory towards conventions of commercial cinema.

Mulvey offers two distinct paths available for the Western hero – outside and inside history – that I want to import as a battle between *power* and *authority* for this analysis so as to calibrate the erotic charge in this masculine universe. Although women do serve as signifiers of society and community, there is enough evidence in a Western to suggest that this pull towards 'history' also forecloses various kinds of homosocial bonds in this time and space that evade conventional representations of sexual difference.

Batwara articulates this homosocial desire as male friendship that dovetails with homoeroticism. The film closes, as we have seen, with the two men riding into death and literally out of history in Mulvey's terms, a closure that betrays the film's inability to offer a place for male friendship and, by the same token, its avowal of the homoerotic desire between the two men. More than any of his other films, *Batwara* highlights the homoerotic possibilities of the homosocial universe staged in the Western, a gesture that also allows us to re-evaluate the representation of women in these films. Not unlike Mulvey or Raymond Bellour's insight on how women are crucial to the narrative of the Western, Dutta's films also employ female characters to halt the snowballing of violence. In *Ghulami*, only one female character directly heightens the class–caste conflict that is already the mainstay of the narrative; in *Yateem*, demands from wife and family puncture the male protagonist's violent actions; wife, mother, and family demands are unable to contain the male protagonist in *Hathyar*, whose violent actions are wholly predicated on a complex network of family honour and Oedipal crisis leaning towards the gangster genre; in *Kshatriya*, mothers threaten to die in a last attempt to end a blood feud; in *Border*, flashback sequences of domestic life with female counterparts tempers the homosocial life of the barracks on the frontier; and in *Batwara*, it is Roop's reminder during Sumer and Vicky's confrontation that arrests their enmity. However varied their location, the female characters in these films only marginally affect the plot, as if to assuage the main homosocial narrative and to occlude homoeroticism that we know the Western genre has masterfully learned to manage and bring to a closure. The management of homoeroticism through conventions of the masculine melodrama and homosociality disturbs the usual assumption that violent actions by men in Westerns are directed against women – rather, these films, particularly *Batwara*, force us to consider how a narrative of estrangement, violent action, and reunion is a way of playing homoeroticism in the shadow of homosocial ties.

Just as Dutta's rewriting of genre films forces us to consider how frontier landscapes aid and abet masculine subjects' relationship to law, so they also advise us to consider how these spaces are an integral part of every national imaginary, and not just American. Addressing the ideological charge of these spaces where notions of history, national taste, ideas of cinematic verisimilitude, and conceptions of state authority are fortified opens an array of addresses initiated by Dutta's films that rightly implores us to consider him as an auteur seated in the interstices of national and world cinema.

Notes

1. See Eve Kosofsky Sedgwick (1985), *Between Men: English Literature and Male Homosocial Desire*, New York: Columbia University Press; Steven Cohan and Ina Rae Hark (1993), *Screening the Male*, New York: Routledge; Peter Lehman (1993), *Running Scared: Masculinity and the Representation of the Male Body*, Philadelphia: Temple University Press.

2. For a thorough survey of the debates on auteurism, see the essays in John Caughie (ed.) (1981), *Theories of Authorship*, London: Routledge.

3. Tom Gunning (2000), *The Films of Fritz Lang: Allegories of Vision and Modernity*, London: BFI; Judith Mayne (1994), *Directed by Dorothy Arzner*, Bloomington: Indiana University Press; Lesley Stern (1995), *The Scorsese Connection*, London: BFI.

4. The review of *Batwara* appeared in *Trade Guide*, 15 July 1989; that of *Yateem* in *Trade Guide*, 4 March 1989.

5. Personal conversation with J. P. Dutta, August 1997.

6. Iqbal Masud (1997), *Dream Merchants, Politicians and Partition: Memoirs of an Indian Muslim*, New Delhi: HarperCollins, India, p. 133.

7. M. K. Raghavendra (1992), 'Generic Elements and the Conglomerate Narrative', *Deep Focus*, vol. IV, no. 2.

8. M. U. Jayadev (1993), 'Polemics of Film Lists', *Deep Focus*, 5.

9. Anil Ranvir Khanna (1993), 'That's Style', *Filmfare*, February, pp. 46–9.

10. Subash K. Jha (2000), 'That Gut Feeling', *Filmfare*, June, pp. 82–5.

11. Quoted in the Spot Poll conducted by Asis Merchant and Deepak Nasta, *Trade Guide*, 5 November 1989.

12. Khalid Mohamed (1986), 'Apocalypse Now', *Filmfare*, 1–15 December; Ajit Duara (1989), 'Where Are the "Mother Indias" of Today?', *Cinema in India*, vol. III, no. 4, October–December.

13. Paul Smith (1993), *Clint Eastwood: A Cultural Production*, Minneapolis: University of Minnesota Press.

14. Mieke Bal (1997), *Narratology*, Toronto: University of Toronto Press.

15. I am grateful to Ira Livingstone for suggesting that I look at Lee Edelman's (1994) book *Homographesis: Essays in Gay Literary and Cultural Theory*, New York: Routledge.

16. Marc Vernet (1983), 'The Filmic Transanction: On the Openings of Film Noirs', *The Velvet Light Trap*, 20, Summer, pp. 2–9; Jacques Aumont, Alain Bergala, Michel Marie, and Marc Vernet (1992), *Aesthetics of Film*, Austin: Texas University Press; and David Bordwell and Kristin Thompson (1993), *Film Art*, New York: McGraw-Hill.

17. See Barbara Creed (1990), 'Phallic Panic: Male Hysteria and *Dead Ringers*', *Screen*, vol. 31, no. 2, Summer.

18. Thierry Kuntzel (1980), 'Film Work, 2', *Camera Obscura*, 5, pp. 6–69.
    Other examples include Marc Vernet (1983), 'The Filmic Transanction: On the Openings of Film Noirs', *The Velvet Light Trap*, 20, Summer, pp. 2–9; Jacques Aumont, Alain Bergala, Michel Marie, and Marc Vernet (1992), *Aesthetics of Film*, Austin: Texas University Press; and David Bordwell and Kristin Thompson (1993), *Film Art*, New York: McGraw-Hill.

19. Stephen Heath (1975), 'Film and System: Terms of Analysis, I', *Screen*, 16, no. 1, Spring.

20. Richard Neupert (1995), *The End: Narration and Closure in the Cinema*, Detroit: Wayne State University Press.

21. I am extremely grateful to Theodore Baskaran for generously sharing these filmic details with me.

22. Miriam Hansen (1991), *Babel and Babylon: Spectatorship in American Silent Film*, Cambridge, Mass.: Harvard University Press; Tom Gunning (1990), 'The Cinema of Attractions: Early Film, Its Spectator and the Avant-Garde', in Thomas Elsaesser and Adam Barker (eds), *Early Cinema: Space, Frame, Narrative*, London: BFI, pp. 56–62.

23. Quoted in Laleen Jaymanne (1992), 'Sri Lankan Family Melodrama: A Cinema of Primitive Attractions', *Screen*, vol. 33, no. 2, Summer.

24. Comments at *Screen* Study Conference, July 1998.

25. Mimi White's paper at the Society of Cinema Studies Conference, Ottawa, April 1997.

26. Anne Friedberg suggests we rethink the way in which films address us as they are aware that our television- and video-watching habits are generously peppered with breaks. I wish to thank Parama Roy for suggesting a link between intervals and television programmes, and Karen Lury for her intimation of the possibilities of a cliffhanger at the interval in Indian cinema.

27. Interview with Salim Khan, *Screen*, 15 July 1988. Also published in Rafique Baghdadi and Rajiv Rao (1995), *Talking Films*, New Delhi: HarperCollins India, pp. 127–37.

28. Interview with Sagar Sarhadi, *Screen*, 11 November, 1988. Also published in Rafique Baghdadi and Rajiv Rao (1995), *Talking Films*, New Delhi: HarperCollins India, pp. 155–61.

29. I am extremely grateful to Patricia White for reminding me of Vertov's *Manifesto*.

30. Annette Michelson (1984), 'Introduction', in Annette Michelson (ed.), *Kino-Eye: The Writings of Dziga Vertov* (tr. Kevin O'Brien), Berkeley: University of California Press, p. xxx.

31. 'Towards a National Cinema', *Movement*, 4, 1969.

32. See 'Coitus Interruptus and Love Story in Indian Cinema', in Vidya Dehejia (ed.), *Representing the Body: Gender Issues in Indian Art*, New Delhi: Kali for Women, pp. 124–39.

33. Among the burgeoning critical industry on masculinity, here are a few books: Paul Smith (ed.) (1996), *Boys: Masculinity in Contemporary Culture*, Boulder: Westview; Fred Pfeil (1995), *White Guys: Studies in Postmodern Domination and Difference*, London: Verso; Peter Lehman (1993), *Running Scared: Masculinity and the Representation of the Male Body*, Philadelphia: Temple University Press; Dennis Bingham (1994), *Acting Male: Masculinities in the Films of James Stewart, Jack Nicholson, and Clint Eastwood*, New Brunswick: Rutgers University Press; Maurice Berger, Brian Wallis, and Simon Watson (eds) (1995), *Constructing Masculinity*, New York: Routledge.

34. Kurosawa's *Seven Samurai* is another favourite master text, remade successfully by Indian film-makers, and recently inspiring Rajkumar Santoshi's *China Gate* (1998).

35. Ted Gallagher (1995), 'Shoot-out at the Genre Corral: Problems in the Evolution of the Western', in Barry Grant (ed.), *Film Genre Reader II*, Austin: University of Texas Press, pp. 246–60.

36. In a structural analysis of Ford's films Peter Wollen offers a master antinomy in the Fordian universe: desert v. civilization. See Wollen (1969, rev. edn 1972), 'The Auteur Theory', *Signs and Meaning in the Cinema*, London: BFI.

37. Madhava Prasad (1998), 'The Absolutist Gaze: Political Structure and Cultural Form', in *Ideology of the Hindi Film: A Historical Construction*, Delhi: Oxford University Press.

38. See Wimal Dissanayake and Malti Sahai (1992), *Sholay: A Cultural Reading*, New Delhi: Wiley Eastern. Also see Ken Wlaschin (1976), 'Birth of the "Curry" Western: Bombay 1976', *Film and Filming*, vol. 22, no. 7, April.

39. Ashish Rajadhyaksha and Paul Willemen (eds) (1999), *Encyclopaedia of Indian Cinema*, London: BFI (rev. edn), p. 94.

40. Personal interview with J. P. Dutta, August 1997.

41. Raymond Bellour's interview with Janet Bergstrom (1979), 'Alternation, Segmentation, Hypnosis', *Camera Obscura*, 3–4.

42. Gerard Genette (1972), *Deceit, Desire, and the Novel: Self and Other in Literary Structure* (tr. Yvonne Freccero), Baltimore: Johns Hopkins University Press.

43. See Corey K. Creekmur's (1995) 'Acting Like A Man: Masculine Performance in *My Darling Clementine*', in Coey K. Creekmur and Alexander Doty (eds), *Out in Culture: Gay, Lesbian and Queer Essays on Popular Culture*, Durham, NC: Duke University Press, pp. 167–82. Creekmur's essay offers a splendid reading of a bar scene in Ford's film as an instance of a gay pick-up scene. He proceeds to unravel the film's regulatory mechanisms that try to establish normal masculinity through the figure of Wyatt Earp.

44. I wish to thank Aditya Behl for fine-tuning the translation of the opening voice-over, April 1997. The voice-over ends on this florid note: 'The world swears by their friendship, theirs is a garden in the midst of these volatile changes.'

45. I once again wish to thank Aditya Behl for correctly translating the Urdu in this scene.

46. *Trade Guide*, 11 March, 1989.

47. Ajit Duara (1989), 'Where Are the "Mother Indias" of Today?', *Cinema in India*, vol. III, no. 4, October–December, pp. 18–21.

48. Telephone conversation with J. P. Dutta, September 1997.

49. See Edward Branigan (1992), *Stagecoach*, London BFI.

50. I concur with Ajit Duara who reads the opening hunting sequence as 'overture to the movie style/theme'.

51. Lynne Kirby (1997), *Parallel Tracks: The Railroad and Silent Cinema*, Durham, NC: Duke University Press.

52. For a reading of trains in Indian novels, see Richard Cronin (1989), 'Indian Trains', in *Imagining India*, New York: St Martin's.

53. Personal interview with J. P. Dutta, Mumbai, September 1988.

54. See Mieke Bal (1997), *Narratology*, Toronto: University of Toronto Press.

55. As an object exchanged in a deal involving family honour and shame, Suman's location is in character with women in Westerns, and her marginalisation from the gangster narrative synchronises with the absence of 'good' women in the latter genre. She and Avi's mother are passive witnesses to an escalating violence in the narrative and stand in contrast to Suman's grandmother who is the linchpin of violence in the village.

56. I refer here to N. Chandra's *Ankush*, Varma's *Satya*, and Chopra's *Parinda*, where this convention is clearly seen.

57. Personal interview, August 1998.

58. Siegfried Kracauer (1995), 'Cult of Distraction', in Thomas Y. Levin (ed. and tr.), *The Mass Ornament: Weimar Essays*, Cambridge, Mass.: Harvard University Press, pp. 323–8.

59. Steve Neale (1993), 'Masculinity as Spectacle: Reflections on Men and Mainstream Cinema', in Steven Cohan and Ina Rae Hark (eds), *Screening the Male: Exploring Masculinities in Hollywood Cinema*, London: Routledge.

60. Frank Krutnik (1991), *In a Lonely Street: Film Noir, Genre, Masculinity*, London: Routledge.

61. For a splendid reading of masculinity in Hong Kong action films, see Julian Stringer (1997), '"Your Tender Smiles Give Me Strength": Paradigms of Masculinity in John Woo's *A Better Tomorrow* and *The Killer*', *Screen*, vol. 38, no. 1, Spring, pp. 25–41.

62. Christian Metz (1997), *Imaginary Signifier: Psychoanalysis and the Cinema* (tr. Celia Britton, Annwyl Williams, Ben Brewster, and Alfred Guzzetti), Bloomington: Indiana University Press.

63. See Itty Abraham (1998), *The Making of the Atomic Bomb in India: Science and Secrecy*, London: Zed Books.

64. Suresh Chabria argues that popular Indian cinema has not 'fully portrayed the village experience' and that it has been left to New Indian cinema to correct a number of myths. Suresh Chabria (1992), 'Images of Rural India in Post-Independence Cinema', in Alok Bhalla and Peter Bumke (eds), *Images of Rural India in the Twentieth Century*, New Delhi: Sterling.

65. Interview published in Rediff on the Internet.

66. Barbara N. Ramusack (1995), 'The Indian Princes as Fantasy: Palace Hotels, Palace Museums, and Palace on Wheels', in *Consuming Modernity: Public Culture in a South Asian World*, Minneapolis: University of Minnesota Press; 'Tourism and Icons: The Packaging of the Princely States', in Catherine Asher and Thomas Metcalfe (eds), *Perceptions of South Asia's Visual Past*, New Delhi: Oxford and IBH.

67. Laura Mulvey (1989), 'Afterthoughts on "Visual Pleasure and Narrative Cinema" Inspired by King Vidor's *Duel in the Sun* (1946)', in *Visual and Other Pleasures*, Bloomington: Indiana University Press.

68. The Fordian universe is also available in Indian cinema, the most prominent example being Ramesh Sippy's *Sholay/Flames* (1975).

69. Interview with J. P. Dutta, *Filmfare*, 1–15 December, 1986.

4

Screening the Past in Mani Ratnam's *Nayakan*

Considered a quintessentially Hollywood genre, analyses of gangster films tend to use historical events such as the Depression as a means to understand studio interests in 'topicals'; dwell on representations of violence; and at times comment on genre's unique iconography.[1] Later cycles of the genre have allowed critics to argue that the peculiar coincidence in the protagonists' struggle against both symbolic law and social authority stages a crisis of masculinity.[2] This move towards problems of masculinity has opened a floodgate of queries on how this genre helps to stage ethnic and class antagonisms, even if the dominant narrative criminalises the immigrant and the unemployed. But these critical essays have little to say about another feature of this genre that also carries a considerable ideological charge: the visual and aural evocation of a past, a period before the protagonists become gangsters. Films in this genre, particularly those produced by Warner Bros. in the 1930s, open with a scene from the protagonist's childhood, a period where the construction of innocence is vital to our understanding of his conversion from lad to gangster.[3]

The 'gangster' film in Indian cinema surfaces as a provisional category within a larger group of films that trade papers refer to as 'action films' or 'police dramas'. Not unlike the Hollywood genre, here, too, protagonists wage war against authority, but with a difference. Often these films spill over the difference between legitimate authority and the brutal power of the state, the latter often represented by corrupt police officers or a biased judicial system. By addressing the state through battles over the difference between authority and power, these films – to use Homi Bhabha's phrase – 'write' the nation state.[4]

In a monumental essay tackling disparate reading strategies, Bhabha extends Benedict Anderson's formulation of 'nation time' by drawing our attention to a continuing negotiation between the *pedagogical* call to 'the people' or 'the nation', and the *performative* that obtains in cultural and literary narratives where more slippery or even shadowy figures of 'the nation' and 'the people' emerge. In a pithy conceptualisation of this tension, Bhabha writes:

> In the production of the nation as narration there is a split between the continuist,
> accumulative temporality of the pedagogical, and the repetitious, recursive strategy of

the performative. It is through this process of splitting that the conceptual ambivalence of modern society becomes the site of *writing the nation*. [pp. 145–6]

Bhabha's literary figuration of nation as narration appears to have no place for the state in the writings of the nation, an analytical figure that haunts so much of contemporary theorisations of power and authority in post-colonial space. Far from being an empirical identity, the nation state in post-colonial state theory is a condensed site that legitimises the symbolic and at times hefty power of the state through the idyllic topos of the nation. Foucault's cautionary remarks on the difference between power and authority help to disaggregate the nation state as a unifying concept, reclaiming a separate theoretical terrain for the nation, while never underestimating the power of the state to bolster the desires and impulses of the nation. The post-colonial modern nation, in short, can never abdicate its continuing negotiations with power and authority while heralding a different space from the colonial.[5]

According to both Benedict Anderson and Homi Bhabha, a nation's past bears considerably on its imaginary.[6] The nation state evokes the past in its official histories, writing its people into a narrative that inextricably links them to a cumulative history from past to present. Yet as Bhabha suggests, this evocation of a continuous past as rightful inheritance can never shake off the performative aspects that underscore repetition. In those annual celebrations of national independence day, for example, we are sutured into the national imaginary of assuredness, yet the repetitious strategy casts a shadow over this imaginary reminding us of the forced idea of unity. Bhabha suggests that this to and fro movement is ideally suited to a reading of continuing negotiation between the pedagogical and performative registers. In a not so dissimilar move, cinema, particularly popular film, is equally available for capturing the 'conceptual ambivalence of modern society' through its endless play with spatial and temporal dislocation within a narrative of past and present.

Of all the genres, the gangster film's obsessions with both the past and brutal power allow us to see it as a site of writing the nation, as well as performing it. Its obsession with the past allows us to see how biographies of gangster protagonists are analogous to biographies of the post-colonial state. Although the vigilante logic of the genre may place it outside the official histories of the nation state, the genre's compulsion to restore law and order at the end does not endorse an anarchic option. Without fail, this genre narrates its past through pre-credit sequences, flashbacks, and period sets, narrative strategies that are at the centre of cinema's own preoccupations with temporality where a past is narrated through forward-moving film images. Focusing on temporality in gangster films encourages us to see how popular genres are equally available for interrogations of memory and history, interrogations that we usually reserve for non-commercial films.

Although images of the past facilitate an enquiry into memory and history, the genre's obsession with spectacular violence cannot override its place within the history of cinema. The idea of film as attraction and shock resonates in early theorisations of cinema and modernity, especially essays by Walter Benjamin, Siegfried Kracauer, and Sergei Eisenstein. As one of the most incisive readers of Walter Benjamin's classic essay 'The Work of Art in the Age of Mechanical Reproduction', Miriam Hansen shows us the ways in which Benjamin sees cinema with its spatial and temporal (even if he was referring exclusively to Eisenstein or Vertov's films) disjunctions, offering us a way to narrate the overwhelming social and cultural transformations brought through industrialisation.[7] Even as Benjamin's own relationship to cinema wavers between castigating it for its shock value and celebrating it for its Utopian possibilities, what emerges is an understanding of cinema's ability to mimic and narrate the spatial and temporal disjunctions that a *flâneur* experiences in his travels through modern urban space. In short, Hansen suggests that for Benjamin 'the peculiarity of cinematic experience rests on an *iconic* relationship between cinema and its referent' (p. 185; my emphasis).

In a provocative recasting of the debates on spectatorship, Anne Friedberg suggests that contemporary contact with films as videos relies extensively on our ability to manipulate narrative time through the rewinding and forwarding options available.[8] Given that cinema coexists alongside video arcades and shopping malls with facades simultaneously simulating past and future, she forces us to reframe the gaze as a 'virtual gaze'. These virtual meanderings through commodity culture, she argues, undermine conventional divisions between time and space, and sunder it from an indexical referent. To mingle Bhabha's theorisation of writing the nation with Friedberg's 'virtual gaze', we can speculate that battles over the partitioning of past and present for the *flâneur*, shopper, or citizen crisscross with cinema's spectator.[9]

These theoretical positions implicitly rely on either avant-garde visual productions or documentary films as ideal cultural products capable of complicating spatial and temporal disjunctions. However, writing on commercial genres draws more extensively on a Metzian model that dwells on secondary identifications and the pleasures of narrative cinema.[10] This bifurcated division of labour between theoreticians of early cinema and classical Hollywood narrative has been addressed in an essay by Laura Mulvey.[11] To Frankfurt School theoreticians, her essay may have a familiar ring from Siegfried Kracauer's theories of distraction or shock, but the originality of the essay lies in its systematic mapping of the points of contact between Marxist and Freudian theories of fetishism. Classical Hollywood narrative, Mulvey argues, thrives on confusing and popularising our presumed borders between these enterprises, a confusion that deservedly charges this cinema for converting cinematic experience into commodity.

When we turn to Indian cinema, we have to frame both theories – cinema of attractions based on spatial and temporal disjunctions, and scopophilia predicated on a tendency towards internal coherence of the narrative – as the only satisfactory method to read its simultaneous use of both kinds of cinematic styles. I argued in the previous chapter that we cannot adequately understand the twists and turns in Indian commercial cinema if we do not consider the interval, a halfway pause in the narrative. Besides this break, Indian commercial films have at least half a dozen, at rare times even forty, song and dance sequences that interrupt the Hollywood style of diegetic continuity.

Whereas Indian films are beholden to the constellation of interruptions for their success, they are not isolated from conventions obtaining in globally circulating commercial genres, such as gangster films, that lean towards internal coherence. For example, Mani Ratnam's Tamil film *Nayakan* (1987), Vidhu Vinod Chopra's Hindi film *Parinda* (1989), and Ram Gopal Varma's *Satya* fit into this genre. *Nayakan* has several visual quotations from Coppola's *The Godfather*, and *Parinda* quotes both *Nayakan* and Kazan's *On the Waterfront*. Both films offer us ways to understand the local manifestation of a globally circulating genre through their continuing tussle with the imagined conventions of Indian commercial cinema. Chopra admits that in *Parinda* he 'appropriated the pillars of Indian cinema and rebuilt the house'. Mani Ratnam openly confesses to experimenting with the limitations of commercial cinema in *Nayakan*.[12] In the absence of reliable documentation on the workings of the film industry in India that may help us draw links between marketing strategies and narrative experiments, I suggest that the legibility of conventions emerges in those films in which both producers and viewers acknowledge the currency of the director.

Methodological Map: the Cross-hatched Grid

This chapter on Mani Ratnam's *Nayakan* and the next one on Vidhu Vinod Chopra's *Parinda* will focus on how narrative time, commodity culture, and masculinity emerge as thematic concerns in these films. Their evocation of the past – a mandatory feature in the gangster genre – allows us consider how they are also strategies of writing the nation, even if they deliberately stage fears and anxieties of declining state authority by displacing the shock of cinematic images on to a narrative of violence. Narrated in terms of individual histories of protagonists battling the brutal power of a corrupt state, a narrative strategy that most commercial films thrive on, these films, nevertheless, are suited to theorising links between writing history and nostalgia for our cultural unconscious. I pay attention to the particular ways in which cinematic mechanisms service this cultural production of nostalgia in a close analysis of both films.

The different intersecting reading strategies in this chapter work as a cross-

hatched grid that guides my reading of the film, using narratology to decipher various differences between story and plot as a way to explore both films' investment
in the past. Mieke Bal (1997) lays out the different relations between the order of
events in the story and their chronological sequence in the fabula. She suggests:

> Differences between the arrangement in the story and the chronology of the fabula we
> call chronological deviations or anachronies. It goes without saying that no negative
> connotations should be attached to these terms; they are meant to be technical only … .
> A conventional construction of a novel is the beginning in media res, which immerses
> the reader in the middle of the fabula. From this point s/he is referred back to the past,
> and from then on the story carries on more or less chronologically through to the end.
> Anachrony in itself, then, is by no means unusual.
>   In popular romances and other popular fiction one encounters all kinds of variants of
> this form. However, anachrony can be used as a means for the realization of specific
> literary effects. I shall discuss three aspects of chronological deviation successively:
> direction, distance, and range. [pp. 83–4]

At the end of a long exposition, Bal moves to the edge of these categories to list a
number of exceptions that are useful to our understanding of song and dance
sequences, both the 'conventional' use of these segments and how we account for its
innovation. She suggests two ways in which we can sight 'achronies' in a narrative:

> To begin with, an achrony is sometimes 'undated,' when it does not indicate anything
> about its direction, distance, or span … . A second possibility lies in the grouping of
> events on the grounds of other than chronological criteria, without any mention of
> chronological sequence … . With this last form of achrony we have exhausted the
> possibilities for structuring the chronological flow within a story into a specific
> sequence. Here, the linearity of the fabula and the linearity of its presentation to the
> reader no longer have any correspondence at all. [p. 99]

Besides attending to the differences between story and fabula, I shall also look at
other temporal ellipses that we find in films – slow-motion shots and dissolves –
and those interruptions particular to Indian cinema, such as the location of the
interval and the timing of song and dance sequences. *Nayakan*'s thrust towards a
linear narrative unfolds through repetition, or more specifically through a doubling
effect that ripples through the film at times inflecting even the song and dance
sequences. This doubling bears an intimate relationship to the Oedipal narrative
that begins the film and surfaces globally as a feature of this genre. Diagonally cutting across the melodrama of the Oedipal narrative, the film celebrates the
gangster genre's long-standing relationship to commodity culture through the

presence of cars in the *mise en scène* as signifiers of authenticity on the one hand, and as disruptions of the linear narrative on the other. The chapter's final section turns to song and dance sequences as the most significant marker of Mani Ratnam's cinematic style that allow us to see the intertextual links between *Nayakan* and his other films. Besides examining the temporal status of these sequences, I also suggest that the iconographic details foreground the ideological charge of his films.

A Narrative of Collaboration

One of the many reasons that Mani Ratnam and Chopra have had the opportunity to rework conventions and command a directorial signature lies in their ability to control the entire production of their films. Nowhere is this clearer than *Nayakan*. Initially financed by Muktha films, Mani Ratnam clashed with his producer Muktha Srinivas who tried to dictate the costs of film-making and pulled out midway through production. The film was picked up by Mani Ratnam's brother G. Venkatesan, who had by then formed his own production company called Sujatha films.

Of all the contemporary directors in India, Mani Ratnam stands out for his cinematic virtuosity and commercial success, a combination that few other directors have matched. Armed, curiously enough, with a business degree, Mani Ratnam entered film-making with a Kannada film, *Pallavi Anupallavi/Pallavi and Pallavi* (1983), followed by a Malayalam film, *Unaroo/Another* (1984). He has made fourteen films in Tamil, *Geetanjali* (1989) in Telugu, and *Dil Se/From the Heart* (1998) in Hindi. He had a retrospective at the Toronto Film Festival in 1995, and his films have become a regular feature at the Washington, DC, International Film Festival. His stock in the national market rose enormously when his smash-hit film *Roja* (1992) was dubbed in Hindi, but it was *Nayakan* that initially won him national recognition. Hindi film director Feroz Khan remade *Nayakan* into the Hindi film *Dayavan/Generous* (1988), though he was unable to reproduce the production quality of the original.

Chastised by intellectuals for churning out glossy products with insidious nationalist messages, Mani Ratnam nevertheless substantially reinvented production conditions by giving equal weight to cinematography and art direction in his commercial films. In several published interviews, cinematographer P. C. Sriram and art director Thotta Tharani have praised Mani Ratnam's style of working, which gave them space to express an individual style.

Graduating from the Madras Film School with a diploma in cinematography in 1979, Sriram had worked on seven films before working with Mani Ratnam on a small-budget Tamil film, *Mouna Ragam/Silent Tune* (1986). However, it was his work on *Nayakan* that catapulted him into the national scene, winning him the National award for cinematography that, Sriram adds, is usually reserved for art-film cinematographers.[13] The chance to collaborate on a period film was an exciting challenge. In an interview, P. C. Sriram details the yellow tint that he experimented with to construct a period look that we associate with sepia photographs:

> We wanted to use a technique calling 'flashing' to reduce the colors. I had another idea. I wanted to give the film a 'period' look. But 'flashing' would have been expensive. So while grading, I played with the analyser to keep the colour to the minimum. Since we print on different negatives, there is no consistency. For the interiors, I decided on top lights which mellow the lights but increase the contrast. What I did with the analyser was only 2 per cent. The rest was achieved by the sets, the costumes, and lighting.[14]

Sriram describes how *Nayakan* also provided him with the opportunity to experiment with underwater photography for the first time.[15] Since this film, he has worked with Mani Ratnam on *Agni Natshatram/Hot Spot* (1988), *Geetanjali* (1989), *Thiruda Thiruda/Thief! Thief!* (1993), and (after a hiatus) in *Alaipayuthey/Waves* (2000).[16] More than any of his other accomplishments in film-making, his place as a star cinematographer is emphasised repeatedly by his fans, who clap thunderously as his name appears on the screen.[17]

Not unlike Sriram, who also runs an advertising company, art director Thotta Tharani is a well-known abstract artist.[18] Working on Tamil, Telugu, and Malayalam films, Tharani identifies the origin of his rise as one of India's best art directors as *Mouna Ragam*, which initiated a long collaboration with Mani Ratnam and continued until *Iruvar* (1996). Likewise, it was *Nayakan* that won him national recognition in the form of the National award for art direction. Tharani erected a huge set simulating the Bombay slum Dharavi in a Madras studio, because 'nothing less than verisimilitude would satisfy him and his director Mani Ratnam'.[19] Newspaper articles celebrating the film's authenticity related how Kamal Haasan worked on his role as the underworld don Velu Nayakan by closely modelling his mannerisms on those of Vardarajan Mudaliar, a real-life Tamil gangster in Bombay.[20] The continuous relay between the extra-cinematic allure of the don and the star actor ensured the film's popularity. The film and Kamal Haasan won numerous awards in 1988 and, in a final gesture of acknowledgement from both the state and the film industry, *Nayakan* was India's official Oscar entry in 1987.

Plot Summary

Based loosely on *The Godfather*, the film tracks the rise of underworld don Velu Nayakan. After killing the policeman who killed his father, a trade-union leader, young Velu flees from Tamil Nadu to the slums of Mumbai (Bombay). First joining a petty smuggler, Velu slowly increases his influence in the underworld. Hailed as a saviour by the Tamil slum inhabitants, Velu eventually becomes Nayakan, or don.

He loses his wife and son in gang wars, but refuses to relinquish his power. His daughter walks out of his house and marries a police officer who is finally responsible for his surrender. At the end, he is shot by his bodyguard who discovers that Nayakan had killed his father, a police officer.

Opening Sequence and Primary Conditions

I argued in the previous chapter that film theory's obsession with opening sequences as condensing properties of the entire narrative fails to match the sequencing pattern in Indian popular cinema, where the idea of the beginning ends at the intermission. In Indian cinema, the first eighty to ninety minutes usually stage the primary conditions of the narrative. *Nayakan*, however, rewrites this convention by favouring the opening segment as the repository of prospective moves.

Nayakan opens with a still shot of a beach, and the camera tracks a boy running on a sand dune. He is suddenly grabbed by a posse of policemen. Cutting to a medium shot, we see the policemen knocking the boy about. They want to know his father's whereabouts. The film cuts to a long shot that places the policemen and boy in the middle of a framed doorway at the end of the dark tunnel. A chief inspector joins the scene. In a medium long shot, we hear the inspector admonishing his subordinates for beating the boy. It is at this moment we learn that the boy's father is a trade-union leader on the run. The film now cuts to a close-up shot of the boy's bruised face. The chief inspector assures the boy that he will not be beaten again and encourages him to convey similar assurances to his father.

Alternating between shots of the boy running through bushes and the police tailing him, we see the boy reuniting with his father at a hideout on the beach. Velu asks his father a series of questions: 'The police claim you and your friends are terrorists. Why do the police want to shoot you? … Is it wrong to be a trade-union leader?' The police sneak into position around the hideout. Grabbing Shakti Velu (hereafter Velu), the father tries to flee, but is immediately shot in the back. Slow-motion shots capture him dying.

We now move to an evening scene where Velu and the police gather around a funeral pyre on the beach. In a series of slow-motion shots, we see the boy running towards a policeman, grabbing his bayonet, and stabbing the chief inspector in the stomach. Velu flees from this scene into a grove of trees, and as he runs into the background the credits roll. On the soundtrack we hear the sound of a moving train, which is soon drowned out by the film's first song, sung by the music director Ilyaraja. Recognisable as a lullaby, the song lovingly soothes a crying baby, wondering who could hurt this prince. As the song takes over the soundtrack, the film moves through iconic images of Mumbai landmarks: Victoria Terminus railway station and the Gateway of India. It breaks briefly when Velu runs into a band of young pickpockets and befriends Selva, a fellow Tamil. The song resumes as Selva introduces

Velu to his extended family of other migrant Tamils – a Muslim called Mustapha Bhai whom the children call Vapa, and his daughter Shakila. The song stops for a moment when Velu asks his foster-parent, 'Vapa, you pray five times a day, whether it rains or shines you go to the mosque, you generously offer money to the needy. Yet you sneak out in the middle of the night to smuggle goods from the sea. Isn't it wrong to smuggle?' Vapa responds, 'It's not wrong to help others.' The song ends with a medium close-up silhouette of both men with the final credits running across the screen. The film dissolves into the next scene, and the camera zooms into a close-up shot of the adult Velu played by Kamal Haasan.

The opening sequence that includes both the pre-credit and credit sequences condenses the different thematic and formal concerns of the film. At the thematic register the relationship between the police, the father, and the son is the principal storyline, a dynamic that strives repeatedly to differentiate patriarchal authority from state power by casting the police as brutal and fathers as innocent. Such primary conditions reveal the film's preference for vigilante justice in the absence of the legitimate authority of the state. This partiality is asserted through a symmetrical logic of violence: the police shoot Velu's father and, in retaliation, Velu kills the chief inspector, both rendered in slow-motion shots. However hard the film works at representing police brutality, Velu's culpability in carelessly leading the police to his father's hideout is never erased from the film's narration and haunts our protagonist's rise in the Mumbai underworld.

The particular manifestation of repetition through a structure of twinning that prospectively inflects the entire film is already intimated through the opening dialogue when Velu questions his father, 'Is it wrong to be a trade-union leader?' and later his foster-father Vapa, 'Isn't it wrong to smuggle?' His father is killed before he can answer the question, while Vapa asserts that smuggling is an honourable means of helping others. This structuring of repetition with difference characterises the narrative temporality of the film, which moves forward by repeating several thematic and formal features twice. The ideological charge of this structuring is blatant when the film refuses to answer Velu's primary question, 'Is it wrong to be a trade-union leader?', but kills the father and chooses to respond to our moral quandary in a dubious manner through the figure of a smuggler. Vapa's answer undercuts the state's authority, but legitimates trading in an unregulated economy. In contrast, in killing the trade-union father, the film erases anticapitalist struggles and forecloses this option for Velu. In both cases, the film enlists our sympathy to see the police as brutal and incapable of delivering justice, a role that Velu better fulfils.

Slow-motion shots and dissolves emerge as formal motifs: shots of Velu's father collapsing into his son's arms and of Velu stabbing the inspector feed into the vigilante thematic of the film; repeated later in the film, they highlight the genre's preoccupation with spectacular scenes of violence. These sequences are a homage to Sam Peckinpah's *The Wild Bunch* (1969), where an expansion of 'real time' returns us to the pleasure and horror of watching violent scenes.[21] After the credit sequences, *Nayakan* uses slow-motion shots twice: first when Velu's wife Neela is gunned down by another mob; and secondly when his demented personal guard, Aji, shoots Velu at the end of the film. Both deaths remind us of the first death in the film, but with a difference. Neela's death dismembers Velu's family, and the film refuses to find an equivalence, even if Velu vindicates her death by killing the three Reddy brothers. However, we can forget Velu's complicity in Neela's death if we instead conceive her death as simple and pure retaliation for usurping the Reddys' domain of activity. Aji shoots Velu for killing his father, Inspector Kelkar, a logic that is formally not equivalent to the scene of Kelkar's own death, but returns us to the film's pre-credit sequence where a young Velu stabs a police officer for killing his father. But the film short-circuits Aji's entry into a filial logic of vengeance by privileging the moment when Velu brutally smashes Inspector Kelkar's head in 'normal speed' and emerges as protector of the migrant Tamils in Bombay. In other words, by formally equating the two filial killings, the film insists that Kelkar's death cannot be avenged because of his brutality against the Tamil community, a logic that justifies Velu's violent actions. By casting Kelkar also as a father, the film retains the melodramatic option of filial revenge as one of the several choices at closure, thus undercutting the logic of gangster films that occupies the central sections of the narrative.

Nayakan also employs dissolves to overcome large disjunctions of real time. Doubling the film's obsession with doubleness, dissolves occur on four occasions: the film dissolves into the post-credit sequence and zooms into the adult Velu; dissolves twice to open Ganesh Chaturti scenes many years apart; and finally once after Velu and Neela's marriage song. In each case it smooths massive temporal and spatial disjunctions and in doing so recalls a typical device of classical Hollywood narrative.[22]

Driving Father's Car

While the pre-credit and credit sequences compress both the film's attempt to juggle different kinds of narrative time by minimising deviations between the story and its chronology, and the Oedipal structuring of melodrama, their relationship to a specific historical referent is rather elusive. The dated uniforms worn by the police are the sole indicators of a referent outside the self-enclosed Oedipal narrative and perhaps point to a period before the mid-1970s. However, the lap dissolve that ends the credit sequence papers over spatial, temporal, and graphic disjunctions and openly engages with conventions of the gangster genre, particularly fortifying the link between two features, narrative verisimilitude and commodity culture. Sketching the protagonist's rise and fall in the Bombay underworld over a period of more than thirty years, the film attempts faithfully to re-create a historical period by care-fully managing different aspects of the *mise en scène*. More than any other detail in the *mise en scène*, automobiles – different models of cars, jeeps, and vans – indicate the passage of time within the diegesis. Employing the presence of the automobile as a road map, I shall drive through the film to demonstrate how they intertwine with the rhythm of twinning, and together both kinds of temporality *perform* the ambivalence of writing post-colonial history that cannot escape completely its own investment in nostalgia.

In his reading of Harmut Bitomsky's film *Reichsautobahn* (1986), Edward Dimendberg points out the intimate relationship between driving and watching films; driving on the autobahn not only affected the speed of moving images, but also encouraged film-makers to replicate the vistas that were now available from above the autobahn. However, genre films have little truck with radical possibilities of changing visual perception, and even Dimendberg implicitly acknowledges this limitation when he closes his essay with a reading of *Plunder Road*, a film noir care-fully presenting details such as speed and distance, but denying us a point of view of the automobile subject except in the opening sequence.

More often than not, cars speed and slide through gangster films as an integral feature of the genre's obsession with verisimilitude: *Nayakan* is no exception.[23] Lit-tered throughout the film, automobiles offer no radical shift in perception, but simply signal the passage of time in the film. Soon after its release, several reviews remarked on the realistic use of cars in Mani Ratnam's films, an impression fuelled perhaps by their otherwise ornamental status in most popular films.

Cars in Indian cinema usually carry singing heroes and heroines across beautiful landscapes, signifying all too often the modern and glamorous aspects of the love story. But this autophilia acquires more deadly dimensions in Feroz Khan's Hindi film *Qurbani/Sacrifice* (1980), where for the first time in Indian popular cinema the camera lingers on a burning (real) Mercedes-Benz. Simultaneously signifying excess and confidence over commodity culture, Khan's film could be said to have set off a huge increase in production costs. The great exception to this unabashed display is Ritwik Ghatak's *Ajantrik/The Unmechanical* (1957), where a car splutters through a landscape marked by nature, mining, and indigenous peoples. Ghatak's film may be the only film ever to problematise the tribulations of owning a Chevrolet in India!

Despite his protestations that he is 'indifferent to cars', Mani Ratnam's films reveal a love for them: in *Mouna Ragam* car problems initiate a comic encounter between a Sikh and a Tamil in Delhi, and another car helps reunite the hero with his wife; in *Thiruda Thiruda* (1993) petty thieves steal cars to make a quick getaway; in *Roja* a new Maruti car symbolises the gap between urban and rural areas; in *Iruvar/Duo* (1997) cars add authenticity to a political drama spanning over forty years in Tamil Nadu and an off-screen car accident kills the female protagonist; in *Bombay* charred cars convey the extent of communal violence; and in *Alaipayuthey*, an interclass love story that is set against a backdrop of suburban trains and motorcycles, it is a car accident that finally reunites the estranged couple. In *Nayakan* cars simulate the linear pressures of the narrative by indicating temporal shifts, but their fetishisation at times unhinges the historical referent and warps the progressive pull of the narrative.

As the film dissolves into the post-credit sequence, we hear the sounds of a truck from an off-screen space, and the film cuts to a moving van with the familiar Tata emblem 'T' on the front grille. Several armed police alight and start aggressively hosing down the Tamil squatters living on the pavements, and other policemen on horseback ride in to frighten them off. As everybody flees from the police assault, the camera concentrates on one man, Velu, standing up to the fierce spray of the police hose and refusing to budge. We see him mouthing an obscenity in Tamil and being quickly detained by Inspector Kelkar; on the soundtrack we hear the sound of a moving train for the second time. Cutting to a close-up shot of Velu's battered face, the sequence moves rapidly to foreground his face and body, with the assaulting police officer and his subordinates in the background. A long shot locating the action in the centre of the frame repeats a shot from the pre-credit sequence, and once again we hear the sound of moving trains on the soundtrack. In the next scene a police jeep – an automobile made in India through a joint venture between AMC and Mahindra and Mahindra that dates back to 1945 – rolls into the central area of the slum and drops Velu's brutalised body in the slushy mess of the preceding night. A number of formal and thematic configurations recall the opening pre-credit sequence – close-up shots, long shots, sounds of trains, and brutal police – but with a difference: automobiles now surface in the repetition. Indexing the 1950s, the Tata police van signals a collaborative relationship between the newly established postcolonial state and large business houses in India.

The film now moves to establish Velu's entry to the underworld, rehearsing another detail from the opening sequence. Velu and Selva offer to take over Vapa's smuggling route for a day while he recovers from a fever. At sea, Velu devises a plan

A police truck enters the slum in *Nayakan*

to hide their booty from the customs, a plan that pays homage to Sergio Leone's *Once Upon a Time in America* (1983).[24] Tying their illicit cargo to large bags of salt attached to rubber inner tubes, Velu and Selva dump them into the sea. The cargo sinks from the weight of the salt, but when the salt dissolves the cargo bobs to the surface – by which time they have passed the watchful eye of customs officers. Their ingenuity turns out to be equally handy when they bargain with the powerful underworld don Dorai. Instead of accepting their standard fee of two hundred rupees, Velu asks for two thousand rupees, threatening to dump the goods into the sea if they are not paid that amount. After this exchange, we cut to a scene where Dorai is livid with his henchman for succumbing to Velu's threat. While Velu and Selva set off to celebrate their earnings at the local brothel, Vapa is captured by the police and is later found hanged in his prison cell. The following morning, Velu finds out that it was Dorai who had ordered the local police officer – the same Inspector Kelkar – to arrest his foster-father.

Vapa's death repeats the events of the pre-credit sequence. Velu hunts down Kelkar, who is drinking with prostitutes, and initiates a fight that ends in the central area of the slum. When Velu is about to deliver the final blow with an axe, the inhabitants of the slum withdraw into their homes, denying us eyewitnesses to the scene and thus indicating tacit approval of Velu's revenge. Departing from the spectacular representation of killing through slow-motion shots, the film posits this murder as the crucial moment when Velu emerges as the Nayakan, or don, for the migrant Tamils. As one woman later explains to the investigating police officer, Raghvan, they are proud there is finally a real man among them to protect them from police brutality. After this second round of filial revenge against the police, Selva addresses Velu using the honorific 'Nayakan', indicating his place as the don.

The film's first ode to private commodity culture occurs when a high-angle shot focuses on three cars – a Morris Minor, a Datsun, and a Plymouth – curving from the bottom of the frame to the top as they drive into the centre of the slum.[25] A Gujarati builder, Seth, arrives with blueprints for a factory worth ten lakh rupees to

Seth's convoy curves into the centre of the slum

be built over the slum. Velu tries to find out from Seth how this is possible, as they believe they live on unclaimed land belonging to the state or, should we say, nobody in particular. Seth asks them to talk to Dorai, a Tamil with considerable influence who brokered the sale. Dorai's response segues into a top shot where we see a car, a late 1930s Packard, curving into the scene. As Dorai steps out, the worried inhabitants crowd around him, expressing their fears of eviction. He first tries to placate them, then argues that they should be grateful for not having paid rent on this land all these years. Velu steps forward and pointedly asks Dorai how much he was paid for selling his own people. Dorai's awkward silence reveals his complicity. Just then Seth pulls up in his car, conveniently offering him a ride out of this confrontation.

Whereas the cars in this segment place the narrative in the 1950s, the next scene undercuts this referent by evoking the present: the film cuts to a medium close-up shot of Seth's construction truck, dumping gravel into the central space. The construction truck is distinctly a product manufactured in the 1980s. Instead of seeing the juxtaposition of objects in the *mise en scène* as a problem of continuity or celebrating it as the film's postmodern gesture where commodities from different eras circulate on the same surface, inserting a contemporary construction truck into the *mise en scène* reveals nostalgia where the point of view of the present impinges on the writing of the past. Furthermore, even as Mani Ratnam chooses cars to delineate discretely the passage of time, automobiles litter the post-colonial consumer landscape in India – models from different periods coexist, a detail that ironically lends verisimilitude to the narrative.

The film detours through Velu's marriage to Neela, the girl he met on his night out at the brothel. The third song in the film moves us through their marriage and Neela's pregnancy, closing with a dissolve that slides over a few years to scenes with their two young children. As Velu Nayakan grows increasingly powerful, the film elaborately describes his entry into the upper reaches of the Mumbai underworld controlled by five families – Lal Bhai, Mustapha, Mahindra, Chandrakant Khosla, and the three Reddy brothers. Once again, the film relies on cars to demonstrate

Velu and his entourage visit Lal Bhai

the wealth of the powerful – a high-angle shot captures two 1948 baby Buicks moving across the frame as they pull into Lal Bhai's driveway for a meeting. This
high-angle shot repeats the shot of cars moving into the slum that we had previously
seen, but with a difference – now the two cars curve from the background to the
foreground. In the driveway we see five other cars, also from this period. As with
most events in this film, here, too, having repeated it, the film loses its interests in
this *mise en scène* detail. This is the last time in the film we see cars made in the
1940s and 1950s used explicitly to historicise the dramatic space.

At the meeting, Velu offers to land illicit cargo held in Mustapha Bhai's ship, a
job usually reserved for the Reddy brothers, who are now experiencing pressure
from vigilant customs officials. The film cuts to the next scene where Velu and Selva
are out at sea. We do not witness the actual transfer of goods from Mustapha's ship
to their boat, but the next shot shows Velu and Selva on their return journey to the
mainland. For the second time, Velu uses sacks of salt to submerge the smuggled
goods in the sea.

In the next scene, Velu struts into Lal Bhai's house, flushed from his nocturnal
success. Velu had driven to the house in a van with a Tamil sign on its bodywork,
the van being part of a fleet of ambulances that Velu Nayakan acquires in order to
take his Tamil neighbours to the hospital. We realise this only in the first scene after
the interval – the ambulance van is unavailable at this moment in the diegesis. (In
a much later scene, the newly appointed assistant commissioner of police commands
his men to seal these vehicles as evidence of corruption in his case against Velu
Nayakan.) Once again, commodity fetishism in this film often undercuts narrative
verisimilitude, even if we believe that they mutually inform each other in genre films.

The Reddy brothers view Velu as a threat competing for their turf in the underworld. The first half of the film closes with the brothers plotting to kill Velu Nayakan
and his family, a moment when melodrama meshes with the violence associated with
gangster genres. Recall that the interval is a crucial punctuating moment in Indian
commercial cinema, often closing off several narrative strands. However, *Nayakan*

Velu arrives with the loot at Lal
Bhai's house

breaks away from this convention by underplaying this moment of disjunction that affects both production and reception of Indian films. Mani Ratnam uses the interval to heighten certain dramatic moments with the promise of continuity when the film resumes, a strategy that is more akin to the location of a cliffhanger in television programming than its deployment in, say, J. P. Dutta's films.[26]

The second half begins with a high-angle shot of a Mumbai road heavy with traffic. Cutting to the courtyard in Velu Nayakan's house, we hear a woman begging for help for her sick child. We see Velu at the hospital threatening the doctor with dire consequences if he does not attend to the sick infant at once. It is at this moment that he asks both Selva and his Hindi interpreter Iyer to buy five ambulances for their neighbourhood so that they do not have to be beholden to the negligent state hospital for transportation. Through the acquisition of these ambulances, the film reinforces Velu's presence as a community leader with these acts of benevolence.

The film cuts from a song and dance sequence celebrating the spring festival Holi to a scene of Velu Nayakan's young family at home. Neela tells her husband that their son Surya is determined to grow up to be like his father. We have already seen the young children, Surya and Charu, play-acting their father's business with their friends. Far from being pleased, Velu hopes that his lowly business will end with him. A woman crying for help from an off-screen space breaks the cosy family moment. The film repeats the high-angle shot of the courtyard where we see once again a woman begging for help at the gates. Emerging from behind the woman is one of the Reddy brothers with a gun. As Neela heads towards the window in response to the cry for help, the woman warns them of the murderous intruder, but it is too late and Neela is gunned down. The sequence closes with Neela falling from a window on the first floor. The slow-motion shots of her death recall the slow-motion shots of Velu's father, but with a difference.[27]

The film cuts to a beach where we see a large imported car (either a Packard or a large Morris) parked in the foreground. Velu orders Selva to kill all three Reddy brothers before Neela's funeral is over. Through a series of intercutting shots, we

Velu at Neela's cremation

move between Velu performing Neela's funeral rites and his men killing the two younger Reddys.[28] The killing scene repeats the structure of twin events in this film: one of the brothers, found in the company of two prostitutes just as Velu found Kelkar, is beheaded; the second brother is garrotted in his car. Finally, Velu himself shoots the eldest brother through the door viewer of an apartment door. The familial dimensions of the killing remind us of the filial cycle of revenge in the opening sequences, as well as the famous intercutting sequence in *The Godfather*. But besides calling on its own rhythm and the intertextual reference to a famous film, the film also traffics in well-worn conventions of urban gangster films by using cars as harbingers of violence. The multiple address in this segment captures the tension in the film as it tries to accommodate two modes: verisimilitude and spectacle.

Neela's death convinces Velu that his children should leave the gang wars of Mumbai for Madras, where they will be in Shakila's care. At the railway station, his daughter asks him if he is responsible for her mother's death. Velu is catatonic, a response that confirms his complicity. Moving through this scene at the railway station, the film cuts to a song and dance sequence that is structured as an external flashback with the opening song playing again on the soundtrack. Rather than a montage of different scenes, this flashback captures one scene when Velu and Neela put their children to bed. Tied to Charu's question, the soundtrack displaces Velu's culpability on to the brutality of the police and renders his memory as pure nostalgia.

The film dissolves to a close-up shot of Velu's face at a public celebration of Ganesh Chaturti, a religious Hindu festival that is celebrated in public spaces in Mumbai.[29] The camera pulls back from the podium, craning up to make room for Nayakan's Ambassador car. In addition to the dissolve, the Ambassador that pulls in with a middle-aged Velu Nayakan marks the passage of time. It locates us in a post-colonial commodity economy where the native bourgeois interests of the Birla industrial house that has manufactured this model since the early 1950s and nationalist sentiments asserting self-reliance have enjoyed a long marriage.

Charu learning to drive on the beach

Velu inaugurates the religious ceremony with a customary prayer for his daughter Charu and the film cuts to another car scene. Charu is learning to drive on the beach. In the centre of the scene is a large American car that we can identify as a 1962/3 Malibu convertible, popularly known as the Impala in India. The Ambassador in the previous scene signals a shift in period, a distinct shift from the reign of English, Japanese, and American imports to domestic production. But Charu's car warps this linear progress, suspending the historical referent in this scene. At this moment, the historical referent of the diegetic universe approximates the 1970s and 1980s: this classic American car from the early 1960s produces the film's only 'pure' retro-effect. This blatant paean to Americanism reveals the film's elaborate investment in commodity fetishism that so far has been disguised as a concern for narrative verisimilitude. From being objects in the *mise en scène* marking and warping time, automobiles slowly move towards actively participating in the dramatic action of the film, mainly through accidents. The cars have moved, in narratological terms, from the status of description to an attribute.

We move to Nayakan's home where his son Surya holds court with the Tamil community on behalf of his father who is praying in an off-screen space. Selva watches Surya take charge of a particular situation: a distressed father recounts how his son, on his way to Dubai, accidentally ran over a boy in a local slum, but, fearing that the repercussions that may impede his departure, he ran away from the scene of the crime. We find out that the son was driving an Ambassador car and the accident occurred in Matunga, a suburb of Mumbai. Surya suggests that the man lodge a complaint with the police, stating that he lost his car three days ago. Turning to Velachami, one of his men, Surya asks him to go to Matunga police station and turn himself in for having run over the boy. Surya promises to support Velachami's family, assuring him of a short stint in jail. Impressed with Surya's deft handling of the crisis, Selva remarks on how it is reminiscent of the young Velu Nayakan. Cars now insert themselves into the filial narrative that governs the emotional drive of the film.[30]

After a transition scene at Neela's propitiation ceremony, performed now for the second time, where Kelkar's widow asks Velu Nayakan to employ her retarded son who wants to be a police officer like his father, the film returns to cars. Sub-inspector Raghvan visits Velu Nayakan to ask a personal favour: his daughter has been raped by the son of a powerful politician, but his superior advises against pursuing his arrest, fearing retaliation from the powerful father. We last saw Raghvan as the officer investigating Kelkar's death. The film calculates this temporal span as twenty years – a figure uttered by Velu Nayakan when he greets Raghvan at his home – a number that neatly divides by two! Nayakan promises to help.

The film cuts to a medium long shot of Charu crossing the road outside Jehangir Art Gallery, Mumbai's well-known contemporary-art museum. As one of the prem-

Nayakan's men assault the
politician's son

ier arbiters taste in India, its façade indicates Charu's social mobility while also
expanding the repertoire of taste in the film from mass commodities to high art. The
film cuts to a black Ambassador driving into a car park, and we see the driver park-
ing his car next to Selva's. Cutting back to Jehangir Art Gallery, we see a shot of a
taxi moving across the frame from right to left. Charu crosses the road after a second Padmini taxi passes in front of her. Already intimating the privileged place of
cars and traffic, the film resorts to a rhythm of intercutting shots. We see Charu
watching Selva and his two companions get out of their car and corner the politician's son. The scene closes with the men using the car door as a weapon to break
the culprit's arm. Moving from being a decorative object in the *mise en scène*, cars
now participate in a brutal beating.

The film slowly speeds the association between cars and violence by tying it
closely to the father–son dyad of the opening sequence. Raghvan visits Nayakan for
the second time, but with a difference – he is now in civilian clothes. The purpose
of the visit is to return a favour. Raghvan informs Nayakan that in court the following day, one of his men, Pandian, will turn state's evidence against Velu in
exchange for his freedom. Surya offers to stop Pandian from testifying while assuring his father that it will be done with finesse.

Cars govern Surya's entire expedition. Outside the court, we see him leaning
against a white Ambassador signalling to his hired killer. Inside the courtroom, just
as Pandian is about start confessing, the hired killer, Ranjan, pulls out his gun. The
film cuts to an establishing shot of the courthouse, and we hear gunshots on the
soundtrack. Ranjan escapes by leaping off the balcony onto a net that is held across
the back of a three-wheeled Tempo pickup. The film cuts to Nayakan's home. Surya
is trying to reach his father from a telephone booth at a petrol station. Ranjan drives
into the petrol station to greet Surya, who is shocked that the former did not change
vehicles as planned. We see a cordon of police jeeps closing around them. Surya tries
to escape, but drives his car into a petrol pump, which explodes. The scene closes
with a long shot of the mushrooming clouds generated from the collision. After

Surya hits a petrol pump and dies
in a ball of flame

Surya's death, the film abandons not only Ambassador cars, but also its obsession with the structuring of twinning. Nowhere is this more evident than at Surya's funeral, where we hear the opening song playing for the third time.

The film, however, does not totally give up using cars to signal the passage of time or foregrounding them as an integral part of the action. At the Ganesh festival, the film signals the passage of time through three different signifiers: a dissolve brings us to the festival celebrated for the second time in the film; Velu Nayakan arrives in a Maruti (a car first manufactured in 1984); and for the second time he offers a prayer for Charu who has abandoned him after her brother's death. Once again, repetition occurs with some difference. Two police jeeps arrive and try to break up the celebration. Selva explodes, ranting about a tradition that has been in place for the past thirty years, another numerical detail that drives home the demise of the twinning structuring dominant so far in the film.

The film heads towards a symmetrical closure mirroring the opening scene. The new assistant commissioner of police is a zealous young officer determined to clean up the underworld. We find out that he is Charu's husband, but realise that he is unaware of this relationship when he raids Velu's various businesses. For the first time we see the city from inside a police jeep, from the point of view of the young police officer. He orders his men to seize Velu's ambulances, seeing them as overt signs of power. Velu drives to the inspector's home in a Maruti van to threaten him, unaware that he is married to Charu. As the police take over the narrative, cars and their ability to reckon historical time fade out, as does the film's fidelity to a cycle of twin events. Velu's supporters riot against the police, and we see a burning police jeep on screen, signifying the charred remains of the film's autophilia. Velu is arrested when performing Neela's annual propitiation rituals for the third time in the film. When the court fails to marshal enough evidence against him, Nayakan is freed, but is killed by Kelkar's son Aji, who closes the filial cycle of vengeance that opened the film.

As the police halt the flow of gangster activity and, by extension, the internal logic of repetition, their role has a familiar place within the conventions of closure employed in this genre. However, this film's investment in questions of temporality that bear on strategies of writing history is hardly generic. As Velu succumbs, the film produces its own flashback of events, breaking all the rules of narrative continuity dominating it so far, a montage of scenes from pre-credit and post-credit sequences: family scenes with Neela and the children, Velu marching towards Seth's home, moments with Selva intermingle haphazardly with scenes that are absent in the diegesis, such as scenes with Nayakan and his adult daughter Charu, and scenes of Nayakan praying.[31] Unlike the two earlier flashbacks, the final moments bear little fidelity to the diegesis. Narrated as the film's own flashback, the segment directs our memory of the film, but, like its own investment in nostalgia, offers us a memory that exceeds our viewing experience. In effect, the final moments return us to consider the relationship between history and memory in cinema that the film attempts to regulate with varying success around the structuring of the Oedipal dyad and autophilia.

Enforced Coherence

The tightly knit narrative in *Nayakan* emerges as one of the most innovative negotiations between local and global conventions of the gangster genre. Simultaneously, Mani Ratnam's cinematic topography opens questions of incoherence that the film cannot completely contain, incoherences that stage some of the unresolved struggles of our social and psychic domains in the post-colonial landscape that films continually exploit. Critics have long taken his films to task for far too skilfully managing his cinematic topography.[32] M. S. S. Pandian and Venkatesh Chakravarthy accuse him of 'commodifying history'; Chakravarthy takes him to task for his seamless editing; and Prasad reads him as encouraging us to surrender to the nationalist–capitalist fantasies of his films. I do not disagree with these critical positions, but my route to them is a little different. Rather than lambast Ratnam for the 'surplus realism' in his films, I suggest we look at those moments of *enforced coherence* as symptoms of his ideological investment as well as the place of social anxieties. In other words, the places of coherence in his films also contain the social anxieties of a nationalist bourgeoisie with global aspirations. Since *Nayakan* more than any of his other films thrives on internal coherence to accommodate interruptions within the structure of the gangster genre, I want to take another look at the ways in which it covers its tracks. The tightly woven rhythm of twinning in the film offers no respite for a different logic of evaluation, yet the film's own investment in continuity touches on the Hindu biases of the secular imaginary that it inhabits. After Velu marries Neela at the Hindu temple, the film decidedly moves towards locating him within a Hindu ethos that had so far been understated – his foster-father was a Muslim and Velu's own religious faith had been absent. This move may explain the film's desire to convert Neela from a prostitute to a good wife, a conversion that cannot completely protect her from the punitive aspects of her violent death, but nevertheless naturalises the relationship between women and domestic ethos in the narrative. Neela's presence in the film rolls back the Muslim presence that was prominent in the film's early sections. Following his marriage, Velu replaces his unmarked clothes with distinctly Hindu markers, such as a white *dhoti* and vermilion marks on his forehead. It is only after Neela's death that Velu sends his children to Madras with his foster-sister Shakila. The melodramatic aspects of this scene fail to explain how Shakila disappears from the film. Chakravarthy also spots a similar disappearance in *Bombay*, when the Muslim wife stops eating meat after she marries her Hindu husband.[33] Slowly erasing the Muslim figure from the narrative or unable to account coherently for Muslims in the narrative touches on the film's culpability in exploiting those aspects of the fundamentalist Hindu social psyche that render the Muslim invisible or too fully present. The jagged representations of Muslims in this and his other films limit the topography of Mani Ratnam's films, reminding us of the provincial reach of his films as they write the nation state.

Song and Dance Sequences

Although the enforced coherence of *Nayakan* foregrounds its ideological investment in a Hindu imaginary, designating the Muslim as an unaccountable figure, we cannot overlook Mani Ratnam's prowess as a film-maker in his relationship to Indian popular cinema, particularly his articulation of the constellation of interruptions. Unfolding through a structuring of twinning predicated on an Oedipal melodrama, *Nayakan* faithfully re-creates several conventions of generic verisimilitude found in gangster films while also enveloping the constellation of interruptions peculiar to Indian cinema. Minimising the weight of the interval as a disruptive moment, the film relegates it to the status of a cliffhanger. Instead of dispensing with song and dance sequences as a risky proposition in a gangster film, Mani Ratnam intertwines them within the discourse of the film so as to mark it as an Indian gangster film.

His deft handling of this interruption in *Nayakan* is not a flash in the pan, but a standard feature of his films, where song and dance sequences are tightly woven into the narrative so as to seem indispensable, a prominent example of his directorial signature. Given their importance in his films, we cannot simply dismiss these sequences as the spectacular excesses of a successful commercial film-maker, but have to reconsider their relationship to the narrative. A close examination of these sequences allows us to see the varied ways in which he handles questions of spatial and temporal continuity, offering us a better means of grasping the peculiar form of the popular film in general as well the place of ideological interest in Mani Ratnam's films.

Although Mani Ratnam's films apotheosise this interruption, it has had a rich presence in the history of commercial Indian cinema, coinciding with the arrival of sound. *Alam Ara* (1930), India's first sound film, included seven songs and set the standard for popular cinema. The first decade of sound witnessed a range of experiments with sound and narrative, including the introduction of a number of songs into films. Musicologist Bhaskar Chandravarkar calls the songs of one minute and forty seconds' length 'songlets' that were rarely heard outside the cinemas and were thus not included on gramophone records of the film score.[34] Referring to such films as *Indrasabha* (1931), laden with seventy-one songs, or *Kalidas* (1931), a Tamil film with fifty songs, Ashok Ranade suggests that not all of them were strictly songs, but more verse-in-tune flowing between prose-based dialogue and a full-blown song, a convention that he suggests emerges from oral-based cultures.[35] Bowing to pressure from the recording industry, songs were standardised to between three and four minutes, emerging as discrete moments in films, a practice that has remained intact for the most part. According to Theodore Baskaran, dramatist P. Sambanda Mudaliyar suggested that 'ideally, song sequences should take about one-fourth of the film's duration'.[36] Along with pressure from the gramophone industry that promised revenues from sales of film song records, experiments in sound recording included pre-recorded song and lip-syncing by playback singers, which encouraged the recognition of film songs as distinct items. Overseeing the composition of lyrics, managing an orchestra, and choosing playback singers strengthened the role of the music director.[37] Allegedly, Nitin Bose's *Dhoop Chaon* (1935) was the first film to use systematically playback singing, under the helm of music director R. C. Boral.[38] Film historians and musicologists suggest that the popularity and persistence of film songs point to Indian cinema's early links with the conventions of nineteenth-century Parsee theatre, as well as folk theatre, which were similarly strung together with a number of songs. Besides these theatrical origins, Chandravarkar and Ranade point to a confluence of musical influences in the hybrid film song: Indian classical, folk, and western tunes.[39] In recent years, in addition to the star music director, choreographers such as Prabhu Deva, Saroj Khan, and Farah Khan have asserted their presence by grafting Indian dance styles with western dance moves.

Although musicologists have written extensively about the synthetic quality of Indian film songs, on the parallel economy of star music directors and singers, there is an absence of literature on song sequences, lending support to the assumption that the sequences are extra-diegetic or in narratological terms achronies, outside the temporal reckoning of the narrative.[40] A flamboyant example of such an instance occurs in S. Shankar's *Indian* (1994), where the film abruptly cuts from Madras to Australia as the preferred setting for the 'Melbourne' song and dance. Declaiming such practices, Baskaran writes: 'The flow of the film would not be affected in the least if song sequences were excised, wholly or partly.'[41] However indulgent song and dance sequences remain, a close analysis of this interruption leads us to explore how they relate to the narrative time of different kinds of films. Even in their most exhibitionistic form, when their presence rarely furthers the narrative and its 'undat-edness' or achrony is most visible in their ability to circulate as self-contained segments on music television or film previews, their iconography is available for a wide range of ideological readings.[42] I have argued elsewhere that the iconography in the song and dance sequences comments on the relationship between the love story and national identity. For instance, the presence and absence of scenes from Kashmir alert us to the ways in which films stage contestations over cartography in the national imaginary.[43]

There is no doubt that the presence of several such sequences is reminiscent of a cinema of attractions found in early cinema, where the spectacular aspects of such scenes override narrative coherence.[44] But they also solicit our interests as tourists, albeit virtual tourists travelling the world within the closed confines of the movie theatre. The coincidence between tourism and cinema is an old one – Lumière-shorts of Egypt are some of the earliest examples – and in Indian popular films these excursions speak to the continued interest in the travel genre, even though a particular film lurches towards a different kind of genre consolidation.[45] So what we often find on screen are hybrid genres: gangster films intersecting with travel genres and so on. This hunt for the perfect or the most exotic locale makes film-makers sound like explorers. Mani Ratnam, too, hasn't been immune from this desire to wander to the limits of the nation-state's imagined cartography, most evi-dent in the sections of *Dil Se* set in Ladhak. In an uncharacteristic move for a director who usually sets his films within the geographical space endorsed by the nation-state, Mani Ratnam uses the sunny beaches of Seychelles as the locale for a song and dance sequence in *Alaipayuthey* without addressing the abrupt spatial leap in the diegesis.

Despite these moments of spectacular excess, song and dance sequences in Mani Ratnam's films reveal his efforts to integrate them into the dominant narrative, forc-ing us to reckon with narrative discontinuity if we extract or overlook these sequence. In other words, Mani Ratnam converts the conventional anachrony of these sequences and their direct address into linear anachrony. Yet, despite their integration into the narrative, they do not totally escape their ability to circulate sep-arately from his films, opening the film text to other economies of production and reception. For example, his films have become ideal vehicles to bolster Ilyaraja and A. R. Rahman's status as star music directors whose popularity tempers the idea of the director as the single author of films.

Rather than performing a uniform function across various films, close scrutiny of these sequences discloses five different means by which he negotiates spatial and temporal continuities, thus soliciting the spectator's interests in equally varied ways. In the first type, the song (and sometimes dance) manages spatial disjunctions within the diegesis. The space of action is clearly spelled out in the film with no abrupt geographical discontinuities. Nowhere is this articulation more evident than in the opening song in *Nayakan*, where we see Velu arrive in Mumbai (Bombay), find a friend, and join a family. Sung by Ilyaraja as a lullaby, the song accompanies our protagonist's flight from the police in Tamil Nadu to Mumbai's migrant Tamil community. Besides the spatial mobilisation, the song prepares us for a narrative conversion from a standard story of police brutality to a gangster narrative generically set against an urban backdrop. Obviously Velu could not have walked from Victoria Terminus to the Gateway of India and finally to the slum in Dharavi within the temporality of the song, but the song assuages temporal disjunctions by highlighting spatial continuity within a recognisable geography of the city. Besides managing spatial disruptions within the geography of the city, the film repeats the song three times on the soundtrack during scenes of personal crisis recalling Velu's life before he became an underworld don, or Nayakan, as well as underscoring the lingering brutality of these dramatic moments ricocheting from his initial battles with the police.

Mani Ratnam deploys this particular form of interruption again in *Thalapathy/ Don*, another gangster film that patterns itself on the story of Karna in the epic *Mahabharata*.[46] As in *Nayakan*, here, too, the song manages spatial disjunctions in the opening sequences: a young, unmarried girl gives birth to a boy and abandons him on a moving train. As the train pulls out of the station, we hear 'Chinna thai aval/'Young mother …' also rendered as a lullaby on the soundtrack of the credit sequence. The train moves along and reaches the next town where a poor washerwoman adopts the abandoned infant. We do not track every minute of a train journey from one town to another; rather, the song highlights particular moments, papering over spatial disruptions. Here, too, the opening number attaches itself to the protagonist, repeating on the soundtrack during melodramatic moments and cueing us to a possible union with his birth mother.

In his love stories, Mani Ratnam deploys a similar technique, but with a difference. Instead of a single protagonist, we find heterosexual couples traversing various spaces. For instance, in *Roja* – the first film in his political trilogy – Mani Ratnam deploys it in the middle of the film. Rishi has been sent to Kashmir on a secret assignment to decode enemy transmissions. His wife Roja joins him, and the trip doubles as their honeymoon. Rishi leads a blindfolded Roja to a craggy edge, and as she opens her eyes we see with her the snow-capped Himalayas. On the soundtrack the duet 'Pudhu vellai mazhai/'New white rain' begins. The song captures several moments of the couple frolicking through the landscape in different clothes and making love in their hotel room. Here, too, the song manages spatial disjunctions so that by the end of the song the film suggests that the once estranged couple are now happily reunited. Notwithstanding its nationalist discourse, the film's use of Kashmir departs from the routine use of this landscape before the period of intense militarisation when film-makers frequented it as the ideal setting for a love song, even when the flight into this space had little diegetic relevance. Mani Ratnam seizes the lovers' paradise in popular cinema as an ideal location for a nationalist narrative, but he also cannot help using the bucolic space for a song and dance sequence, though he does so diegetically.

In *Bombay*, the second of his films in the political trilogy, Mani Ratnam regulates spatial discontinuity not through standard images of well-known spaces, but through architectural styles. The film opens in an imaginary town in the Tirunelveli district of Tamil Nadu. A Hindu boy, Shekar, falls in love with a Muslim girl, Shaila Banu. Shortly after a brief encounter with her, Shekar attends a local Muslim wedding and spots her again. The film does not suggest that our protagonists have left the village, but the wedding takes place in the Tirumal Nayak palace in Madurai, miles away from the village in Tirunelveli. Rebuilt in the seventeenth century by Tirumala Nayak, architectural historians see it as a fusion of several styles that broadly fit under the rubric of Indo-Saracenic.[47] The wedding song 'Kannalanae'/'With my eyes …', initiated by her, moves the narrative forward so that we understand that by the song's end their desire is mutual. The spatial disruption in this sequence is assuaged within the geographical imaginary of the film, which metonymically extends the architectural synthesis of styles to the intercommunal couple.

In the above form, the song and dance interruption papers over spatial disjunctions, propelling the narrative forward. However, in the second type, Mani Ratnam uses the interruption to smooth temporal shifts in the narrative where the distance of the anachrony may be several years, a length of time that suggests significant changes in the life of the protagonist. In *Nayakan*, his most overt attempts to convert the achrony of this interruption to anachrony surfaces in the marriage song following Velu and Neela's wedding. The song 'Ne uru kadal sangeetham'/'You are a love song' indicates changes in the protagonists' life by stringing together scenes from their marriage, including Neela's pregnancy. By the end of the song, we have moved through a dissolve from their wedding to the next segment where we see their two young children, Surya and Charu. He uses this device again in a similar marriage segment in *Bombay*: the 'hulla gulla' (also known as 'Poovukenna pootu'/'You cannot close a bloom') song takes us through Shekar and Shaila Banu's marriage, pregnancy, and the birth of twins. At the end of the song, we see the two five-year-old boys. Condensing large temporal shifts in the narrative through a song and dance sequence foregrounds the use of this interruption as a device that serves the narrative, in the process domesticating the anachrony status of song and dance sequences within the dominant generic logic of a film.

The third type of song and dance sequence approximates the Hollywood subgenre of the backstage musical, in which our relationship mirrors the audience in the film serving as our proxy.[48] In *Nayakan*, the second song, 'Naan sirithal …'/'When I smile ...', replays this arrangement. Set in a brothel bearing signs of a decadent, landed gentry, this sequence through its retro-gestures refers to the 1950s when Muslim socials flourished in the Bombay film industry.[49] As Velu and Selva's outing after their first big score, the scene not only circumvents the parenthetical status of this interruption by providing it with narrative purpose, but additionally regulates the exhibitionism imbuing these spectacular sequences by further augmenting the *mise en scène* of the period. Here we are encouraged to see a coincidence between performance time on screen and real time, a coincidence that converts the anachrony of this interruption by weaving it into narrative time. Both songs and cars in this section signify a cinematic memory of a period between the 1940s and 1950s, bolstering the film's desire for verisimilitude.

Mani Ratnam's most blatant attempt to regulate the anachrony of these sequences while retaining the splendour of the spectacle occurs in the 'Andhi mazhai megham'/'Rain clouds' segment celebrating the spring festival Holi. Dousing them with coloured water, revellers ambush Velu Nayakan's family in the centre of the neighbourhood, the centre where Seth's men were measuring land, where Velu killed the inspector, and so on. This sequence recalls the Holi sequence from Ramesh Sippy's *Sholay*, where the celebration of spring works as a buffer for the prospective violence. Here, too, the focus on Nayakan's picture-perfect family is gingerly squeezed between the Reddy brothers' threat and their eventual execution. In terms of its relationship to the chronology of the narrative, the span of time in this sequence is very much like the second song, 'Naan sirithal'/'When I smile', where the idea of entertainment within the diegesis dominates the rationale of this spectacle. However, this desire to regulate the narrative from within peculiarly impacts on questions of realism. By setting the sequence against the backdrop of monsoon rains, Mani Ratnam alters the seasonal and festival calendar in such a way that the very distinct moments of Holi (in March) and monsoon rains (in June) are fused together. In terms of conventions, this reordering of two different calendars offers an ingenious method to deal simultaneously with conventions of rain and festival songs that have great currency in popular cinema. However, we have to consider how Mani Ratnam's preoccupation with narrative verisimilitude rests on delivering an improved and altered reality to his viewers.

In *Thiruda Thiruda/Thief Thief*, Mani Ratnam manages the anachrony of this sequence through a hybrid form of the backstage musical. Set against the backdrop of the Madras Museum, an Indo-Sarcenic building, the 'Chandralekha ...' (also known as 'Koncham nilavu'/'A ray of moonlight') song takes the form of a performance piece by one of the protagonists, Chandralekha, who is both a dancer and a thief. As in the backstage musical, the audience in the film serves as our proxy. The spectacle of the entire performance with top shots of swirling skirts and groups of men is reminiscent of S. S. Vasan's spectacular film *Chandralekha* (1948), especially the famous drum dance choreographed over acres of ground.[50] A close scrutiny of the actual sequence reveals several spatial disruptions that only film can easily assuage: Chandralekha moves from the performing floor to the tower in the space of one cut, an agility that only a film cut can deliver. Notwithstanding these temporal ellipses, this sequence fits into the third type of song and dance sequence in which we find a close fit between performance time and real time.

Another spectacular example of this type surfaces repeatedly in his *Iruvar/The Duo*, a film that is explicitly about the intimate relationship between cinema and politics in Tamil Nadu. As a thinly disguised biopic of M. G. Ramachandran – a popular star who governed as the chief minister for twelve years – the film has several song and dance sequences that are inserted into the narrative with dramatic spatial disjunctions exploiting the film's thematic preoccupations. The extravagant monochromatic re-creations of song and dance sequences from MGR's films in *Iruvar* are technically vastly superior to the original, a film-making strategy calculated to impress upon us that this narrative of return upstages the original, the quotation more splendid than the original. Of all the song and dance sequences in *Iruvar*, only one approximates the hybrid backstage musical – 'Hello Mr Edhir Katchi'/'Hello Mr Opposition'. Through shot/reverse shots we watch this sequence from the point of view of the protagonist Anandan and his wife in a studio theatre. Closely resembling sequences from American musicals, our viewing time matches Anandan's viewing time within the film.

In all four examples of the Indian backstage musical, the song and dance interruption manifests itself as a delaying device: in the 'Naan sirithal' song it offers a breathing space from the violence in a gangster genre; the Holi song delays the Reddys' threat; in *Thiruda Thiruda* the 'Chandralekha' song delays police work; and in *Iruvar* the love story. Note that, of all the types, this one, with the audience watching the performance within the film, has tremendous currency in popular cinema, surfacing in practically every film, whether organised as a marriage song, a high school celebration, or a festival song. In *Hum Dil De Chuke Sanam/I Have Fallen in Love with You* (1999), Sanjay Leela Bhansali authenticates a regional Gujarati ambience by setting his song and dance sequences around several local rituals, an obsession that finally throttles the international love story. Its wide use in several films allows us to read this type as a means to understand the ways in which cinematic construction of the quotidian boomerangs into the extra-cinematic so that the borders between the two blur. Conversely, these celebrations in life extensively imitate cinematic conventions of choreography, costumes, and timing.

The fourth category carries all the spectacular elements of the previous type, but, instead of being demarcated from the rest of the narrative through show-stopping spectacle, we find a more deliberate attempt to link it to the narrative. In *Nayakan*, it is tied to Velu and Selva's smuggling trip on the open sea. Selva brings along a dancing girl to amuse them, and she sways to the 'Nila athu vaanathu mele'/'Look at the moon' song. The cabaret-style dancing and singing recall a standard convention of exhibitionism in Indian commercial cinema, in which the camera's investment in fragmenting and sexualising the female body has little narrative relevance. Here, however, instead of pure sensory excess, Mani Ratnam ties the song to the narrative by also using the sequence for an encounter with the coastguard. The girl continues to dance around the police as they search the boat for smuggled goods. Christian Metz's commentary on metaphor and metonymy is useful in nuancing the relationship between the dancing girl and the police search: the dancing girl is a metaphor placed in a paradigm. Besides bolstering the reckless confidence of the two men by swaying along the boat, she also stands in for their illegal activities, a suggestion that the film has already mobilised in the 'Na serachi' song that was set in the brothel, the place where Velu found his wife Neela. Repeating with a difference, this song and dance interruption replicates the twinning rhythm structuring the film where in the first instance the prostitute is converted into a wife.

In his other films, Mani Ratnam modulates this particular form of metaphor in a paradigm by bifurcating the two-part paradigm through intercutting. In *Roja*, on Rishi and Roja's wedding night, we watch a dance number led by a group of old and young dancers heaving and thumping to the song 'Rukmini! Rukmini!' Dovetailing the wedding, we are encouraged to read this number as a surrogate for the sexual energy of the newlywed couple, an impression that is reinforced through the intercutting between the couple's wedding bed and the dancers. In the final moments of the sequence, intercutting gives way when Rishi and Roja join the dancers. With no *a priori* explanation for these dancers except for the convention of wedding songs on the one hand, and censorship prohibitions on showing explicit sexual scenes on screen on the other, Mani Ratnam exploits the limits of one convention by using another.

He resorts to a similar intercutting strategy in the 'Humma! Humma!' song (also known as 'Antha Arabi Kadaloram'/'By the Arabian Sea') in *Bombay*. An endless stream of guests from the landlord's home prevents Shekar and Shaila's sexual union. When the guests finally leave, they derive their sexual energy from a location outside their home – the red-light district! Greeting the prostitutes, Shekar walks home with Shaila, and as the couple enter their home the song begins in the off-screen space. Intercutting between their bedroom and the red-light district, the song unfolds with frenetic energy supplied by the dancers. Instead of serving as a pure metaphor where the two scenes have no diegetic connection, the film connects them explicitly, showing Shekar looking at the dancers and the newlywed couple mimicking their movements. In the final moments of the sequence, the film abandons the couple altogether, focusing instead on the dancers whose energies gather a metaphoric meaning through a blazing fire in the background. I concur with Ravi

Vasudevan, who reads this sequence as mobilising another level of prohibition in the cinematic representation of a sexual union between a Muslim and Hindu.[51]

In the fifth category, Mani Ratnam resorts to the most familiar form that critics usually assume characterises this interruption – as extra-diegetic sequences. Given the tightly knit internal structuring of *Nayakan*, the film does not permit such an occasion in its narrative, but we do see extra-diegetic sequences in his love trilogy – *Roja*, *Bombay*, and *Dil Se* – where songs abruptly break the spatial continuity of the narrative. In *Roja* he moves abruptly from a chase sequence in Kashmir to a pastoral setting in Tamil Nadu. On the soundtrack, the song 'Chinna chinna asai'/'Little desires' replaces the sound of a gun. We see a girl bathing, conventionally evoking wet-sari songs, but with modesty. Only in the next scene do we find out that the dancer is one of the protagonists in the film. This abrupt juxtaposition, according to Madhava Prasad, leads us to anticipate a steady corruption of the pastoral scenes by the aggressive militarism opening the film.[52] However manipulative Mani Ratnam is for insinuating such a meaning, it is equally important to see how he uses the spectacular aspects of the song and dance sequence to *prospectively* offer a narrative purpose.

In *Bombay*, the 'Kuchi kuchi rakkama'/'How are you, little one?' song articulates a similar function. The Hindu and Muslim grandparents have arrived after the outburst of the first communal riots. The grandfathers fight over the grandsons; exasperated by their bickering, the boys rush into their parents' bedroom. Playfully, Shekar suggests that they send their boys away to have a little girl. Shaila coquettishly refuses, permitting the film to cut suddenly to a lush, hilly landscape. Dressed as a gypsy, Shaila leads a chorus of young girls who refuse the advances of a group of men led by Shekar and his sons. The sylvan landscape provides a respite from the communal antagonisms in Bombay, but using tribal folk in the dance displaces Hindu–Muslim antagonisms on to their bodies, a move that cannot help reminding us of their tenuous place in the Indian national imaginary. Tribal settings are not infrequent in song and dance sequences, metonymically extending associations of primitiveness to the narrative. *Bombay* is no exception, where it appears that the sexual energies of the couple now have to re-route through such a landscape when faced with the threat of communal riots.

Mani Ratnam's first Hindi film, *Dil Se*, has two songs that undercut continuity in different ways. The first song, 'Chaiyya chaiyya', abruptly cuts from a night scene at a remote railway station in India's northeast to a 'jaw-dropping' spectacle set on the roof of the train seen from the point of view of the male protagonist.[53] The sequence evokes a loose graphic match between the railway station and the train as a way to regulate the rampant spatial discontinuity conveying the sexual exuberance of the male protagonist. Although spectacular, the spatial disruption of this song infects the ensuing love story, which stalls and fails to provide a happy ending. The disruption exhibits the male protagonist's desire, but not the woman's. Mani Ratnam resorts to this form in the 'Jiya jale jaan jale'/'The heart burns, my life burns' song, when the film cuts from an engagement ceremony in Delhi to a boat scene in Kerala, forcing the interruption to carry the weight of sexual energy that he cannot muster in scenes between the male protagonist and his new girlfriend. Rather than working as a compensatory structure, retrospectively we can read this song once again as a symptom of a failed union between this new couple. In my interview with Mani Ratnam, he suggested that *Dil Se*'s box-office failure may be attributed to the song and dance sequences that adversely tampered with the pacing of the narrative.[54]

These varied experiments do not and will not exhaust the interruption's formal shape in his future films or its manifestations in other directors' films. Rather than see these categories as *langue* that are etched in stone, I consider them as articulations of *parole* that, read retrospectively, reveal the structuring of *langue*. Moreover, as my reading of *Nayakan* demonstrates, genre structuring weighs in on the rhythm of these sequences, sometimes expunging the extra-diegetic form of this interruption. In a similar vein, the interval also organises the number of song and dance sequences: in *Nayakan* there is only one song after the interval; in *Bombay*, after the interval, the love song is replaced by an extra-diegetic family song and the film finally closes on its theme song on communal harmony. Each of these intersections with other interruptions directs us to read song and dance sequences within the narrative logic of the film, as well as within the cinematic discourse that goes beyond attending solely to textual operations.

Even as I map the various possibilities in Mani Ratnam's films as a working template to better understand the form and function of this interruption, other film-makers have found additional ways to either tie them into the narrative or exaggerate their spectacular disruption. Rajiv Menon's *Kandukondain Kandukondain/I Have Seen You!* (2000) exaggerates the spatial disjunctions by initially cutting from a lush landscape typical of southern India to a desert. Within the song and dance segment, the film splices props from the desert landscape of India, but sets them against an Egyptian desert. While maintaining the desert as the dominant motif, as the chosen place to articulate love, the spectacular incorporation of elements from different geographical spaces in one song sequence showcases experiments in this form, as well as innovations towards genre consolidation in popular cinema.

More than any other film-maker, Mani Ratnam carefully choreographs these sequences to heighten the viewing pleasure of these attractions as well as their function within the narrative. Rather than flatten the language of Indian cinema by expelling these sequences, his films confidently assert their presence, which reminds one of the films made by Guru Dutta and Raj Kapoor. His tremendous facility with these sequences, as well as their success, has allowed other film-makers, music directors, and dance choreographers to experiment extensively with its iconography, however excessive at times. In the face of the sweeping globalisation of cinematic styles led by the rampant distribution of American films, Mani Ratnam's films offer us the possibility of a distinct national style that celebrates such interruptions and demands that we acknowledge their presence in our readings.

My attempt to offer a structural reading of the song and dance interruption thinly disguises my cinephiliac obsession with these sequences. Recognising the formal elegance of Mani Ratnam's films does not necessarily mean that our critical eye should turn away from reading its ideological interests. What I am offering is a more ambivalent relationship that reads the contradictory moves in his films while recognising my own seduction. Such an ambivalence epitomises our critical relationship to popular films that speak to our different desires through a constellation of interruptions, producing a constantly shifting relationship to the text.

Notes

1. A representative collection of these enquiries include Nick Roddick (1983), *A New Deal in Entertainment: Warner Bros. in the 1930s*, London: BFI; Colin McArthur (1972), *Underworld USA*, New York: Viking Press; and Frank Krutnik (1991), *In a Lonely Street: Film Noir, Genre, Masculinity*, London and New York: Routledge.

2. See Peter Lehmann (1993), *Running Scared: Masculinity and the Representation of the Male Body*, Philadelphia: Temple University Press.

3. This device of beginning in childhood is a familiar trope that is well developed in the *Bildungsroman* novels where the elaborate linear unfolding of the protagonist's life is the main thrust of the novel.

4. Homi Bhabha (1994), 'DissemiNation: Time, Narrative and the Margins of the Modern Nation', in *The Location of Culture*, London and New York: Routledge.

5. See Itty Abraham (1998) on state theory in his *The Making of the Indian Atomic Bomb: Science and Secrecy*, London: Zed Press.

6. Benedict Anderson (1991), *Imagined Communities* (rev. edn), London: Verso.

7. Miriam Hansen (1987), 'Benjamin, Cinema and Experience: "The Blue Flower in the Land of Technology"', *New German Critique*, 40, Winter, pp. 179–224.

8. Anne Friedberg (1994), *Window Shopping: Cinema and the Postmodern*, Berkeley: University of California Press.

9. In a concurrent argument using documentary films, Philip Rosen argues that the indexical impression of cinema – a line of enquiry that competes with the iconic point of view – arises from its very inception and includes notions of the 'document' and evidence, notions that shape modern historiography. Rosen's analysis offers yet another story of interrelatedness between writing the modern nation and cinema. See Philip Rosen (1993), 'Document and Documentary: On the Persistence of Historical Concepts', in Michael Renov (ed.), *Theorizing Documentary*, New York: Routledge, pp. 58–89.

10. Christian Metz (1982), *The Imaginary Signifier*, Bloomington: Indiana University Press. See also his essays in *Screen* since the late 1970s.

11. Laura Mulvey (1993), 'Some Thoughts on Theories of Fetishism in the Context of Contemporary Culture', *October*, 65, Summer, pp. 3–20.

12. See interview with S. Shivkumar in *Stardust*, February 1999, pp. 54–61.

13. Profile by K. Ram, 'Through the lens, darkly ...', *Aside* (n.d.).

14. Interview with P. C. Sriram (1988), 'Images More Eloquent than Words', *The Hindu*, 22 July, p. 7.

15. Personal interview with P. C. Sriram, September 1994.

16. On the long hiatus with Mani Ratnam, see his interview in *Aside*. Sriram explains: 'We just decided to give each other a bit of mental ventilation' (p. 36).

17. P. C. Sriram has made his own forays into direction: *Meera* (1992) and *Kurudhippunal/ River of Blood* (1995). A remake of Govind Nihalani's *Drohkaal* (1994), *Kurudhippunal* won a number of regional awards and was India's official entry for an Oscar award that year. Sriram and Mani Ratnam worked together on *Alaipayuthey* (2000), which skilfully experiments with digital photography to narrate a love story.

18. On Tharani's art, see Geeta Doctor, 'One Artist, Two Lives', and Aditi De, 'How He Gives "Force" to his Drawings'. From Thotta Tharani's personal archive. Date not available.

19. See R. Bhagwan Singh (1990), 'Myth and Magic', *Sunday*, 25–31 March.

20. See 'Cinema', *Sunday*, 21–27 February 1988.

21. See Paul Seydor (1980), *Peckinpah: The Western Films*, Champaign: University of Illinois Press. See also Michael Bliss (ed.) (1994), *Doing it Right*, Carbondale: Southern Illinois University Press.

22. David Bordwell's comments on the dissolve are particularly pertinent here:

    The dissolve, the most common indication of duration, affords us an instructive example of how classical narration does its temporal work. Visually, the dissolve is simply a variant of the fade – a fade-out overlapped with a fade-in – but it is a fade during which the screen is never blank. To the layman or the average theatregoer, a lap dissolve passes unobtrusively by on the screen without his being aware that it had happened. A lap dissolve serves the purpose of smoothly advancing the story. The dissolve was quickly restricted to indicating a short, often indefinite interval, if only a few seconds (e.g. a dissolve from a detail to a full short). This makes the dissolve a superb way to soften spatial, graphic, and even temporal discontinuities. [pp. 46–7]

    David Bordwell (1985), 'The Classical Hollywood Style, 1917–60', in David Bordwell, Janet Staiger, and Kristin Thompson, *The Classical Hollywood Cinema: Film Style and Mode of Production to 1960*, New York: Columbia University Press.

23. On automobiles and cinema, see Edward Dimendberg (1995), 'The Will to Motorization: Cinema, Highways, and Modernity', *October*, 73, Summer, pp. 91–137.

See also Kristin Ross (1995), *Fast Cars, Clean Bodies: Decolonization and the Reordering of French Culture*, Cambridge, Mass.: MIT Press.

24. I wish to thank Carl Bromley for drawing my attention to this intertextual link.

25. I wish to thank Richard List for a wonderful afternoon of autophilia, June 1998.

26. In my interview with Mani Ratnam, he acknowledged the place of the interval in his films, and admitted to carefully crafting his films to exploit this punctuation.

27. Certain DVD copies of *Nayakan* have deleted the slow-motion shots of Neela falling out of the window.

28. The intercutting editing style in this sequence distinctly recalls the famous baptism scene in *The Godfather* where Michael orders his men to kill Sonny's killers as he participates in the baptism of his sister's child.

29. See Ram Gopal Varma's *Satya*, where a killing scene takes place amid celebrations on the last day of this festival in Mumbai.

30. On the erotics of car crashes, see David Cronenberg's *Crash* (1996). See also Iain Sinclair's (1999) reading in his *Crash: David Cronenberg's Post-Mortem on J. G. Ballard's 'Trajectory of Fate'*, London: BFI.

31. P. C. Sriram told me how, in the final version of the film, Mani Ratnam cut an entire song and dance sequence between Velu and Charu. The whereabouts of this sequence are unknown, perhaps lost in a studio vault or more likely destroyed in a fire.

32. See Madhava Prasad's (1990) essay in *Ideology of the Hindi Film*; M. S. S. Pandian and Venkatesh Chakravarthy (1996), '*Iruvar*: Transforming History into Commodity', *Economic and Political Weekly*, 21 December; Venkatesh Chakravarthy (1988), 'Eliminating Dissent: The Political Films of Mani Ratnam', *Toronto Review*, vol. 19, no. 3, pp. 19–32.

33. Chakravarthy, 'Eliminating Dissent', p. 29.

34. Bhaskar Chandravarkar (1981), 'Growth of the Film Song', *Cinema in India*, vol. 1, no. 3, pp. 16–20.

35. Ashok Ranade (1981), 'The Extraordinary Importance of the Indian Film Song', *Cinema Vision India*, vol. 1, no. 4 , pp. 4–11.

36. S. Theodore Baskaran (1996), 'Songs in Tamil Cinema', in *The Eye of the Serpent*, Madras: East–West Books, pp. 38–61.

37. According to Baskaran, *Ambikapathi* (1937) is the earliest Tamil film to have a credit for a music director.

38. See the entry for R. C. Boral in Ashish Rajadhyaksha and Paul Willemen (eds) (1999), *Encyclopaedia of Indian Cinema*, London: BFI (rev. edn). See also Terri Skillman (1986), 'The Bombay Hindi Film Song Genre: A Historical Survey', *Yearbook for Tradition Music*, vol. XVIII, pp. 133–44.

39. See a series of articles by Bhaskar Chnadravarkar, 'The Tradition of Music in Indian Cinema', *Cinema in India*, vol. 1, no. 2 (April 1987) to vol. 3, no. 3 (July–September 1989).

40. We still lack a complete analysis of sound, technology, song writers, and music directors that will help us better understand the relationship between sound and image in Indian popular cinema.

41. Baskaran, *The Eye of the Serpent*, p. 48.

42. A good recent example is Sashilal Nair's *Kabhi na Kabhi*, where a sequence forms a separate system independent of the narrative.

43. Lalitha Gopalan (1997), '*Coitus Interruptus* and Love Story in Indian Cinema', in Vidya Dehejia (ed.), *Representing the Body: Gender Issues in Indian Art*, New Delhi: Kali for Women, pp. 124–39.

44. See Jane Fuer (1993), *The Hollywood Musicals*, Bloomington: Indiana University Press; and Tom Gunning on early cinema (see Bibliography).

45. On the travel genre in early Euro-American cinema, see Charles Musser (1990), 'The Travel Genre in 1903–1904: Moving Towards Fictional Narrative', in Thomas Elsaesser with Adam Barker (eds), *Early Cinema: Space, Frame, Narrative*, London: BFI.

46. K. Hariharan gave a talk on the structural relationships between *Thalapathy* and *Mahabharata* (unpublished), Philadelphia, March 1995.

47. On architectural styles, see Thomas Metcalf (1989), *An Imperial Vision: Indian Architecture and Britain's Raj*, Berkeley: University of California Press.

48. On backstage musicals, see Jane Feuer (1993), *The Hollywood Musical*; Rick Altman (1989), *The American Film Musical*, Bloomington: Indiana University Press. Altman describes the backstage musical in the following manner:

    In the backstage musical … the film audience not only watches the theater audience watch the show, but it also observes the theater actors rehearsing the show. The show itself thus loses its primacy, making way for the new primary concerns of observing the show and making the show. [p. 205]

49. On courtesan dramas, see Sumita Chakravarthy (1993), *National Identity and Indian Popular Cinema*, Austin: University of Texas Press.

50. See a description of this sequence in Erik Barnow and S. Krishnaswamy (1980), *Indian Film*, New York: Oxford University Press (rev. edn), p. 174.

51. Ravi Vasudevan (1996), 'Bombay and Its Public', *Journal of Arts and Ideas*, 29 January, pp. 44–65.

52. See M. Madhava Prasad's (1998) excellent reading of this juxtaposition in his essay 'Towards Real Subsumption: Signs of Ideological Reform in Two Recent Films', in *Ideology of the Hindi Film: A Historical Construction*, Delhi: Oxford University Press, pp. 217–37.

53. The phrase is from the Washington, DC, Film Festival Brochure, 1998.

54. Interview with Mani Ratnam, Chennai, August 2000.

5

Memory and Gangsters in Vidhu Vinod Chopra's *Parinda*

Mani Ratnam's *Nayakan* closes with a montage highlighting the film in no particular linear order, a montage that also contains scenes between Nayakan and his daughter that we have not been privy to in the diegesis. Ending on a flashback undercuts the narrative's dominant linear temporality and urges us to attend retrospectively to the enforced linear temporality of its own narrative, broken on only one other occasion in the entire film. If *Nayakan* is resolutely not about memory, but rather about progress within a linear narrative, its closing sequence solicits our ability to remember the film, to recall crucial moments. Emerging as a supplement questioning the tightly ordered linear progression of the film, the closing sequence of Ratnam's film gestures towards other temporalities of storytelling that have not by any means been exhausted in this film, a gesture taken up by Vidhu Vinod Chopra's *Parinda* (1989). Rather than surfacing at the closing moments and recalling our memory of the narrative retrospectively, Chopra's film evokes the flashback as a cinematic device to present a memory of past events that impacts on the entire crime narrative. In sharp contrast to the linear tale of rags to riches in *Nayakan*, *Parinda* plays with temporal discontinuities to justify the violent actions between gangsters. In this film, too, we find its temporal discontinuities serving as a model for writing the history of the modern nation that is less developmental and progressive. If the nation is the all-encompassing imaginary within which we locate our reading, a more circumscribed frame of reading *Parinda* allows us another occasion to see the interplay between the constellation of interruptions and the logic of the gangster genre available internationally.

In *Nayakan* we saw how the film harnesses the temporal disruptions mobilised by song and dance sequences, as well as the interval, by subjugating them to the linear temporality of the film. In fact, Mani Ratnam's directorial style is most visible when he minimises the temporal and spatial disjunctions produced by these two interruptions. In a not so dissimilar manner, temporal disjunctions in Chopra's films emerge as a legible sign of his cinematic style. For instance, in his thrillers *Sazaye Maut/Capital Punishment* (1981) and *Khamosh/Silence* (1985), Chopra abandons song and dance sequences, but liberally employs flashbacks to solve a crime. In *1942: A Love*

Story (1994), Chopra moves away from masculine genres such as thriller and crime films to a historical love story, but continues to experiment with temporal discontinuities to shore up the tensions between politics and love. In *Kareeb/Near By* (1998), temporal discontinuities move and halt a love story ridden with class differences.

Parinda marks Chopra's first entry into the world of Indian commercial cinema, where we see a distinct engagement with the constellation of interruptions that is now yoked to other kinds of temporal and spatial disruptions. Reviewing *Parinda*, Iqbal Masud quotes Chopra: 'I have taken the pillars of Hindi popular cinema and built the whole edifice on them. Then one by one I have removed the pillars hoping that the edifice won't collapse.'[1] Recognising its close kinship to American-style gangster films, Masud ends on this note: 'The script of *Parinda* is placed in *Godfather*-land. But its heart is not there, its heart is in the highlands – the highlands of Raj Kapoor and Guru Dutt romanticism.'[2] In a review in *Deep Focus*, placing *Parinda* within the genre of the American gangster film, Babu Subramaniam admits: 'The film's intelligent use of the medium as well as its romanticism, notwithstanding its glib quality, together place *Parinda* far above films in this genre in popular Hindi cinema.'[3] Both reviews acknowledge a certain directorial competency over film-making that Masud rightly identifies as emerging from Chopra's training at the Film and Television Institute of India: 'but the point to be noted here is Chopra, like Ketan Mehta and Saeed Mirza, fellow FTII graduates, is trying to build a bridge from what

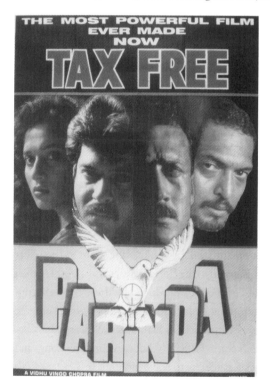

Wall poster for *Parinda* (courtesy of the National Film Archive, Pune)

is called "art" cinema to commercial/popular cinema; *Parinda* has to be judged by the stretch of that ambition'.[4]

Unlike the other directors discussed in this book who have had no formal training in film-making, Chopra's years at the FTII appear to have taught him that cinema includes competency over both editing and cinematography – his editor Renu Saluja and cinematographer Binod Pradhan, who also graduated from FTII, regularly double as his associate directors. Before her death in August 2000, Saluja was well known for her non-linear editing style, nost noticeably in Govind Nihalani's *Ardh Satya/Half Truth* (1983), Shekhar Kapur's *Bandit Queen* (1994), Kamal Haasan's *Hey! Ram* (2000), and Harish Dayani's *Godmother* (1999). In an advertisement on the Internet for Avid editing, the firm Reel-Image uses a quotation from Saluja, an editor who seems to have effortlessly moved from flatbed editing machines to digital editing, to market its editing equipment.[5] Besides the consistent use of flashbacks that we attribute to Renu Saluja's editing prowess, Binod Pradhan's cinematography textures Chopra's films in a different way: his crane and tilt shots that finally rest as top shots in crucial scenes emerge as a motif in this film. In *Parinda*, the top shot mimics the bird's-eye view in several scenes as the camera moves from the claustrophobic close shots to an establishing shot of an action scene. Saluja and Pradhan's

Chopra on the set of *Parinda* with his editor Renu Saluja (courtesy of Vidhu Vinod Chopra)

contributions to Chopra's films shift the focus of commercial film-making from stars and producers to star technicians, a feature that we usually associate with alternative films in India. In addition to the laudatory reviews, *Parinda* gained both the National Award and *Filmfare* Award for Best Film; Renu Saluja received the National Award and *Filmfare* Award for Editing; Chopra received the award for Best Director from *Filmfare* and shared the honours for Screenplay with Shivkumar Subramaniam. And *Parinda* was India's official Oscar entry.[6]

As we fetishise Renu Saluja's predilection for flashbacks or muse over Pradhan's quirky use of top shots, the irony is not lost on us when we realise that all three, including Chopra, were trained at the FTII on the implicit understanding that once they graduated they were expected to produce quality, non-commercial cinema. To amplify the dissonance between state-ordered dictates on quality cinema and the commercial viability of films, we find *Parinda* has been principally backed by the National Film Development Corporation (NFDC), which was formed to support experimental, small-budget films.[7] However, given the shifting and changing intentions of the NFDC over the years, we can say that *Parinda* belongs to that period following a series of recommendations made in a 1984 report that, according to the *Encyclopaedia of Indian Cinema*, took the following form:[8]

> The NFDC sought to institutionalise a confused desire for 'good' cinema measured mainly in terms of national film awards and international film festival exposure, that should be able to make a profit in a market where it could not compete with the industrial cinema's levels of expenditure on exhibition, production and promotion. [p. 162]

High-angle, bird's-eye shot of the brothers meeting (courtesy of Vidhu Vinod Chopra)

Under these new conditions of 'confused desire', *Parinda* does not appear to be a misstep in the chronicle of the NFDC's shifting relationship to popular cinema. Its technical virtuosity, star cast of actors, gangster narrative, and conventions of Indian commercial cinema characterise the paradoxical role of the NFDC in the production of commercial films. Obviously, the film's formal elegance owes much to the history of the post-colonial state's desire for quality cinema that includes the formation of the FTII as well as the NFDC, a desire that wavers between wanting a realist aesthetic and an experimental form. However varied these films, they do reflect the changing relationship between the state, industry, and audience as a series of accommodations that inflected the form of Indian popular cinema at the interstices of global and national cinematic styles.

Plot Summary
Chopra's Web page offers the following plot summary:

> The story is about two brothers left to fend for themselves in the brutal city of Bombay. Kishan (Jackie Shroff), the elder brother, is forced to join Anna (Nana Patekar), an underworld don, to sponsor younger brother Karan's (Anil Kapoor) education in the USA. Back from America, Karan, who is not aware of his brother's profession, witnesses the murder of friend Prakash (Anupam Kher), an honest police officer. Prakash is murdered by Anna's hit-men. He dies in Karan's arms. Paro (Madhuri Dixit) is extremely disturbed by brother Prakash's murder. Her state of mind and Karan's desire to revenge his friend's death take Karan into the underworld, where he discovers the other side of his brother's life. Karan is caught in a dilemma between revenging Prakash's death and guarding Kishan's interests.[9]

Karan eliminates Prakash's killers, but dies in the process. Kishan is the sole survivor of the bloodbath.

Besides opening the text to a wide range of readings, the hallmark of *Parinda*'s innovation emerges from Chopra's ability to build on the 'edifice of Hindi popular cinema', an edifice none other than the constellation of interruptions unique to Indian cinema. Rather than simply transposing the American crime film to an Indian scenario, *Parinda* rewrites the structuring of anticipation in crime and gangster films by exacerbating the temporal and spatial disruptions mobilised by both the flashback and the constellation of interruptions. This chapter attends to the temporal discontinuities in *Parinda* as a way of coming to terms with local and global conventions that frame our reading of the Indian gangster film. Hence, my concern is to explore how the flashback intersects with the interval and song and dance sequences and how, at times, its temporal and spatial disruptions are regulated by these interruptions. I shall also reveal that the film demonstrates a strengthening of certain thematic features that surface in Indian gangster films, such as fraternal bonds and the precarious yet necessary place of heterosexual romance, through its finessing of interruptions.

Although the unfolding of these temporal and spatial disruptions forms the mainstay of the chapter, I want momentarily to draw the reader's attention away from the strict genre considerations and suggest a series of intertextual relays that render *Parinda* as a more polyvalent text. For instance, *Parinda* undoubtedly relies on the metaphoric possibilities of its title that translates as 'bird' signalling the protagonists' desire to fly as freely as birds, away from the web of gangster activities that each and every one of them has stumbled into. Yet the title also delivers a literal meaning. We have several scenes where birds flutter across the cityscape, and one of the protagonists, Prakash, is shot at a fountain used by flocks of pigeons. Both title and *mise en scène* texture the ornithic meaning of the film, sealing its intertextual relationship to both *Nayakan* and *On the Waterfront* (1954).[10] In *Nayakan* we see pigeons fluttering, with the Gateway of India in the backdrop, and roosting in the courtyard, and Velu tending to them on the rooftop. Elia Kazan's *On the Waterfront* uses pigeon coops on the roof of an apartment building as a crucial place of the film's drama – death, romance, police investigation, and male bonding are all set in this space. However, *Parinda* departs from these films, fusing the birds and cinematic apparatus in such a way that birds screech on the soundtrack while the high-angle shots frequently employed as establishing shots appear to be from the bird's point of view. Its play on the ornithic camera reveals this film's intertextual relationship to another

Birds take wing by the fountain in *Parinda* (courtesy of Vidhu Vinod Chopra)

text – Hitchcock's *The Birds* (1963). Slavoj Žižek argues that Hitchcock's propensity for establishing shots urges his spectators to play God while playing on their voyeurism.[11] But in *The Birds*, he argues, Hitchcock destabilises our complacent voyeurism by converting this establishing shot to a bird's point of view which, in this film, is the point of view of the aggressor. When I interviewed Chopra and suggested that his film evokes *The Birds* through both the title and point-of-view shots, he was quick to admit to multiple influences, even though he was not particularly conscious of them when making his films.[12] Although the birds in *Parinda* carry none of this horrifying or aggressive charge, the high-angle shots work as establishing shots that slowly start standing in for point-of-view shots of the birds or the omniscient narrator's point of view, which, the film suggests, is the criminal's point of view. Like Hitchcock, Chopra exploits our complicity when watching these scenes that, while granting us God-like powers, do not acquiesce to our status as witnesses of a crime. For instance, immediately after Prakash's death, the film cuts to a morgue where we see Paro identifying her brother's body. The film cuts to a high-angle shot, and we hear the police officer telling Paro that Karan invited Prakash to the fountain with full knowledge that Anna's men would kill him. We see Karan walking into the frame at that very moment. The high-angle shot at this time is no longer an establishing shot from the point of view of an omniscient narrator, but is associated with a bird's-eye view, an association that Karan confirms later in the film when he tells Paro that he is haunted by sounds of birds fluttering from the scene of Prakash's death. When it repeatedly surfaces in familial and romantic scenes, the high-angle shot encourage us to remember the other scene of the film, the criminal narrative. There is no doubt that, in the factory scenes, the high-angle shot relays the point of view of Anna's office that stands guard over the activities in the space below, but at other times we are aligned with the camera to perch over scenes like birds on a wire surveying the scene below.

In the first half of the film, *Parinda* deploys the high-angle shot to evoke the dominant criminal narrative, a motif that is subsumed by a rhythm of intercutting in the second half. Among the several high-angle shots in the film, the most sinister one takes place when Karan tries to reconcile with Paro after Prakash's death. He arrives at the temple, and we see Paro feeding pigeons in slow motion. On the soundtrack we hear the childhood romance theme song, 'La, la, ho, ho' set to the tune of Leo Sayer's song 'I love you more than I can say'. As the camera closes in on her, the song cuts off as Paro spots Karan. A bird's-eye view spots her walking across the temple courtyard towards the stairs at the exit. Karan corners her to explain that Kishan was responsible for Prakash's death. The camera registers the couple's reunion in the temple through three zoom-in shots in slow motion with the childhood romance song on the soundtrack: the first one zooms in below the stairs towards Karan; the second zooms from above heading towards Paro; and the final zoom is from a long shot of the couple in profile towards a medium long shot. Instead of a flashback, the soundtrack recalls the past through repetition.

The romantic reunion is broken by another set of looks. The camera cuts to a high-angle shot of Iqbal (Anna's former henchman) and Abdul, one of Anna's associates, on the edge of the frame looking up towards us; Karan returns their look through a close-up shot, recognising Abdul as one of Prakash's killers. Abdul, in turn, registers Karan's look and flees down the flight of stairs. As Karan runs after him, the camera pulls up to a bird's-eye view of the chase down the flight of stairs, emphasising its criminal point of view. Abdul fights off Karan in a medium long shot, and the camera pulls up again to provide us with a bird's-eye view of the chase with Paro following the two men. The sequence is intercut with extreme close-up shots of running feet and frontal shots of the two men, with music hitting a crescendo on the soundtrack. Abdul scrambles into his white Ambassador car swiping his gun at Karan. The scene closes with a high-angle shot of Karan reeling to the ground in pain.

The sequence at the temple condenses one of the film's narrative tasks: how to account for romance in a gangster genre. Formally, *Parinda* retains bird's-eye view shots for criminal strands and accentuates this association by assigning Abdul as the organiser of the point-of-view shots in the couple's reunion in this sequence. The sequence also sets the template for romantic scenes in the film, which are repeatedly interrupted by the dominant criminal narrative so as to produce a structuring of back and forth rhythm between the two that finally meets a deadly end.

The film's more pointed engagement with Hitchcock occurs in the second half when Francis, one of Anna's men, and Karan are sent to kill Anna's arch enemy, Moosa, in his hotel room. As the two men enter Moosa's room, we hear screams from the film showing on the television set in the foreground. And the film showing on television is none other than Chopra's own *Khamosh*. In a fabulous series of intertextual relays, Chopra chooses the scene from his other film that parallels this one in *Parinda*: the protagonist Shabana Azmi, who plays a star in the film within a film, is taking a shower and on the television at her hotel we watch the notorious shower scene from Hitchcock's *Psycho* (1960). In a classic Hitchcockian wink at the audience, Chopra uses the scene from *Khamosh* as a red herring, to lead us on a false trail. This dense quotation from *Khamosh* recalls both Hitchcock and Chopra's other film, and within the text it provides the anticipatory structure for the ensuing killings in this sequence.

The film revels in rehearsing other configurations relaying our identification with the cinematic apparatus. For instance, when Karan tries to tell Kishan that he wants to help the police find Prakash's killers, the older brother protests, insisting that Karan go to Delhi. The irreconcilable differences between the brothers end with a fade-out. The next scene opens with an extremely long shot of a sunset, and the camera pulls back to a medium close-up shot of Karan's face. A dissolve moves us into a close-up shot of Karan, where the camera fuses with the character: Karan is on a mobile base moving from left to right of the frame, with apartment buildings in the background. The camera breaks this fusion, tilting up as Karan's mobile suddenly changes its horizontal movement and heads down. Perched up like a bird, we see the top of his head, and on the ground a flock of pigeons fly into the air. More than any other movement in the film, this fusion between character and camera indicates the film's desire to jolt us from our passive voyeurism of commercial genres.[13] Mesmerised by the mobile camera on a cricket dolly, I revelled in the film's confidence to offer, perhaps even smuggle, a cinematic spectacle that would lift us from the plane of genre regulations. It is at such moments that we are witness not only to the murders in the narrative, but also to Chopra's prowess as a film-maker, Renu Saluja's editing, and Binod Pradhan's cinematography that outweigh the film's compliance within a commercial genre.

Opening Sequence and the City

Although its flamboyant use of camera angles and shifting points of view wrench the film from a straightforward relationship to genre films, it is equally beholden to several aspects of the gangster film genre including gangland loyalties, gory scenes of violence, and the *mise en scène* of the city. Nowhere else are the film's thematic and formal preoccupations better captured than in its opening credit segment, 'For my brother Vir', a dedication that is sustained in the film as a narrative strand structured around fraternal love. The following two frames cut from 'Vidhu Vinod Chopra's' to 'PARINDA'. On the soundtrack, chirping birds slowly interrupt the production of 'silence'. Moving from a shot of a luminous twilight, the film cuts to a night landscape of Mumbai that stretches from high-rise buildings to huts on the beach; we hear Aaron Copland's *Fanfare for the Common Man* (1942) on the soundtrack, and the credits roll. Incorporating in total five shots of the city, the credit sequence captures the spectrum of difference in wealth: the shot of huts and high rise apartments yields to two shots of a brightly lit Marine Drive – the nerve center of Mumbai's wealth. The sixth shot of the credit sequence is a still, frontal shot of a mansion.

We are immediately transported into a narrative that we expect will be set in the depths of night in Mumbai. The five opening shots recall the genre of city films made in the 1930s across Europe, as well as film noir and gangster films produced in Hollywood in which we find similar homages to the cityscape in the opening segment.[14] In all three genres, shots of a city or movement through city spaces recall the historical and conceptual coincidence between the film spectator and city-dweller that lies at the heart of the formulations of modernity. Walter Benjamin's essays, for instance, suggest that the immobile film spectator's relationship to the film screen

paradoxically replicates the *flâneur*'s wanderings through the city because of cinema's ability to produce an illusion of movement through spatial and temporal
disruptions.[15] Although the critical literature influenced by Benjamin has served our
readings of the iconography of the Euro-American modern-city films, often these
positions implicitly suggest a conjunction between the development of genre cinema
and modern city spaces in our imaginings. For instance, certain Hollywood genres,
such as gangster, crime, and film noir, are etched in our memory mainly as narratives of New York, Chicago, or Los Angeles, most visible in the opening shots or the
panoramic shots of cityscape punctuating their narratives.[16]

By contrast, the city has had a covert presence in Indian popular cinema. We have
several stories of city-dwellers in Chennai, Mumbai, and Calcutta, but besides stock
images of certain landmarks, we would rarely think of, for instance, Raj Kapoor's
Awara (1951) as a Mumbai film or S. Shankar's *Kaadalan* as a Chennai film. Calcutta, however, is more legible in smaller films: Satyajit Ray's *Mahanagar* (1963),
Mrinal Sen's *Ekdin Pratidin/And Quiet Flows the Dawn* (1979), Aparna Sen's *36
Chowringhee Lane* (1981), and so on.[17] In one of the few published essays on the
relationship between films and cities, Amrit Gangar argues that, as Mumbai was the
first city where films were exhibited and the first to produce films, it seems likely
that it should serve as a backdrop for urban and urbane narratives.[18] He suggests,
quoting Kumar Shahini's well-known essay 'Politics and Ideology: The Foundations
of Bazaar Realism', that commercial cinema serves up enticing scenes to cushion the
frenzied lifestyle of the industrial working class. Gangar seems to argue that it is only
the alternative cinema of Kumar Shahini, Mani Kaul, and others that grasps the
more searing and realistic aspects of urban life in Bombay.[19] What he implies, but
does not fully develop, is Benjamin's formulation on how cinema captures urban life
not because of a perceived coincidence in their histories, but rather by the very composition of the cinematic medium through innumerable shot compositions that
represent the fragmented nature of modern urban life. Concurrently the smoothing
over of these shots through movement of frames at a regular pace blunts their
abruptness, a technique that also extends to the shock of urban living where the
wretchedness of everyday life vies with the sensory pleasures of moving through an
urban landscape that often works as compensation for drudgery.

Gangar's observation that the city as a space evokes anxiety, or neurasthenia, has
a long history in Indian films, where, for instance, the poor farmer migrates to the
city in *Do Bigha Zameen/Two Acres of Land* (1953), facing endless days of wretched
labour that finally kill him. The city as a benign space that serves a realist commercial genre such as the gangster film has been slow to develop in Indian cinema,
perhaps hinting at both the lack of reinforcement of such genres and a lack of cinematic presence for Indian cities. However, there are exceptions. We have seen that
in J. P. Dutta's film *Hathyar*, the cityscape consolidates the film's move towards the

gangster genre prominently epitomised by the presence and absence of suburban trains in the film. In *Nayakan*, the protagonist's move from a beach in Tamil Nadu to Mumbai is captured through a montage of the city. However, after this point, the film relies on frontal shots of monuments such as the Gateway of India and the Jehangir Art Gallery to convey the urban Mumbai. Most of the action in this film takes place in the central space of a slum or in the interior of Velu's home. There are two occasions when the city space occupies the entire frame, once in the opening scene after the interval and the other after Surya's car goes up in flames. The edge of the city is marked by the water, but we never see shots of the city from the sea. Evoking familiar tourist sites, the film does not abdicate its narrative of an ethnic Tamil hero struggling to find a place in alien Mumbai.

In contrast, Chopra's *Parinda* revels in the various representations of Mumbai, soliciting our spatial familiarity of the city that exceeds that of a tourist's. Unlike Dutta or Ratnam's films, which begin in non-urban settings, *Parinda* opens with a panoramic view of the Mumbai landscape, immediately transporting us into the iconography that we associate with urban crime films. In other words, the opening credit segment allows *Parinda* to uproot itself from rural dacoit genres, firmly anchoring itself within the internationally circulating gangster film genre. *Parinda*'s opening segment prefigures Ram Gopal Varma's gangster film *Satya* (1998), which also uses this segment to pay homage to Mumbai through images of the Victoria Terminus, while a voice-over eulogises the city.

The last and sixth shot of the credit sequence cuts to a still, frontal shot of a mansion. Abruptly, the film cuts to an extreme close-up of a wind-up toy, focusing on its movement until a hand enters the frame to stop it. We see a man picking up the toy and moving towards a garlanded family photograph. He strokes the infant's image and kisses the frame. A high-pitched female voice singing on the soundtrack matches the images. The man answers the telephone, saying 'Anna'. We gather that someone from another gang has been caught. Ordering the caller to keep the victim alive until he arrives, Anna puts down the telephone. As he leaves the frame, the camera moves into the photograph. A scream on the soundtrack moves us to a close-up profile of a man's face coming down to hit the floor with a thud. Through an elegant composition of shots that move from static close-up to tilts, we know that there are three men each wielding a hammer, a knife, or a gun. We hear the sound of a gun. Abdul informs Anna that the victim belongs to Moosa's gang. Anna orders them to pack the body and send it to Moosa. He is visibly upset.

We hear police sirens on the soundtrack as the camera tilts a full 180 degrees to finally rest on a top shot of the entire scene, which works as the establishing shot of the factory floor of a coconut-oil press. The men hurriedly hide the dead body in a pile of coconut shells. Police Inspector Prakash rushes into Anna's office looking for a man. Abdul roughs up Prakash, but Anna stops him with a mocking admonition that he should defer to the uniform that keeps India alive. As the police leave, Anna instructs Abdul to send Kishan over to meet Moosa.

The film cuts to a day scene where we see Kishan driving a Padmini,[20] curving around an enormous tank on the edge of the city. As he gets out of the car, he successfully fights off two men on the tank and later two swordsmen on his way to meet Moosa. Making a showy entrance, Moosa walks up a flight of stairs and stands against a backdrop of a slum interspersed with high-rise buildings signifying his domain. After a brief exchange between the two men, the film cuts to Anna's office, where we see Kishan with Moosa's 'token of his pleasure', a white handkerchief. Anna scoffs at Moosa's disingenuous call for truce.

The compact opening segment immediately moves into the structures of anticipation that we associate with gangster films, both thematically and formally. Having propelled us *in media res* of the narrative, the film assumes our familiarity with the structuring of expectations in the Indian gangster genre which no longer needs to stress the protagonist's origins. Instead, we abruptly enter the middle of the inter-gang war unravelling across the landscape of Mumbai spearheaded by the gangs' respective heads, Anna and Moosa. Anna's three men – Rama, Francis, and Abdul – kill one of Moosa's men; Kishan, his lieutenant, tries to negotiate peace with Moosa. The police, represented through Prakash and his men, appear to be a step behind the activities of the underworld, and from Anna's insinuation we gather that Moosa had tipped them off.

Although the film does not traffic in communalising gang warfare, it meanders through a Hindu habitus reminding us that some of the most common Hindu spaces and practices provide ideal settings for a gangster genre, a use that is not so different from similar religious evocations in Francis Ford Coppola's *The Godfather*, Ratnam's *Nayakan*, and Dutta's *Hathyar*.[21] In the first scene of the post-credit sequence, we see a garlanded family photograph in Anna's office. From the cultural convention of displaying photographs in India, we infer that the two other figures in the garlanded photograph – wife and child – are dead.[22] Later in the film, we see Anna performing Hindu propitiation rituals for his wife and child, an occasion that also alerts us to his pyrophobia. Several Hindu temple scenes in the film play on the genre's preoccupation with the difference between religious and social authority. At the same time, however, Anna's three henchmen (Abdul, Rama, and Francis) neatly fit into the film's idea of a plural secularism in the underworld. His nemesis Moosa has too brief a role for us to make enough of his religious faith; however, from the stereotypes that circulate in commercial cinema, we can infer from his clothes and name that he is a Muslim.

Just as opening *in media res* relies on our long familiarity with genre films, the film also relies on our ability to read the logic of cinematic images that exceed our familiarity with genre narratives. For instance, the abrupt cut from Anna talking about

Kishan in his office to a day scene where we see Kishan driving into Moosa's territory is riddled with rapid cuts that function as a delaying mechanism, delaying the arrival of the star actor Jackie Shroff, who plays Kishan. Although paradoxically he plays the part of a beleaguered man pushed into gang life because of circumstances beyond his control, his ostentatious entrance signifies his star status and exceeds genre concerns. Whereas the structure of anticipation built around Shroff's entrance eases the rhythm of rapid cuts, there is no doubt that, through the logic of the cut, the film demands and, at times, acknowledges our familiarity with the logic of cause and action that we associate with action genre films. Yet its experiments with a fast-paced editing rhythm surpass the structuring of anticipation and expectation in genre films and remind us of the rhythm of cinema itself that is predicated on producing an illusion of movement through discontinuous images separated by cuts. Genre films, *Parinda* suggests, are one way of coming to terms with the cinematic cut by displacing it on to a narrative logic of cause and action.

There is another element in the *mise en scène* fermenting the movement of cuts, which is none other than the telephone: Anna, for example, answers the telephone to receive news from his men about having successfully kidnapped one of Moosa's men. The film does not opt to stage this scene as an intercutting sequence to arouse narrative tension as horror films love to do, but uses the telephone to connect us to this off-screen space. Later in the film, we see similar stagings: Kishan begs Anna on the telephone not to harm Karan; Kishan receives calls at the bar; Paro receives calls at the school; Karan calls Moosa, and so on. The film leads us to see the telephone as a link between two spaces, as a stand-in for the off-screen space that soothes the pile of cinematic cuts unreeling in front of us by providing a narrative rationale.[23]

Flashbacks and Memory

Just as this accelerated jump into the narrative distances *Parinda* from *Nayakan*, we find a looser fit between the events of the story and the fabula. Like other gangster films, *Parinda*, too, is invested in exploiting the protagonist's past as the impetus for violent actions, but here the film moves away from a logic of linearity. Rather, the film recalls the past through a series of flashbacks that take us to the antecedents of this contemporary life of crime, functioning as prelapsarian moments in the protagonists' lives. Flashbacks puncture and encourage the narrative of violence in this film and, at the same time, intertwine with the constellation of interruptions peculiar to Indian cinema. The interval changes the content and form of the flashback, effecting stylistic shifts in the film, and the song and dance sequences absorb flashbacks even if they, in turn, are interrupted by the criminal narrative. In short, the flashback emerges as one of many experiments in the spatio-temporal continuities in the film.

Tracing the history of the flashback from early silent cinema to classical Holly-wood narrative via European and Japanese films, Maureen Turim presents an impressive array of its functions: reordering narrative elements, surfacing as mem-ory, and finally as a temporal disruption in Alain Resnais's films with no particular character assignation.[24] Considering the flashback as a device, Turim suggests that a close scrutiny of it reveals a complicated relationship between film and memory. Flashbacks are not uncommon in Indian films and are used particularly to resolve a narrative enigma. For instance, as an external flashback – not seen in the diege-sis before this point – in S. Shankar's Tamil film *Gentleman* (1993), it provides us with clues to the protagonist's behaviour. At other times, an internal flashback – repeated as a segment seen earlier in the diegesis – directs us to make sense of the protagonists' actions, as in the pre-credit sequence in *Yaadon ki Baraat/Procession of Memories* (1973). Flashbacks as memory of a traumatic event in the past seem particularly well suited to explain gangster motivations while simultaneously evok-ing nostalgia for a time before the protagonist has fallen into criminal ways. All Chopra's films betray his fondness for flashbacks that surface regularly as memory: in both *Khamosh* and *Saazye Maut*, he uses flashbacks to solve murders; in *1942*, *Kareeb*, and *Mission Kashmir*, films that tie the love story to social and political antagonisms, flashbacks bolster character motivation for revenge as well as longing for the loved ones. However, it is only in *Parinda* that he exploits flashbacks to their fullest extent, weaving them into the structuring of the interval and song and dance sequences.

From its beginning, *Parinda* refuses to assign a singular point of view to the flash-back, thus departing from its conventional use as a protagonist's memory in both classical Hollywood narrative and Hindi popular cinema. Nevertheless, the film mobilises an economy of circulating memories between characters that variously motivate their actions and structure their relationships. Kishan appears in Anna's office with Moosa's truce proposal; Anna wants to corner Prakash, who he says is responsible for initiating the recent exchange of corpses between the two gangs. Kis-han withdraws from the initiative, and Anna immediately remembers that Kishan's brother, Karan, is returning from America that day. As Kishan and Anna walk across the frame from left to right, the latter reminiscences about the first day they all met, the day Kishan's father died. The camera zooms in on the frosted glass of the office door and dissolves into an open sky with birds flying across the frame. The flash-back opens with a long shot of the open sea with birds flying, and the camera tilts down to a young Kishan and Karan watching a group of teenagers, including Anna, playing cards and eating. Kishan placates a hungry Karan with promises of food. In the next scene, Karan befriends a young girl called Paro and her brother Prakash, who is selling birdseed. As the four bond, Anna storms into them, taking a swipe at Prakash's birdseed. Kishan intervenes, but Anna replies by daring Kishan to steal and challenging them to enter into the rough and tumble street life of Mumbai. Karan goads Kishan, who finally runs off at great speed after having grabbed a shopper's purse. Through a dissolve, we return to the film's present, where Anna remembers how fast Kishan ran that day, adding that Karan and Prakash were always steadfastly close. Anna orders Kishan to use Karan to stop Prakash's policing. From the contents of the flashback we can say that the span is a day and its distance from the main narrative is incalculable; in short, this external flashback provides us with information of a time in the past.[25]

Although Anna is the last to leave the frame before the flashback commences, we cannot assign it to either one of them as the film presents an empty frame for a few seconds before the dissolve. At the end of the scene, through a dissolve, we return to wooden blinds in Anna's office as he re-enters the frame from the left, suggesting that the flashback may have been from Anna's point of view. Given the lack of a dissolve from a close-up shot of a character's face, it is tempting to see the flashback as belonging to the film's own narrative, or as a shared memory between the two men. However, as Anna is the last to leave the frame and the first to return, he dominates the segment by exerting his power over the allegedly common past, drawing in Kishan to see it from his perspective. Kishan's inability to participate fully in the structuring of the flashback points to the power struggle between the two men: not only is Anna Kishan's boss in the underworld, but he also controls Kishan's memory. It is only after Karan's death that Kishan calls on a past scene to destroy Anna.[26]

Parinda initiates the second flashback through a song and dance duet between Karan and Prakash, doubling the play of temporal disjunctions. Their reunion follows closely on the heels of a segment that moves rapidly through Prakash raiding Anna's factory, Anna's meeting with Meerani (an informer in the police force), and Anna's plans to kill Prakash when he meets Karan. Dominated by speeding cars, a dollying camera, high-angle shots of roads heavy with traffic, and intercutting scenes between the brothers' reunion and Anna's hit men, the segment conveys the frenzied logic of cause and action in a gangster film represented by moving vehicles that heighten the rapid cuts. Not heeding Kishan's warnings against leaving the apartment, Karan slips out in his brother's car to meet Prakash. Kishan tries in vain to stop him and to his dismay spots Abdul following Karan in his Ambassador. The song 'Jo yaar ki kushi vo kushi hai hamare'/'We revel in our friend's happiness' begins with a long shot of the sea with birds in flight that then proceeds to alternate between Karan and Prakash in their respective vehicles, an editing strategy that overshadows the anachrony of the sequence. Using a set of traffic lights as a graphic match, the film moves from the present to a scene in the past in which we see young Prakash, Paro, Karan, and, at times, Kishan, who is gambling with other adolescents. The alternating sequence not only switches between two discrete spaces – Prakash

Anna, Kishan, Karan, Prakash and Paro as children in *Parinda* (courtesy of
Vidhu Vinod Chopra)

and Karan on the different roads – but also between two temporalities – the present and past. Unlike the first flashback, the span of this flashback is as
indeterminate as its distance from the main narrative, but it does function as an
external flashback. Mirroring the opening close-up shot of the segment, the flashback and song close with Karan, yet its content encourages us to enter a regime of
a collective past shared by both men rather than being singularly attached to one
character.

   Not unlike the first flashback, here, too, the friends share memories, but with a
difference: the song celebrates their reminiscing, which conveys their equality.
Embedded in a song sequence, the flashback cannot help acquiring some of the
characteristics of the convention – a sequence of attractions on the one hand and
as a delaying device on the other. In both manifestations, the flashback bolsters the
song and dance interruption and, in effect, foregrounds the temporal disruptions
that inflect both devices so as to build anticipation.

   The song celebrates friendship, but we cannot help tempering our sentiments, as
we know that Anna's men are waiting for Karan to meet Prakash, an appropriate
occasion to kill Prakash. Although Karan is unaware of Anna's designs, Paro will
later force him to recognise his culpability in Prakash's death. Several aspects of the
mise en scène hint at impending doom for Prakash: he drives through a 'No Entry'
sign singing and waving his identity card at the local traffic cop, and his jeep bumps
over a speed breaker as if to slow his speeding automobile from its fatal encounter.

Karan arrives first and watches the pigeons clustering before taking off on short flights around the fountain. Prakash's arrival sparks a fond reunion, initiating an intercutting segment between the friends and an approaching white Ambassador.[27] Set as a frontal medium close-up shot of the two men, we see the car moving in the background. As Prakash ventures to tell Karan about Kishan, Karan cuts him off to show him the engagement ring he bought for Paro. The traffic and automobile motifs of the preceding song now continue to simulate a wipe as the Ambassador car moves behind Prakash's jeep. At the cost of temporal and spatial continuity, we see the three car windows wind down to the dominant sound of birds anxiously fluttering. Abdul, Rama, and Francis shoot Prakash in the back as he collapses into Karan's arms. Reaction shots capture Karan's shocked response. The scene closes with slow-motion shots of Prakash collapsing into Karan's arms and a close-up shot of Karan looking at an off-screen space beyond the camera lens.

Through a rhythm of intercutting, the scene pits gangland killing against male friendship. Killing a police officer is standard fare in gangster films, which the narrative will exploit by representing it as one of the most transgressive acts. In *Nayakan*, Velu becomes the don after one such act, and, in *Hathyar*, Avinash is expelled from the city to the countryside after killing a police officer. In *Parinda*, however, the rhythm of intercutting consolidates the link between death and friendship on the one hand, and on the other suggests the precarious place of heterosexual

Rama shoots Prakash (courtesy of Vidhu Vinod Chopra)

A wounded Prakash collapses into Karan's arms (courtesy of Vidhu Vinod Chopra)

love in a gangster film. Moving away from an innocent recall of the past, the flash-back now functions as a premonition of death, an association that the film progressively strengthens. In the sections after the interval, the film uses scenes from Prakash's death as the motivating drive for Karan's murders.

If the film has so far employed flashbacks to evoke the protagonists' memory of a childhood as it stands at the threshold of gangsterism and love, *Parinda* now uses a flashback to impress upon us Anna's fearful violence. The temporal and spatial dis-junctions in this segment move between Iqbal, one of Anna's former henchmen, recounting his crimes and Anna's home, where he is performing the annual propiti-ation ceremony for his wife and child. The scene begins at the temple where Iqbal, who is now a lemon seller, warns Karan not to pursue Paro. As Karan turns to Iqbal to explore the implications of his warning, we see Rama watching the scene. He rushes off on his scooter to Anna's home, where he waits for Anna to return from his rituals. The film cuts to a scene where the priest lights a match, and sounds of a woman screaming engulf the soundtrack which until then had Indian drumbeats. Anna looks behind him to catch a glimpse of a burning figure rush up the stairs. As the priest lights a mound of camphor, Anna goes into a screaming fit that only Kis-han can calm. Finishing the ceremony, Anna rushes downstairs to confer with his men. Rama whispers into his ear, and Anna orders his men to threaten Iqbal with dire consequences. Towards the end of this meeting, with little prompting, Anna claims he was a passive spectator watching his wife set fire to her son and then her-self. His account of their death is immediately challenged by the film as it abruptly cuts back to Iqbal's narration, where he tells Karan that Anna lied about their death and that, in fact, it was he who set fire to them. When we return to Iqbal, we hear him tell Karan of his brutal encounter with Anna. Suspecting him of defecting to Moosa's camp, Anna flings Iqbal onto an industrial drilling machine and proceeds to run the drill through his knees. The film narrates this moment by focusing on Anna – a low-angle, medium close-up shot. Instead of returning to Iqbal, the film cuts to the next scene, where we see Anna seated at his table talking on the telephone.

Meandering through several spaces – Iqbal at the temple and different spaces in Anna's house – the film ties Iqbal to Anna through a structure of intimacy and betrayal that characterises the gangster film.[28] With Iqbal's flashback, the film introduces another meaning to the system of flashbacks – Anna's old crimes are ren-dered more frightening when located as an external flashback. In equal measure, *Parinda* shows that external flashbacks of childhood appear more tender. In both evocations, they supply the viewer with additional information to better compre-hend the antagonisms unfolding in the narrative. Nestled in Iqbal's rambling flashback is a peculiar moment when Anna sees a burning apparition, pushing the limits of genre verisimilitude. Unlike the spatial discontinuity mobilising the stan-dard flashback, this one points to cinema's long history regarding magic, a link that we see extensively displayed in horror films and mythological genres through the use of special effects.[29] In both genres, we are accustomed to seeing 'unreal' subjects in the *mise en scène* – dragons, flying beings, cyborg monsters, and the like – that are spatially continuous with realist action. Similarly, emphasising spatial continuity in *Parinda*, the fleeing apparition seems to be available to both Anna and Karan, a composition that encourages us to consider how Anna's criminal acts outmanoeuvre temporal discontinuities even if he is cast as an hysteric.[30] In short, although Anna is hysterical, Kishan does not doubt him, thus reaffirming his own powerlessness in this relationship. Towards the end of the film, when Kishan kills Anna by setting fire to his office, we see the burning apparition from Anna's point of view, a difference that finally releases Kishan from his boss's clutches.

The next flashback sequence elaborates on brotherly love, a thematic concern that opens the film. The scene begins with Karan telephoning Kishan at Anna's office, asking to see him. As Karan confronts his brother about his involvement with Anna's nefarious activities, Kishan defends his own entry into the criminal underworld as the only means available of caring for his sibling. As Karan accuses him of murdering Prakash, Kishan defends himself by recalling his steady entry into underworld activities: when Karan needed books for school, Kishan sold marijuana in the streets; the day he sent his brother to boarding school, he sold liquor; the day he sent Karan to America, he pimped five women on the streets. When Kishan asks, 'Do you remember?' both men are in close-up shots in one frame. As the film dissolves into a flashback, we see the two brothers walking the streets of Mumbai where the younger one is whining about feeling hungry. Kishan says, 'Don't worry,' and the film cuts back to the present scene in the apartment where we see an over-the-shoulder shot of him – conventionally used as a reaction shot in classical Hollywood narrative. The scene is so carefully crafted that at no point in the series of flashbacks is it exclusively from Kishan's point of view – the only character who has had no access to flashbacks and the only one to survive the bloodbath at the end.

We could retroactively read these scenes from Kishan's point of view but, as the film dissolves from the two in the same frame, we cannot unilaterally attach it to him. When Karan says he was very young, the film replays the same pickpocketing scene, which is now rearranged: instead of Anna challenging him and Karan prodding him, we cut to Karan goading him towards the shopper. This flashback, like the earlier one in the sequence, dissolves with the two brothers in the same frame, even though it is Kishan who begs Karan to recall. Given the lack of a distinct point of view from either brother, we enter an economy of circulating memories that the film requires the protagonists to recall differently, underlining its preoccupation with the changing relationship between memory and truth.

Juggling romance and crime, the film now heads towards the last sequence before the interval, choosing to stage the tensions between gangster activity and

fraternal ties. Effectively, the narrative of fraternal bond competes with the romantic narrative, emerging as a convention of Indian gangster films where romance is
gingerly located alongside other repressed erotic economies. Kishan breaks into
Paro and Karan's romantic scene, whisking off his brother to his yacht to talk him
out of being a police witness; Karan is expected to identify Abdul in a police line-
up the following morning.

Abdul, Rama, and Francis watch Kishan board his yacht at the Gateway of India.
On the yacht, Kishan flatly tells Karan that if he identifies Abdul at the police line-
up, both he and Paro will be killed. Karan stoically responds that Kishan will face a
similar dilemma some day – a murderous death of those close to him. Karan ignores
Kishan's advice, threatening him with a death sentence if he had participated in
Prakash's death. Kishan fires his gun in frustration at the thought of his brother con-
doning his death. Karan and Kishan leave the yacht with little agreement on how to
respond to Prakash's death – Kishan wants Karan to flee to Delhi before being
caught in a net cast by the police, whereas Karan wants to help the police. Kishan
finally insists on giving Karan a gun to protect himself from Anna and his men. The
film alerts us to a prospective chase when it abruptly cuts to Abdul playing his flute
on the soundtrack. As Karan walks through the dark streets of downtown Mumbai,
he spots a white Ambassador car revving up. He starts running towards Kishan, but
the car gathers speed with Francis shooting at the two men. The scene cuts to slow-
motion shots of Abdul shooting Kishan in the back. Wounded, Kishan collapses into
Karan's arms while continuing to shoot at the car. On the soundtrack we hear *Fanfare for the Common Man*. The film cuts to a bird's-eye view of the scene as the
camera cranes up to the arch of the building, away from the bloody scene. The film
fades out to an intertitle declaring 'Intermission'.

After the interval, *Parinda* resumes on a fraternal note – Karan and Kishan are
holed up in their apartment with a doctor attending to Kishan's wounds. The film
underscores their besieged state by signifying any changes in this scene as intrusions:
the doctor leaves, allowing the film to cut to a space outside the apartment where
we see Anna huddled with his men. The shrill ring of the doorbell links the fright-
ened brothers inside the apartment and Anna's men outside, building a structure of
suspense that steadily amplifies in the film. The first ring intercuts between the
brothers inside the apartment and Anna's three henchmen outside. But with the
next two rings the film breaks away from the previous pattern of intercutting to show
us Kishan warning Karan not to open the door. Despite Kishan's cautionary injunc-
tions, Karan opens the door and we see the attending nurse outside. The doorbell
rings again after the nurse injects Kishan. She offers to answer it, but Kishan forbids her, and it is Karan who opens the door for Paro. It is at this moment that we
hear Karan express doubts about the police being able to protect them. Paro nevertheless persuades him to go to the police station.

In the next scene Iqbal, Paro, and Karan are at the police station. Iqbal tells them that Anna burned his wife and son, hence his pyrophobia. As Karan checks the police line-up, we hear the strains of a flute, an audio cue that prepares us for Abdul. Abdul threatens Karan with Kishan's death, an act that can be easily accomplished, he adds, with the help of the nurse who works for him. Karan flees the line-up and runs into Rama and Francis, who rough him up. Reaching the apartment he finds his brother alone – the nurse, we are told, has stepped out. The doorbell rings again, and Anna and his men burst in to talk to Kishan; Karan rushes out of the apartment to meet Iqbal who turns up with Paro's engagement ring, bearing her message of disappointment at Karan's cowardice. Karan's brief encounter with Anna is their first meeting as adults in the diegesis. As Anna and his men leave, Abdul corners Iqbal and threatens to kill him. The film fades out, and we cut to the balcony where Karan tells Kishan that he will start working for Anna.

Unlike Ratnam's *Nayakan*, which attempts to smooth the disjunctions caused by the interval, Chopra's *Parinda* embraces the interval as a punctuation that mobilises changes in the narrative. At the interval, the film closes to the sounds of Copland's music, recalling the opening sequence of the film and thus establishing a symmetry between the opening and closing sequences of the first half. Francis's attack on Kishan recalls the opening dedication to Chopra's brother Vir, nudging us to return to the fraternal drama. After the interval, the film ceases to refer to external flashbacks of the protagonists' childhood, shifting towards a revenge narrative spearheaded by Karan, a shift manifested by replacing temporal discontinuity with spatial intercutting. In a concurrent move, the film circumscribes the role of the police by expelling them from the intercutting rhythm dominant in the second half. In short, the interval rearranges motivations in the narrative by foreclosing minor strands where both the security of the police and a memory of an innocent childhood no longer seem sufficient to combat Anna's machinations. Turning to the unravelling of the logic of justice in the underworld, the film juggles fraternal loyalties, romance, and gang warfare by resorting to a rhythm of intercutting between different spaces as an editing alternative that produces a series of binary oppositions: fraternal bonds versus gang loyalties; romance versus crime.[31] Besides exerting its influence on the form and content of flashbacks, the interval neatly bifurcates the number of song and dance sequences in the film – two in each section of the film.

Frenetic intercutting in the second half emerges as a motif exacerbating narrative tensions by supplanting, though not completely, the high-angle shot dominant in the first half of the film. A different rhythm of intercutting shots heightens the tensions between the two brothers. After Karan tells Kishan that he plans to work for Anna, the film cuts to Anna's office at the factory where Kishan rushes in to dissuade Karan from joining the ranks of the underworld. As Anna appeases Kishan the camera dollies left to locate the two men in one frame, and to reinforce this newly grafted relationship we see welding in progress – a metallurgical cliché for the new alliance. The film intercuts between Anna's office and the factory floor, where we see Abdul guiding Karan to his first test: to kill a man with a handgun. Giving Karan a pistol, Abdul pushes him into a dark room with instructions to kill the captive, who is none other than Iqbal. Karan is mortified, but Iqbal spells out his options: if he fails to shoot Iqbal, Anna will kill him. Unable to convince Karan, Iqbal shoots himself. In Anna's office, Kishan's claim that Karan can never kill rings false as we hear a gunshot reverberate from an off-screen space.[32] Kishan and Anna rush to the factory floor. The film cuts to a bird's-eye view of the scene, and on the soundtrack we hear the music of the *Fanfare for the Common Man*.

Convinced of Karan's conversion, a despondent Kishan returns to his yacht. It is only when Karan calls Kishan about his imminent wedding that the film stages a reunion between the brothers in a song and dance sequence set in their apartment. Sung as a duet between the two brothers, the 'Sehre me dulha hoga'/'The bedecked groom' endorses the genre's obsession with fraternal love as it emerges in Hindi cinema, a love that also carries the possibility of betrayal. Within the representational system of the film, this song repeats the intensity of the song between Karan and Prakash, but with a difference: rampant spatio-temporal discontinuities rationalised as flashbacks govern the first song, whereas the second song maintains spatial and temporal continuity. Close to the bachelor-party festivities found in Indian popular cinema, including similar sequences in Dutta's *Ghulami* or the more gloriously joyous 'Goli mar'/'Shoot!' song in Varma's *Satya*, this sequence emphasises homoeroticism in the homosocial world of masculine genres, even if it is between brothers. Besides borrowing from a recognisable convention in Hindi cinema, what is particularly salient about this sequence within the representational system of the second half is the continuity of action in one space, instead of resorting to the preferred intercutting, an absence that may suggest an easier fit of such song and dance sequences in the masculine genres. It must be noted that the brothers' reunion takes place only after Karan has completed his killing spree and made amends with Paro, conditions that underscore the violence underpinning homosocial reunions in masculine genres.

The film's romantic strand struggles to survive in the crime-ridden narrative, squeezed between narratives of crime. In the first half of the film, zigzagging through Anna's factory where Kishan attacks Abdul for assaulting his brother, the film segues into Karan and Paro's romance, which takes place as a domestic scene in Kishan's apartment. The film will repeat the structure of interrupted romance in the 'Tumse mil ke'/'Having met you' song and dance sequence. Employing a prominent signifier of romance, the film resorts to commercial film conventions, but manages the achrony or discontinuity of such sequences by setting it against the backdrop of Paro cooking. Maintaining the film's propensity for flashbacks, the romantic sequence also undergoes temporal and spatial disjunctions. As she stirs the pot, the film dissolves into a scene at a fair where a young Paro and Karan are on a merry-go-round. We hear the replay of the same dialogue that was established in the first flashback, which we saw from Anna's point of view. The lights suddenly go out, and Paro screams, 'Karan, you must promise never to leave me,' and Karan obliges. Thus Prakash and Karan's flashback extends as a common memory to include Paro. The scene closes on a distressing note: the telephone rings and a stone breaks the window, interrupting the love scene. The film cuts to Kishan, who is trying to reach Karan from his yacht.

While the crime narrative interrupts the romance by literally halting the song midway, we return to a day scene at the flat where Karan and Paro continue their duet as they repair the broken window. Between the two parts of the song and dance sequence, the film digresses through a police station where Iqbal, Karan, and Paro identify Abdul in a portfolio containing photographs of criminals, then to Anna's office where he learns of Karan and Iqbal's visit to the police station. Splitting the same song in two parts – night and day – offers us an innovative film-making strategy to regulate the anachrony or discontinuity of this interruption that mimics its codes. By subsuming the interruption into the meanderings of the narrative, the song and dance sequence not only loses its status as pure spectacle, but also makes it impossible for us to consider it as a discrete segment.[33] Furthermore, Chopra inverts the sequencing of this interruption: the dominant crime narrative interrupts the romantic song and dance sequence instead of the reverse. In short, instead of its routine status as a delaying device, the song and dance interruption faces cuts and delays brought forth by the regulatory mechanisms of a gangster film. Such a reversal in sequencing not only relegates the romantic strand of the narrative to the status of a sub-plot in a dominant gangster narrative, but also comments on the status of the song and dance interruption as a metaphor.[34] Instead of its iconography and words commenting on the dominant narrative, in this particular reversal the film comments on the fragility of heterosexual romance in a crime narrative through interruptions. This peculiar reversal in its status heightens the romantic significance of the song and dance sequence, a detail that this segment demands we acknowledge.

The intermission bears no significant impact on the romance narrative, but inflects the film's move towards genre consolidation. Paro breaks off her engagement with Karan when he fails to identify Abdul at the police line-up. The film delays reuniting the estranged couple until Karan goes on his avenging way. After killing Francis, Karan tries to reach Paro at her school. Called to answer the telephone while teaching, Paro slams down the receiver after hearing Karan's voice. When the telephone rings again, she shouts into the telephone, 'There's nobody called Paro here …'. As she leaves the office, the film cuts to a high-angle shot of the room, reminding us of the criminal narrative that continues to influence their romance, thwarting their reunion. This pressure heightens when the film cuts from this scene to Karan collaborating with Moosa. It is only after Karan frames and kills Rama that the film entertains the idea of a possible reunion.

Dispensing with the telephone, Karan arrives at Paro's school, whisking her away from a rehearsal of a Christmas pageant. Recounting Iqbal's courageous act and his own calculated entry into the underworld, Karan confesses to two murders, committed because he could no longer stand being haunted by the sounds of gunshots and fluttering birds following Prakash's death. Paro bursts into a song, 'Pyar ke mod par, chodoge jo baahaen meri'/'On the road to love, forgive my excuses ...'. As in the two previous love songs, here, too, love competes with crime: Karan drives away in his car, interrupting the love song. After killing Abdul, Karan arrives at Paro's apartment. The earlier love song, interrupted by Karan's departure, now resumes as a duet: the male singer begins singing and is joined later by the female singer. Karan slips the engagement ring on Paro's finger. Using Karan's killing spree as the dominant strand in the narrative that splits the love song between her and his sections points to the film's attempts to subsume romance under a narrative of crime. Chopra resorts to a similar sequencing of the song and dance sequences to convey the fragility of the love story in *1942: A Love Story* and *Kareeb*. Bifurcating song and dance sequences in this manner integrates them into the dominant narrative through an intercutting strategy rather than setting them apart as separate modules of pure spectacle. At the same time, it alerts us to genre pressures inflecting the form of song and dance sequences: crime separates the song in *Parinda*, and anti-colonial struggles split the sequence in *1942*.

However, the film fails to nurture the romance narrative in a gangster film. Karan and Paro's wedding suffers from digressions: Kishan leaves the ceremony at the temple, and the film wanders through Anna's factory before returning to the temple. Interrupting the marriage scene, the crime narrative asserts its provenance over the presumed stability of the heterosexual union, as well as working as premonitory signal for forthcoming attacks. The most spectacular attack on the heterosexual union unfolds on the night of their wedding. Kishan, unaware of Karan's murders or of Moosa's tip-off to Anna on the identity of the killer, lends his yacht to them on their wedding night. Karan and Paro's love scene intercuts with Anna sneaking on to the yacht with throw-away scenes of revellers ushering in the New Year in downtown Mumbai. The segment begins with a high-angle shot of revellers at the dock, cutting to a long shot of Anna and his men wading through the crowd to get to their boat. Cutting to the yacht, we see Paro and Karan preparing to make love. The sex scene intercuts with scene of revellers – a bird's-eye view of the crowds first, then extreme long shots of the Gateway of India presumably from Anna's motor boat. As Karan and Paro make love, we hear *Fanfare for the Common Man* on the soundtrack which intercuts with *tabla* beats as Anna climbs aboard the yacht. The scene depends on the intercutting between these two visuals and soundtracks to heighten the polarised difference between the two scenes. Karan ends their orgasm uttering 'Siddharth', Kishan's name for their son. The door bursts open and Anna machine-guns the couple in their sexual ecstacy. The film cuts between a close-up shot of Anna firing and a high-angle shot of the bed, an angle that progressively goes up to simulate a bird's-eye view. Anna finally shoots down the bed that is held up by ropes before leaving the room. In slow motion, Karan falls off the bed and Paro rolls towards him; on the soundtrack we hear the first love song. The camera pulls up to a high-angle shot of the bloody scene with one rope from the wedding bed wildly swinging in the air. The scene closes with Kishan's late arrival. Pursuing a logic of interrupted romance colouring the entire narrative, Anna's orgy of violence offers a deadly conclusion to the logic of intercutting. Killing the couple immediately after their orgasm, *Parinda* explodes any idea of a safe place for a heterosexual couple in a gangster genre that is more routinely managed through homosocial bonds.

It must be noted that the interval neatly bifurcates the four song and dance sequences into two: we have a love song and a song between the men in each half. In each instance, Chopra subjects them to the turbulence of the crime narrative by further magnifying the spatio-temporal discontinuities: the love songs are interrupted by crime in both halves of the film; the song between Karan and Prakash is rife with flashbacks that anticipate the latter's death; and the song between Kishan and Karan delays the final showdown.

Flashbacks and Revenge

While the film resorts to a flip-flopping structure of intercutting to exaggerate the differences between brothers and lovers in the second half, the dominant criminal narrative of murder and vengeance returns to the preoccupations of the first half: flashbacks recur to punctuate Karan's killing spree. The interval substantially revises both the form and content of flashbacks in the second half by dismissing external flashbacks narrating scenes of childhood in favour of internal flashbacks driving the revenge narrative. In a section already riven by rapid intercutting between different spaces, providing few clues regarding character motivation, the flashbacks anchor Karan's conversion from a witness to a protagonist. Intimately tied to Karan, the flashbacks recall Prakash's death as the primary scene inflecting his motivation to kill, conditions that provide the impetus for the narrative, moving it decisively towards the logic of a gangster narrative.

Having convinced Anna – and, by extension, us – of his desire to join his gang, the film cuts to a night scene at the fountain with Karan holding a gun to his head and weeping, thinking of Prakash's final moments. Keeping pace with the intercutting rhythm structuring fraternal relationships, the film cuts to Kishan's troubled soliloquy on his yacht about somewhere away from gangland full of children and birds. At the fountain, Karan is haunted by an earlier exchange with his brother, who asserts that Anna rules out all legitimate options. Karan then resolves to avenge Prakash's death. As he washes his face, the film twice inserts scenes of birds flying by day. We recognise them as scenes from the first half, minutes before Prakash was gunned down, minutes after a buoyant reunion between Karan and Prakash. In a 180-degree flourish from the ground to the skies, the camera tilts to reveal Karan standing at the balcony of the flat. Similar to the tilt in the first half, when we were aligned with Karan's point of view after Prakash's death, the film highlights difference through repetition: despondency now transforms to revenge. The thematic continuity focusing on birds unites the brothers. It also drives a wedge between them by marking different scenes of birds: Kishan's pastoral scenes with no visual image jarringly matches Karan's recall of Prakash's death. Maintaining its obsession with flashbacks, the film replaces external flashbacks with internal ones, suggesting a shift towards the gangster narrative. As in the first half, here, too, flashbacks function as a protagonist's memory, albeit a traumatic one that acts as a precipitating moment in the revenge narrative obtaining in the second half. Through Karan, the film will steadily recall Prakash's death, underscoring Karan's trauma, as well as justifying his murders.

Intimately linked to Karan's actions, the film distributes bits of the original scene of Prakash's death to lend motivation to Karan's crime. Offering to kill Moosa, Karan is escorted to Moosa's hotel. Abdul drops Karan and Francis at the hotel with explicit instructions that it is Karan who should pull the trigger. In a series of Hitchcock-style red herrings, the level of suspense increases in this scene: Karan points the gun at Francis twice, the murder scene from *Khamosh* playing on the television in Moosa's room, and finally a series of close-ups of a gun being passed under the table between Karan and Francis. Karan claims the trigger is stuck, but Francis realises the safety is on. Although building up the suspense, none of these moments ends with Francis's death, which the film reserves until Moosa's arrival. However, we receive intimations of Karan's action in a series of intercutting scenes recalling Prakash's death: a close-up shot of a fizzing beer bottle intercuts with scenes of Prakash's shooting. This time, the flashback elaborates beyond the initial fluttering of birds: we see Francis lowering the window and aiming his gun and a wounded Prakash collapsing into Karan's arms. Intercutting twice between the beer bottle and the internal flashback, the segment conveys the full weight of the flashback as memory from Karan's point of view. In effect, through the figure of Karan, the film rearranges the system of motivations, no longer retaining the flashback as a nostalgic return to an innocent childhood, but rather as a brutal memory of a friend's death. Dissolving from Karan's face into the scene at the fountain, the film replays a scene we know cannot be from Karan's point of view. Rather, the film converts the

High-angle shot of the factory floor – Karan offers to kill Moosa (courtesy of
Vidhu Vinod Chopra)

scene of Prakash's death from an omniscient narrator's point of view into a psycho-
logical memory of one of its protagonists. As the scene replays we are well aware
that the flashback exceeds Karan's memory, but, closed through a dissolve, it now
decidedly converts into one.

Having won Moosa's trust by killing Francis, Karan joins with him to kill Rama,
double-crossing Anna. Karan frames Rama receiving money from Moosa, then
offers to kill him for Anna. Unlike the structuring of Francis's death, the film refrains
from visually recalling scenes from Prakash's death. The camera tilts down to show
us Rama's corpse sliding down the conveyor belt. The scene closes with the film's
preferred high-angle shot for crime scenes, reminding us of Iqbal's murder in the
same space.

Orchestrating a meeting between Meerani and Abdul, Karan heads towards his
final act of revenge. Shot at night at the fountain, the scene is stacked with revelations: Abdul finds out that Karan killed Francis and that Meerani double-crossed
him. As Abdul reels from this information, Meerani leaves the scene. Karan confronts Abdul about Prakash's death, a scene that the film articulates through an
internal flashback – from his point of view. The flashback commences as a clean cut
from a close-up of Karan: the window winds down in the Ambassador and we see
Rama, Francis, and, finally, Abdul. We must remember that on the initial occasion,
except for a shot of Francis, we were not privy to Karan's sighting of the other
two men. At this moment, however, the film fills that gap in our information by

rearranging the scene from Karan's point of view, a view that so far we have only been able to infer. As Abdul pulls out a knife to threaten Karan, a white car honks and as the window winds down he spots Moosa with one of his men sitting in the back seat. Abdul tries to flee, but Karan shoots in his direction, hitting the fence. The film reverts to another internal flashback with a different sequencing rhythm: Rama, Francis, and Abdul replaced by Abdul, Rama, and Francis. The birds fly up, and the scene dissolves to Karan shooting Abdul. Abdul charges at Karan with his knife. Karan shoots him for the second time, a scene that we now witness from Moosa's point of view. Grabbing Abdul, Karan tells him that, as they shot Prakash three times, Abdul, too, will be shot thrice. As the third shot goes off, the film cuts to the initial shooting scene where Prakash collapses into Karan's arms. Cutting back to a high-angle shot, we see Karan dropping Abdul's body into the pool at the base of the fountain, and, through a close-up shot of Karan's face, we cut to another high-angle shot from a greater height. Moosa walks in and encourages Karan to start anew, promising not to breathe a word about the shooting.

After the interval, flashbacks undergo a substantial revision in their content. Unlike the first half, where the external flashbacks circulate as collective memory with little or no attachment to an individual protagonist, in the sections after the interval flashbacks manifest distinctly as character memory. Such a move, from considering the flashback as a temporal past with no particular character affiliation towards a more definite anchoring of these temporal displacements as individual memory, consolidates the film's more overt engagement with a Hollywood-style

Karan regards Abdul's corpse in the fountain (courtesy of Vidhu Vinod Chopra)

Anna guns down Karan and Paro on their wedding night (courtesy of Vidhu Vinod Chopra)

genre driven by character-centred plots and individualised flashbacks. In retrospect, the first half of the film presents us with a more expansive version of the temporal displacements that we see in non-Hollywood films, whereas the second half marks a distinct move towards the gangster genre.[35]

After Karan's death, the film relinquishes its focus on Prakash's death and moves instead towards the final showdown between Anna and Kishan. Their encounter is marked with flashbacks reorienting Kishan's relationship to Anna and his own past. Arriving too late to intercept Anna's killing rampage that guns down Karan and Paro, Kishan rushes through the revellers to Anna's home. The soundtrack heightens the mood of revenge. As Kishan enters Anna's room, the latter bends down to check for weapons, removing a knife tucked into Kishan's boot. Anna offers him a drink, reminiscing about Karan. As Kishan mourns, Anna reasons that in this business there is no place for sentimental bonds between brothers, or between father and son. Kishan breaks a bottle, brandishing it as a weapon. Anna retaliates swiftly, threatening to kill him, but stops when Kishan flicks his lighter – Karan's gift. And on the soundtrack we hear Karan's last vow to kill Anna in the same way that he killed his wife and child. Grabbing Anna, Kishan sets fire to the drinks trolley and flings liquor

Anna surrounded by flames (courtesy of Vidhu Vinod Chopra)

bottles around the room. Anna is hysterical and finally runs to the safety of the swing. Fire engulfs the room and, in the last high-angle shot in the film, we see Anna standing on the swing with blazing fire swirling around him. At this moment, we see from Anna's point of view the screaming figure of his wife rushing across the room – a deranged recall of a similar moment in his past as he is torched. As Kishan leaves the room, the film incorporates a few shots from Anna's murderous moment on the yacht. Though the scene cuts from a close-up of Kishan, we know that he never witnessed the shooting, only its aftermath. Kishan pulls out a gun and shoots the ropes holding the swing, dropping Anna into the swelling flames. Anna's family photograph also drops into the fire.

From the fire in Anna's home, the film cuts to the cremation fire. On the soundtrack, the film replays the first song, 'Jo Yaar ki kushi', from their childhood, choosing that moment when Kishan joins Karan, Paro, and Prakash in play. We hear a young Karan cajoling his brother to give up his strong-arm tactics and choose the path of love. Kishan looks beyond to a different scene – we see young Paro and Karan playing on the beach among birds. As if responding to Karan's words from the past, he flings down his gun and the film finally closes with a freeze shot of silhouettes of the two children.

The film's closure deploys a fraternal rationale for the killings, restoring the symbolic place of the family. Kishan avenges Karan's and Paro's death with Karan's gift – a cigarette lighter from America. Anna's death finally ends the snowballing violence in this film, which had been ruled by his logic of gangland loyalties that undercut familial ties. As the legitimate authority of the state has had a marginal role since the interval, the film's final homage to social authority harks back to an external flashback, a device associated with death in the film. In the final scene, recalling his brother's words, Kishan flings his gun away and, in effect, abandons the never-ending cycle of violence perpetrated in the gangster genre. Kishan's relationship to these flashbacks has been ambiguous in the film. However, by associating them with the last living figure in the narrative, *Parinda* offers the only available Utopia that is available in the gangster film. If the protagonists resisted submitting to the authority of the state, they are guaranteed a nostalgic return to childhood. Such a recall does not overturn the authority of the state, but returns to the options set in motion in the diegetic universe of this film.

As we have seen in the avenging women chapter, the last-ditch attempt to restore the authority of the state by the sudden appearance of the police does not undercut the vigilante logic of the film, as the narrative depends on our understanding of corrupt state power. Madhava Prasad points to the late arrival of the police in Hindi films as a symptom of the weakening legitimacy of state power, a sympton that popular cinema has ably exploited in its various closing strategies.[36] Rather than resort to the sudden arrival of the police, *Parinda* seeks to end with an external flashback, an ending that arises from options rehearsed earlier in the film's narrative, an attempt that draws us back into the film.

To grasp the import of this ending, I should like to evoke Richard Neupert's four categories of endings: in the *closed text*, a hallmark of classical Hollywood narrative, the story is resolved and the discourse is closed; in the *open story*, the story is unresolved and discourse is closed; in the *open discourse* film, the story is resolved, but the narrative discourse avoids a strict closure of its strategies; and the *open text* leaves both narrative levels open. The last three categories, according to him, 'challenge classical notions of resolution, completeness, or even unity in ever more dramatic and radical ways'.[37] We may call *Parinda*'s ending an open discourse, where 'the story is resolved but the narrative discourse avoids a strict closure of its strategies.'[38] We know that Anna and his men are dead, but Moosa is still alive; Kishan loses both Karan and Paro, but his own ability to live is undercut by evoking a flashback of a scene in which he played no part. The open discourse ending draws us back into the film's discursive conditions that obsessively play on temporal displacements and shifting points of view that complicate the status of flashbacks as either an individual protagonist's memory or the film's play on chronology. The sections after the interval draw an intimate relationship between flashbacks and death: protagonists recalling their past finally face death as the narrative recall prepares them for their quietus. Kishan's relationship to his own flashback remains ambiguous – often tied to either Anna's or Karan's – but at the end, the film closes with a flashback from his point of view, but not necessarily his own. Given the film's tendency to place a death sentence on the recalling protagonist, we, too, expect Kishan to meet a deadly end, but the film ends short of that scene. Thus, although the story is resolved, the film retains an open discourse, a feature that also marks its departure from the Hollywood genre in which, as Neupert suggests, we expect to find a resolution to both story and discourse.

Heeding Neupert's suggestion that 'film viewing is a double process involving expectation and retrospection', *Parinda* appears at the crossroads of genre cinema.[39] Its open discourse ending seals its difference from the usual gangster film, but after the interval the film decidedly unravels along the lines of general gangster films through a logic of revenge. The first half, however, bears all the iconography of an Indian gangster film, but at the same time the tenuous relationship between temporal disjunctions and flashbacks anticipates the ending of an open discourse film. The hybrid cinematic styles in *Parinda* address a cinephile whose memory evokes the temporal disjunctions in Alain Resnais's and Akira Kurosawa's films, as well as the gangster genres of Hollywood and Indian cinema. Perhaps the film closest to Chopra's preoccupation is Sergio Leone's masterpiece *Once Upon a Time in America* (1983), a film replete with flashbacks.[40] According to Adrian Martin, the scrambled chronology in Leone's film does not prop up standard preoccupations, but explores what happens to gangsters after their rise in the underworld, an exploration that flirts with genre features without fully taking them on board. Although *Parinda* bears a close kinship to Leone's film, its engagement with the constellation of interruptions in Indian cinema supports a different approach that suggests revising our routine reading strategies of genre film to include its covert relationship to art-house productions. As in Dutta's masculine genres, the interval rearranges our genre expectations by initiating a series of internal flashbacks that are wound around a revenge narrative. The song and dance sequences, however, delay and interrupt the crime narrative and, in the process, become (as in Ratnam's *Nayakan*) an integral part of the narrative. Rather than neatly reproducing a Hollywood genre, *Parinda*'s hybrid cinematic style, like *Once Upon a Time in America*, is 'part pulp, part art' and solicits our memory of global cinemas. It reminds us that globally circulating genres such as the gangster film have local or national signifiers through their accommodation of a constellation of interruptions. The consolidation of genre films in non-Hollywood sites such as Mumbai cinema can produce unruly and promiscuous projects with little deference to studio narratives of the West. Above all, as the film conveys a shifting allegiance to the gangster film genre, it exposes those weak links or impasses in genre films where we often find ourselves rationalising narrative disruptions as purposive. For instance, the shoot-out between gangs in a gangster film not only takes up a considerable amount of screen time, but also often evokes an army of strangers that we never encounter in the diegesis. As viewers, we often justify such lapses in continuity by calling on the logic of the genre that routinely subverts spatial and temporal continuity.[41] However, when a film such as *Parinda* attempts to rewrite genre films without forsaking the constellation of interruptions peculiar to Indian cinema and evoking a different history of global cinema, the temporal and spatial disruptions cannot be simply justified within the logic of genre films. Rather, we have to turn our critical eye to local conventions.

Notwithstanding its varied experiments with revising genre features, the spatial and temporal continuities and discontinuities structuring the film return us to the early histories of narrative cinema as it moved from single-shot to multiple-shot stories. Writing on early cinema, Tom Gunning proposes four cine-genres characterising this period: narratives completed within a single shot; a genre of discontinuity consisting of at least two shots; a genre of continuity composed where discontinuity is de-emphasised by action at the story level; and finally the genre of discontinuity in which the action is continuous at the story level though disruption is caused by editing at the plot level.[42] As narrative increased story time, a single film could have several of these genres at various moments. In a similar fashion, it is instructive to think of the various experiments with space and time in *Parinda* as meditations in cinematic time and space, and as being composed of several cine-genres: Anna on the telephone evoking an off-screen space; Anna seeing a burning figure that allows us to see the magic in cinema; intercutting between the beer bottle fizzing and Prakash's death permits us to see links between two disparate spaces; and so on. Gangster genre emerges as the peg on which we can hang the different spatial and temporal disruptions in the film, but it would be foolhardy to see it exhausting its various experiments.

Conclusion: Writing History

I now want to re-evaluate the questions posed in the beginning of this section, which attempted to link the evocation of the past in the gangster film genre as a project of writing history. My readings of the structuring of repetition and nostalgia in *Nayakan* or the question of retroversions in *Parinda* touch on the different styles of storytelling available in Indian popular cinema. It appears that the Oedipal dyad takes precedence in *Nayakan*, whereas fraternal bonds challenge the logic of violence in *Parinda*. How these differences inform us of greater cultural patterns of behaviour seem beyond the scope of this book; rather, it seems reasonable to speculate that these differences in narrative structure point to certain differences in storytelling between the two industries in Chennai and Mumbai, though this, too, will have to be substantiated through further empirical research on crime films in the two film-making centres.

Being located within an international genre of gangster films, both films rely on a certain rendering of social authority, however corrupt or illegitimate it is at times. It is this evocation of both social authority and psychic law that draws on the spectator's desire for realism, or even hyperrealism, in part explaining the popular response of films dealing with the breakdown of the authority of the state. Uncovering these spectacular productions of realism leads us to the narrative structuring of these films, throwing up the ideological differences between them.

Our reading of *Nayakan* teased out the intimate relationship between commodity culture and cinema, a relationship that relies on the credibility of the *mise en scène*. *Nayakan*'s reception has frequently touched on the teamwork ethic established among Mani Ratnam, his cinematographer P. C. Sriram, and art director Thotta Tharani. My own interviews with Sriram and Tharani reveal their investment in adequately delivering a realist cinema, a position that sees the bulk of Tamil cinema as unrealistic. These views on the production of such an aesthetic are not without their ideological baggage, but we have to ask how such a realism is coloured by class, caste, and gender interests. Even as these film-makers learn to account for these differences, Ratnam's cinematic style is characterised by its investment in the production of pro-filmic. Contrary to traditions of cinéma vérité where the pro-filmic has an indexical quotient, Ratnam's films deliver a much improved and altered reality. Nowhere else is this clearer than in the Holi song in *Nayakan*, where we are presented with a reconstructed festival and seasonal calendar, or in *Iruvar*, where Ratnam produces a retro-future so that our memories of sequences from MGR's films are vastly improved. It is these aspects of his oeuvre that draw him closer to consumer economies of nostalgia and taste, aspects that are more akin to advertising. We have also seen how *Nayakan* subjugates the spatial and temporal disjunctions brought to the fore through the interval and song and dance sequences into its dominant preoccupation with a linear narrative.

Parinda, however, exploits these spatial and temporal disjunctions by privileging post-production work on the film, especially editing. The highly wrought narrative of flashbacks, cuts, intercutting, and high-angle shots abandons the pro-filmic, calling instead on our histories of film viewing and ability to decode cinematic language in various ways. The expansive use of spatial and temporal disjunctions in Chopra's first big commercial film, *Parinda*, paradoxically marks the most legible sign of his directorial style. Rather than abdicate his fondness for flashbacks that shape the narratives of his early small films, he incorporates it into both the interval and the song and dance sequence in *Parinda*. In *1942: A Love Story*, Chopra continues to deploy the flashback and the bifurcation of the song and dance sequence into his and her sections, and uses the interval to introduce a love triangle; in *Kareeb,* he chooses a more linear narrative style with less aplomb, but the song and dance sequences bear his signature. Not only do we find a repetition of the bifurcation in the song and dance sequence, but flashbacks are incorporated into one of the songs to signify loss of the loved one as well. Since *Parinda*, his film-making style has emerged as a twin movement between the desire to produce an internally coherent diegesis and trying not to abdicate the constellation of interruptions. This particular puzzle, as I have discussed in the other chapters, also afflicts the film-making style of J. P. Dutta and Mani Ratnam, who have similarly tried to regulate or exaggerate the spectacle of attractions arising from the song and dance sequences or manage the disruption in the diegesis caused by the interval. In each case, the result is not simply a riposte to Hollywood genre films, but a fully worked synthesis of local and global conventions where the legible sign of directorial style is most visible in an ability to control the constellation of interruptions. Such an assertion of a national aesthetic in the age of sweeping globalisation deserves another look, even if the narrative reform tightening internal coherence in these films tends to service capitalism.[43] For me, the assertive place of a national aesthetic in these films works against the rampant homogenisation that we are used to, holding out hope that such assertions will also give way to more confident subversions of dominant narrative forms.

Notes

1. Iqbal Masud (1989), 'The Pillars Are Borrowed', *Cinema in India*, October–December, vol. III, no. 4, pp. 16–17.

2. Masud, ibid., p. 17.

3. Babu Subramaniam (1990), 'Whirlpool', *Deep Focus*, vol. III, no. 1, pp. 97–8.

4. Masud, op. cit., p. 17.

5. www.reel-image.com. Site visited on 31 May 2000.

6. See Vidhu Vinod Chopra's website www.vinodchopra.com. Checked on 30 May 2000.

7. See Madhava Prasad (1990),'The Moment of Disaggregation', in *Ideology of the Hindi Film: A Historical Construction*, Delhi: Oxford University Press, on the history of the Film Finance Corporation and the NFDC and its engagements with mainstream popular cinema.

8. See the entry on the National Film Development Corporation in Ashish Rajadhyaksha and Paul Willemen (eds) (1995), *Encyclopaedia of Indian Cinema*, London: BFI (rev. edn).

9. www.vinodchopra.com, 16 May 2000.

10. I am grateful to Ranjani Mazumdar for telling me about a conversation she had with Javed Akhtar on how Chopra's script was inspired by Kazan's film.

11. See Slavoj Žižek (1992), '"In His Bold Gaze My Ruin Is Writ Large"', in Slavoj Zizek (ed.), *Everything You Always Wanted to Know About Lacan (But Were Afraid to Ask Hitchcock)*, London: Verso, pp. 211–72.

12. Interview on the telephone with Vidhu Vinod Chopra, January 2000.

13. During my telephone conversation with Vidhu Vinod Chopra, he explained that the actor Anil Kapoor was standing on a cricket dolly.

14. See essays in David B. Clarke (ed.) (1997), *The Cinematic City*, London: Routledge. See also David Reid and Jayne L. Walker (1993), 'Strange Pursuit: Cornell Woolrich and the Abandoned City of the Forties', in Joan Copjec (ed.), *Shades of Noir*, London: Verso.

15. Walter Benjamin (1960), 'The Work of Art in the Age of Mechanical Reproduction', in Hannah Arendt (ed.), *Illuminations*, New York: Schocken.

16. On representations of the city in European cinema, see Myrto Konstantarakos (ed.) (2000), *Spaces in European Cinema*, Exeter: Exeter Intellect, 2000.

17. A conference in Copenhagen by scholars working on Indian cinema focused on the city, June 1999.

18. See Amrit Gangar (1995), 'Films from the City of Dreams', in Sujata Patel and Alice Thorner (eds), *Bombay: Mosaic of Modern Culture*, Bombay: Oxford University Press. Gangar lists exhaustively a number of films set in Bombay.

19. For an alternative perspective on the relationship between modernity and the city, see A. G. Krishna Menon (1997), 'Imagining the Indian City', *Economic and Political Weekly*, 15 November.

20. A car manufactured by Premier Automobiles and commonly referred to as the Fiat, an allusion to the company's long association with the Italian automobile manufacturer.

21. On habitus, see Pierre Bourdieu (1984), *Distinctions: A Social Critique of the Judgement of Taste* (tr. Richard Nice), Cambridge, Mass.: Harvard University Press.

22. For a stimulating discussion on photographs, see Christopher Pinney (1997), *Camera Indica: The Social Life of Indian Photographs*, Chicago: University of Chicago Press.

23. For a marvellous reading of the telephone and parallel editing, see Tom Gunning (1991), 'Heard Over the Phone: *The Lonely Villa* and the De Lorde Tradition of the Terrors of Technology', *Screen*, vol. 32, no. 2, Summer, pp. 184–96. See also Gunning (2000), *The Films of Fritz Lang*, for his reading of the telephone in Fritz Lang's *M* (1931).

24. Maureen Turim (1989), *Flashbacks in Film: Memory and History*, New York: Routledge.

25. For the sequential ordering of the fabula, see Mieke Bal (1997), *Narratology*, Toronto: University of Toronto Press, pp. 99–110.

26. I should like to thank Madhava Prasad for pointing out the power struggle in this flashback.

27. The Ambassador is manufactured by Birla and resembles the British Morris Minor.

28. On betrayals in gangster films, see William D. Routt (1989), 'Todorov among the Gangsters', *Art and Text*, 34, Spring, pp. 109–26.

29. On special effects, see Sean Cubitt (1999), 'Introduction. Le Reel, c'est l'impossible: the Sublime Time of Special Effects', *Screen*, vol. 40, no. 2, Summer, pp. 123–30.

30. At a different register of film production, the fleeing, burning figure in this scene recalls the economy of stunt men who appear in various films and use asbestos to protect their bodies as they play body doubles. On the work of body doubles in Hindi cinema, see Malavika Rajbans Sanghvi (1988), 'Where Doubles Dare', *Sunday*, 13–18 November, pp. 76–80.

31. On intercutting, see Andre Gaudreault (1990), 'Detours in Film Narrative: The Development of Cross-cutting', in Thomas Elsaesser with Adam Barker (eds), *Early Cinema: Space, Frame, Narrative*, London: BFI, pp. 133–50.

32. In the middle of this intercutting a peculiar incident takes place between Anna and Kishan that is tied to the temporal ellipse of intercutting: Anna offers Kishan a cigarette and the latter lights it with his lighter – Karan's gift from America. When we return to Anna's office from the factory floor, we see him stubbing out his cigarette and Kishan playing with the lighter. At this point, it is not clear if Kishan ever smoked his cigarette or lit one for Anna, given the latter's pyrophobia.

33. Bhaskar Chandravarkar observes a similar strategy in P. C. Barua's *Devdas* (1935):

> *Devdas* opens with title music that must have appeared to be very lyrical to the audiences then. The orchestra is small and is led by violins (strings) and two wind instruments, clarinet and flute. This is followed by a songlet. The couplet of the words a *thumri*-style lyric, 'Balam aye baso moray manamein'. This is where Parvati is walking with a pitcher, in a outdoor scene. After the couplet we find a cut that reveals Saigal (Devdas) sitting under a tree singing the same song, but the song is modulated, i.e. the tonal centre has been changed now. Again the song is interrupted. After some dialogue it is resumed. I find this a fascinating use of sound. The song seems to have been used almost like a visual. You can cut away from the song without cutting away from the visual. The continuity of the visual is maintained but not that of the tonal centre, or even the song. When the song is resumed after a bit of dialogue it moves to an *antara*, 'Suratiya jaki matwari'. Some improvisation – something like a *badhat* – of this *antara* takes place. We return to the *mukhada* and end with a convincing *tihai*. The pattern that is so natural and beautifully naive is used for the song. This kind of a film song is probably better integrated with the film than the module-like song in later films that be kept or removed.

    Bhaskar Chandavarkar (1987), 'Growth of the Film Song', *Cinema in India*, vol. 1, no. 3, p. 18.

34. For an elegant reading of tenor and vehicle, see Linda Williams (1981), *Figures of Desire: A Theory and Analysis of Surrealist Film*, Berkeley: University of California Press, pp. 56–105.

35. Maureen Turim (1989), 'Disjunction in the Modernist Flashback', *Flashbacks in Film: Memory and History*, New York: Routledge.

36. For the conjunction of police and endings in Hindi cinema, see Madhava Prasad (1990), *Ideology of the Hindi Film*.

37. Richard Neupert (1995), *The End*, Detroit: Wayne State University Press, p. 33.

38. Neupert, op. cit., p. 32.

39. Neupert, op cit., p. 31.

40. For a stunning reading of Leone's film, see Adrian Martin (1998), *Once Upon a Time in America*, London: BFI. I should like to thank Carl Bromley for insisting on a link between these two films.

41. On genre and cultural verisimilitude, see Steve Neale (1990), 'Questions of Genre', *Screen*, vol. 31, no.1, pp. 45–66.

42. Tom Gunning (1990), 'Non-continuity, Continuity, Discontinuity: A Theory of Genres in Early Films', in Thomas Elsaesser with Adam Barker (eds), *Early Cinema: Space, Frame, Narrative*, London: BFI.

43. On narrative coherence, see Madhava Prasad's reading of *Roja* in his 'Towards Real Subsumption?: Signs of Ideological Reform in Two Recent Films.' *Ideology of the Hindi Film*, pp. 217–37.

6

Conclusion: Digital Imaginings in Indian Popular Films

How does one conclude a book on Indian cinema arguing for a close scrutiny of interruptions? In the preceding chapters I have suggested that interruptions rule the narrative of Indian films: song and dance sequences work as a delaying device; the interval defers resolutions, postpones endings and doubles beginnings; and censorship blocks the narrative flow, redirects the spectator's pleasure towards and away from the state. In each meditation, film endings seem elusive and distant, suggesting a rather perfunctory status in my analysis. However, I know from my most cherished ritual of waiting for the very last frame of the film before exiting the theatre that the lights do come on, the stream of light from the projector ceases, and the film does end. Reading my desire to wait for the very last frame of Ram Gopal Varma's *Satya* three days in a row as reluctance to leave, the theatre manager at the now defunct Manhattan Twin suggested jokingly that I could always come back the following day to see the film again. Obviously he, too, understood that repeat viewings offer the assurance of a loop journey for the cinephile. Checking the same images again and again reassures me that I can recall them, yet repeat viewings also promise new ways of seeing the movement between frames. As we leave the theatre, different moments of a film shepherd us into the world outside promising to brand our experiences for a long time: the virtuosity of the opening credits in *Satya*; an extreme close-up shot in Terrence Malick's *Thin Red Line* (1998); the kinetic energy of an action sequence that has me darting from one end of the screen to the other in *The Matrix* (1999); or the lingering, slow-motion shot that simulates longing. At other times, I also remember feeling relieved it all came to an end in S. Shankar's tiring *Jeans* (1998) or sad that Hansal Mehta's *Dil Pe Mat Le Yaar/Don't Take It To Heart* did not last longer. At still other times I am reassured that the provisional ending will generate sequels, urging me to return to the theatre once again. In a similar spirit, I wish to see this concluding chapter as a way of closing the argument and opening possibilities for future research.

Proposing that we read Indian popular cinema as a cinema of interruptions, this book suggests that this cinema is not only structured around spatial and temporal discontinuities, but also celebrates them. Whereas the particular configuration of these interruptions and the relationship between them emerge as a hallmark of popular Indian cinema, differentiating it from other national cinemas, I argue that its address is global rather than confined to national, regional, or local audiences. Even if in large part our viewing pleasures of this cinema emanate from its spectacular excess that mocks temporal and spatial continuity, there is no doubt it equally betrays a tendency towards recognisable genre formations available in commercial films internationally. Juxtaposing various kinds of cuts that include spectacular excess characterised by song and dance sequences, abrupt endings heralded by the interval, or lost footage caused by censorship regulations, Indian popular films are equally invested in assuaging the discontinuity accompanying these cuts by resorting to generic logic. In other words, for instance, in a film such as *Nayakan* with more than six song and dance sequences, we can also identify a gangster film narrative that draws us away from the spectacular excess into the diegesis.

Each chapter has grappled with this double focus, exploring how a well-worn, internationally available genre is reconfigured in Indian cinema by attending to local cinematic conventions such as censorship regulations, the interval, and song and dance sequences. The avenging women genre, I argued, although shadowing the rape–revenge Hollywood B genre, is equally beholden to Indian censorship regulations re-routeing the spectator's pleasure into an orbit of heady negotiations between the state and the film industry. Rather than randomly breaking the flow of the narrative, the ubiquitous interval in J. P. Dutta's films refurbishes his riposte to masculine action genres in such a manner that they cease to be straightforward copies of the Western, gangster, and war films. In my discussion of Mani Ratnam's film *Nayakan,* I isolate his attempts to regulate the interruptions, especially the interval and song and dance sequences in a gangster film, as a sign of his directorial signature. In a different way, my reading of Vidhu Vinod Chopra's *Parinda* comments on the film-maker's peculiar engagement with a temporal discontinuity that abounds in non-commercial films – the flashback. Whereas the flashback redirects the generic logic of this gangster film by calling on the past, it also informs the flow of the song and dance sequence and the place of the interval.

The main thrust of this book has been to offer a theorisation of the popular Indian film form, but it also joins forces with film critics who have been arguing against the global dominance of Hollywood-style genre films. For instance, David Desser offers us a structural reading of Japanese samurai films that parallels with the Western yet is marked by a different articulation of time and space that we are made to read as 'Japaneseness'.[1] In a similar way, critics writing on Italian spaghetti Westerns identify similarities with the American Western, yet argue for their uniqueness stemming from a separate set of historical conditions. Although available for readings within the rubric of the Western, both the samurai and spaghetti Westerns have not only revived the sagging generic narratives of the American Western, but have also sharpened our understanding of the nationalist and imperialist undertones of these films. In contrast, although Indian film-makers have long been poaching from American genre films as well as Japanese samurai films and spaghetti Westerns in their attempts to remodel the action genres, their influence on other national films takes a different route, a route that touches on the very constituents of genre films. Halting the film at the interval, cutting away for a song and dance sequence, or censoring scenes that are deemed explicitly sexual or overtly violent, popular Indian films rail against the perceived naturalised, internally coherent form of the American studio genres, underscoring the national characteristic of both kinds of cinemas.

Through the play of interruptions we can also see how genre films across the world harness both movement and spectacle, which form the bedrock of cinema. From Lumière and Méliès to Eisenstein and Vertov we have learned that cinema is constructed through shock effects of movement, cuts, and spectacle. Over the years, narrative cinema has routinised the shock effects so that we have learned not to be taken aback by the peculiar arrangements of movement and spectacle. But remnants of both movement and spectacle continue to haunt genre cinema, most notably in action genres. In a more regular manner, the interruptions in popular Indian cinema are not simply signifiers of a national cinematic style; they take us to the beginnings of narrative cinema where the relationship between movement and spectacle were far from regulated.

Hence, readings of Indian popular film allow us to see traces of early cinema, as well as drawing attention to correspondences with other cinemas of the world. For instance, the triptych structure we find in *Chungking Express* (1994), *Before the Rain* (1994), or *Amores Perros* (1999) reminds us of the interval in Indian cinema; the song and dance sequences in *Dancer in the Dark* (2000) and *Moulin Rouge* (2001) remind us of similar spectacular segments in popular films; the inert narratives of indirection of contemporary Iranian cinema highlight the workings of film censorship in other nation states.[2] Of course, I hear my fellow academics in the wings whispering how all this was always available in early American films: discontinuity, singing cowboys, and pre-code films. But if we can stop the urge to write histories of world cinema into the American Hollywood omnibus, we can see the trajectories of different experiments in commercial world cinemas rather than flattening these processes within the tired formulation of Hollywood domination across the world. Perhaps the most ambitious aspect of this book is to identify points of intersection between different national cinemas or between different language cinemas, points of intersection that acknowledge the global circulation and influence of different cinematic styles.

As much as the book underscores a national cinematic style, I am equally aware that the nation as a viable concept is under duress: the breakdown of the former nations of Eastern Europe and the Soviet Union has paradoxically produced a rich cinema: transnational film-making that uses actors from one place, post-production in another, and distributes the finished product through a different circuit; and diaspora film-makers who flirt with the idea of home without committing to any one location.[3] For their part, Indian films now include works by directors living in Canada, the USA, and the UK; Indian directors use post-production facilities in the West and East; and their narratives acknowledge a global audience. Besides the changing political economy of film that has curbed the dominance of any one national cinema, the most significant change affecting the ontological status of film has been the advent of digital technologies. Film-makers increasingly edit celluloid film on non-linear editing systems such as Avid, Quantel, and so on, a choice that has decreased post-production costs, pointing to the hybrid nature of contemporary audiovisual production.[4] At other times, entire features are being shot on digital camera and edited digitally, a reality most recently acknowledged in the inaugural digital film festival in March 2001[5] and more extraordinarily in a forthcoming film that has dead stars M. G. Ramachandran and Raj Kapoor starring with Aishwarya Rai. Even if we cannot assess completely the impact of digital technologies on narrative cinema and its audience, there is no doubt that their domination in contemporary global cinema introduces realms of space and time that were imagined in cinema's first century, but never fully achieved their potential. Digital technologies undoubtedly enhance the exhibitionist and spectacle nature of cinema – the action genres from Hollywood to Hong Kong bear testimony to this influence. In a similar vein, we can hazard that the new digital technologies will accentuate the spectacle of the song and dance sequences in a way that would not substantially revise their function as spectacular distractions. Yet, as Michelle Pierson persuasively argues, we cannot see the presentation of new technologies in film as pure spectacle, but rather it is also an assertion of cinema's historic preoccupation with technological effects.[6] It is no surprise that Pierson reviews the CGI (computer-generated imaging) effect in Hollywood through the science-fiction genre in which we see a celebration of technology as part of the diegesis. Lacking a fully developed science-fiction genre, Indian cinema has been absorbing CGIs and non-linear editing in different genres not only for their straight-forward spectacular effects, but also, more interestingly, for various experiments in narrative continuity: S. Shankar's *Indian* (1996) uses digital technologies to enhance his historical narrative; Chopra's *Mission Kashmir* (2001) uses digital effects in fight sequences, bolstering the black-wire stunt sequences. These and other films suggest that Indian popular cinema with its constellation of interruptions is well suited for forays into digital technology: the interval allows for an easy grafting of different effects; the song and dance sequences can now exploit the virtual journeys offered by reworking backgrounds; and state censorship may have to catch up with the subversive possibilities inherent in digital technologies.

As a way of imagining the future (the sequel to my argument), I should like to offer a preliminary reading of digital technologies' impact on popular Indian cinema, and here I include Avid editing and CGI, by turning to Mani Ratnam's *Alaipayuthey/Waves* (2000) and Kamal Haasan's *Hey! Ram* (1999), films that are clearly beholden to digital technology: Mani Ratnam's film was edited on Avid editing systems and Kamal Haasan's film gained a number of awards for its innovative use of digital effects.[7] Although different in their narrative preoccupations, both films resort to digital technologies to animate the relationship between space and time, in effect opening them to more incisive interrogations on the relationship between cinema and history, as well as initiating shifts in the narrative.

Alaipayuthey (hereafter *AP*) is a vintage Mani Ratnam-style love story particularly reminiscent of his *Agni Natshatram* (1988), *Mouna Ragam* (1986), and *Pagal Nilavu* (1985), films in which we find a similar structuring of class difference as the crucial transgression in the love story. Produced after the resounding failure of *Dil Se* (1998), the last film in his political trilogy, in *AP* Mani Ratnam plays down overtly nationalist preoccupations, amplifying instead class difference as an obstacle that hinders the lovers' union and subsequently spoils their marriage. In his political trilogy, Mani Ratnam ties the love story to political antagonisms challenging the legitimacy of the state, so that the couple's reunion parallels a statist resolution to incursions: the military captures the militants at the end of *Roja* (1992); the reunion of communities is fractured by communal antagonisms in *Bombay* (1995); and the annihilation of the suicide bomber earlier in *Dil Se*. Each of these films stages the problem of a heterosexual couple in the national imaginary, a narrative tack that also informs the 'foundational fictions' of other nations.[8] Except for the flashback describing the military's invasion of the female protagonist's home in *Dil Se*, all three films rely on a linear narrative to resolve progressively the antagonisms between the couple and the national imaginary, highlighting temporal progression as the preferred temporal locale for the love story.[9] By resorting to non-linear storytelling, *AP* chooses instead to explore the fragility of a marriage whose murky hopes for the future rests on a romantic past, quietly rupturing Mani Ratnam's preferred mode of tying the temporality of the love story to a linear narrative of the nation.[10] In no small measure, Mani Ratnam's facility with Avid editing programs has made it possible for the film to move between the past and present through extensive use of flashbacks marking a shift in his filmmaking style.

Although *AP* relies extensively on the possibilities offered by non-linear editing to narrate the shift between hope and despair, it also ties these experiments to the constellation of interruptions (as we have seen in Chopra's *Parinda*, a film that uses the interval to organise the articulation of flashbacks). In contrast, Mani Ratnam's film retains the use of the flashback as a source of information that drives the narrative forward on the one hand and uses the interval to offer a preliminary closure to one phase of the love story on the other. At the interval, Shakti and Karthik's marriage is no longer a secret from her parents: Shakti's father confronts Karthik at the railway station; the film cuts back to the present, where we see Karthik waiting for Shakti at Nungambakkam Station. The sections after the interval, while retaining the back and forth movement mobilised by the flashback, decisively frame the setting in a new space – the newlywed's appartment. However, the film uses the interval to change the composition of the song and dance sequences in a way that heightens the bifurcation between 'love story' and 'marriage'. The two song and dance sequences in the first half exploit the class difference between the couple by playing with spatial discontinuity: in the song 'Pachai nirame'/'Green colour', the film cuts from the urban milieu to sylvan landscapes; in the 'Rahasya snehadai'/'My secret friend' song, the film cuts from the newlyweds' secret rendezvous to monuments in northern and western India. Frolicking and lip-syncing through these spaces, the lovers unite, overcoming their class differences. This spatial discontinuity spills over into 'Yavano oruvan'/'There was somebody', which is composed as a background song set in Kerala, following close on the heels of the lovers' decision to part after a disastrous encounter between the two sets of parents. Shakti is at a medical camp in Kananoor, and Karthik goes in search of her, braving bad monsoon weather. Although we are well prepared by information provided in the diegesis to expect Karthik's journey through a rain-drenched, wind-blown landscape, the song sequence nevertheless enhances the idea of lovers travelling through both real and imagined landscapes to reunite. These spatial disruptions prefigure in the wedding song 'Yaro yarodi'/'There is somebody' (where Karthik and Shakti first meet), which ensues when the film cuts from Karthik waiting at the suburban station to a rural setting in the opening sections of the film. Although not strictly the first song in the film, the sudden cut to sylvan landscapes orients us to the film's preferred scene of desire.

In sharp contrast to the abrupt spatial disruptions in the sections before the interval, the two songs after the interval insist on spatial continuity even though, paradoxically, they do not particularly enhance our understanding of the plot. Set in the couple's apartment, 'Kaadhal sadugudu'/'Love game', the first song after the interval, maintains spatial continuity even though different costumes indicate that the segment compresses several disparate moments to convey the highlights of the early months of marriage, a thematic repetition from the 'You are a love song' sequence in *Nayakan*. The second song, 'September maadam'/'In September', set against the backdrop of a beach picnic, similarly maintains spatial continuity, even though the film uses the convention of recruiting well-known female dancers to infuse the plot with sexual desire, notwithstanding the fact that their relationship to the diegesis is distant.

Although this relational paradigm between the interval and song and dance sequences remains one of the most novel aspects of the film's articulation of interruptions, I want to return to the film's experiments with non-linear chronology in a love story. Peppered with slow-motion shots in the song and dance sequences, the film asserts familiarity with digital editing, but its most innovative use of this technique does not rely on linking it to interruptions as a way of doubling the quantity of attractions. Instead, the film chooses other sections of the narrative to calibrate the speed of moving frames, thus producing a self-consciousness about the ideological impact of these technologies.

Besides flashbacks dominating the conception of movement, the film also employs dissolves to suggest temporality. As a very familiar device from narrative cinema to control temporal disruptions, dissolves move us out of the Nungambakkam railway station to the past. Although seen less frequently in Indian popular films, in this film the dissolves tie together two frames to suggest a certain spatialisation of time. In a more innovative manner, the film refurbishes the fade-out by converting it from the standard circular dot to a receding square fading in the background. What we see on screen is often a frame within a frame, a technique that is akin to split-screen devices used in commercial television programmes: the credit sequences of one programme roll into the next programme or when two television programmes appear on one screen. In *AP*, one frame slowly recedes to the background giving way to another, clearly choosing to maintain the spatial coexistence of the past and present over a neatly cut progressive narrative.[11] At times, the film finds diegetic relevance for this technique by suggesting that Karthik is watching his past through a format resembling a television or computer screen.

Although these innovations suggest that *AP* revises several conventions of the

Passing trains at Chennai – *Alaipayuthey*

love story, the film presents us with another love story by recalling an older love story in the history of narrative cinema. The new love between narrative cinema and digital images recalls film's old love for moving trains to simulate movement on screen. The film opens with Karthik waiting for Shakti at Nungambakkan Station. Through flashbacks the film chronicles their love story, which began at a wedding, in the 'Yavano oruvan' song: he was with the groom's party and she with the bride's. The rural setting in this song does nothing more than lend a certain pastoral eroticism to the couple that needs the city to flourish. From the wedding scene we cut to an overhead shot of neatly lined government railway quarters in Tambaram. Karthik and Shakti catch a glimpse of each other through the open doors of the moving trains speeding in opposite directions. He registers his pursuit by keeping track of the trains from Tambaram that may carry Shakti; trains not only unite the couple, they also reunite Shakti with her mother and sister. Although the film seeks to provide the full spectrum of transport options in Madras as a sign of class difference – Karthik rides a motorbike, Shakti and her sister Purni use public transport such as the train and bus – its repetitive focus on moving trains urges us to consider narrative film's archaic yet long-standing love affair with trains to simulate movement.

When Karthik and Shakti catch a glimpse of each other from moving trains on opposite tracks, the film prolongs the movement of trains through digitally doctored slow-motion shots. Although slow-motion shots here and in the song and dance sequence call on our understanding of longing and pleasure between the lovers, I suggest that the slow-motion shots of trains allow us to read cinema's long affair with moving trains, producing, in effect, a palimpsest frame with traces of the past and gestures towards the future on this enduring scene of movement in cinema. As Lynne Kirby argues, tracing the history of moving trains from the Lumière brothers to the rushing trains in early American cinema, the kinetic energy produced by moving trains along with a whole host of technologies associated with modernity allowed cinema to mimic and replicate the thrill of speed.[12] Using slow-motion shots of trains as transition shots between the past and present, or even between scenes, *AP* opens the narrative preoccupations of the love story to include an understanding of film history that dwells on cinema's long-standing use of trains to stimulate movement on the screen. It is as if digital slow-motion shots were allowing us a peek into the various experiments in movement studies characterising early cinema on the one hand and, on the other, by returning us to this period they allow us to rediscover lost options that we now uncannily realise with the advent of digital technologies. When Walter Benjamin extolled the virtue of changing perceptual consciousness in cinematic technologies, he believed that the cinematic apparatus was the most promising instrument to affect our optical consciousness. However, it has taken us a hundred or more years to realise the options that were long available but not actualised in film. The digital 'scanning' of images does not altogether

Shakti is brutally knocked down in traffic

dispense with the gap between frames – another interval – but does suggest that the standardisation of frame speed in film production suppressed other degrees of movement between images.

Whereas the focus on movement and trains in the film opens the question of movement in cinema, *AP* does not abandon its attempt to intertwine the movement of the love story with that of the train for diegetic purposes. Take, for instance, the scene when Karthik successfully tracks down Shakti and effusively says, 'I love you.'[13] Unflustered but feigning incomprehension, she asks him if love means he would jump off a moving train for her. Towards the end of the film, we return to this remark in the hospital when Shakti wakes up from her coma and says, 'I love you' to Karthik. This time he asks her if it now means that she would jump off a train for him. The film ends on this last question. Associating trains with death and undying love, the film uses other characters to ventriloquise this sentiment: Shakti's mother curses her with death on the tracks. Nevertheless, the film does not exploit associating death with trains, although it uses it to signal movement, but instead returns to Mani Ratnam's pet object of mobility – the car. As in *Iruvar* and *Nayakan*, here, too, he uses a car accident as the precipitating moment in the narrative: a car runs into Shakti while Karthik waits at the suburban railway station. By resorting to a car accident, shot in digital slow motion, as the crisis to reignite Karthik and Shakti's love, the film numbs the shock effects produced by images of rushing trains, but retains their spectacular image of movement that exceeds their narrative function, to signify erotic longing. In effect, the digitally mastered slow-motion shots of moving trains in a love story reinvigorate the old love story between movement and spectacle that forms the bedrock of cinematic subjectivity.

In contrast to the intimate spaces of a love story and marriage in *AP*, Kamal

Haasan's *Hey! Ram* (1999) tackles a nationalist narrative of epic proportions, including the partition, Gandhi's assassination, and contemporary communal politics in India. Rather than working as part of the backdrop, the film intimately ties these political and social events to the fate of the male protagonist, Saket Ram. The twin preoccupations of the film produce an unruly narrative that avoids a resolution of the knotty issues that it sets in motion, yet it urges us to consider the inextricable links between cinematic and national histories. Keeping pace with the narrative, the film deploys a number of formal strategies, including monochromatic sequences for the contemporary scenes, digital images akin to video games, and a rich tapestry of quotations from world cinemas: elephants from D. W. Griffith's *Intolerance* (1916) and Pastrone's *Cabiria* (1914); dream sequences from Luis Buñuel's films; *mises en scène* from *Indiana Jones* (1981); and so on. Simultaneously, it evokes these references to world cinema within a nationalist narrative and in effect revisits similar coincidences of interests in Griffith's *The Birth of a Nation* (1915), to a lesser extent in Mehboob Khan's *Mother India* (1957), and more overtly in S. Shankar's *Indian* (1996), a rich set of associations encouraging us to consider Mikhail Iampolski's suggestion that quotations in films gesture towards the past.[14] *Hey! Ram* reconfigures the melodramatic aspects of these nationalist narratives by focusing exclusively on the male protagonist's relationship to the nation, a focus that dwells on the slow conversion of the South Indian Brahmin from a distant observer to a militant subversive by deploying digital technologies.[15]

To the consternation of critics lamenting the invasion of digital technologies, there is no doubt that digital morphing as a technique vastly improves the use of dissolves and cuts to suggest corporeal transformation on screen – wolf to man, man to woman, and so on.[16] A similar pre-digital history obtains in Indian cinema where cut-and-paste devices achieve the metamorphosis of a woman into a snake, especially the genre of snake films that includes *Nagin* (1954) and *Nagina* (1986), or grafting two separate frames maintains the illusion of the multiple roles played by the same actor. In an instrumental sense, digital technologies advance the making of these illusions by rendering seamless transformations of screen and, in effect, uniting us with the diegesis of the story. Yet this pull into the narrative cannot completely repress the history of innovations in digital technology overlapping with military experiments that are similarly plagued with time and space structuring the narrative of target practice.[17] It is therefore not surprising that we should find the most spectacular use of digital technologies in conquest narratives such as *Independence Day* (1996) and *The Matrix* (1999), heightening the relationship between cinematic and military modes of representation. Although *Hey! Ram* underplays military prowess, the film's use of digital technology to simulate a different story of origins consolidates the nationalist narrative and cannot help but remind us of the militant aspects of nationalism.

Not unlike *AP*, Kamal Haasan's film also scrambles linear chronology by moving back and forth between 1999 and the period between 1946 and 1948. We see Saket Ram, a Tamil Brahmin, working as an archaeologist in Mohenjodaro in 1946; with his first wife Aparna in Calcutta during communal riots, a scene that ends with her death in 1946; a respite in Chidambaram and Madras, where he marries Mythili a little before independence in 1947; visits to Maharashtra and joining ranks with right-wing Hindu militants between 1947 and 1948; and denouement in Delhi when he tries to assassinate Gandhi in 1948. The temporal scrambling matches the spatial journey through pre-partition India, allowing the film to draw a continuum from communal antagonisms during partition to contemporary tensions set in motion after Hindu militants demolished the Babri Masjid on 6 December 1992. Saket Ram's conversion proceeds from a disinterested scholar who becomes a militant Hindu nationalist after encountering the gorier aspects of communal riots in Calcutta and finally turns into a Gandhian pacificist by the end, a conversion narrative that rescues the film from wholly aligning itself with Hindu nationalism. Yet it is the middle sections, the parts spelling out Ram's entry into the ranks of the Hindu right, that are replete with the film's mastery over digital technology, especially morphing, relaying its own conversion from analogue to digital images.

One of the most flamboyant exhibitions of digital morphing takes places during Ram and Mythili's visit to a kingdom in Maharashtra – marking his definitive sympathies towards the right-wing Hindu party Rashtriya Sevak Sangha (RSS) – when the local king at the behest of Abiyankar (a right-wing Hindu zealot whom Ram encounters during the riots in Calcutta) draws him into a scheme to kill Gandhi. After fortuitously meeting up again with his old friend Lalvani from Karachi, Ram and Mythili join the Ram Lila celebrations on the palace grounds where Abiyankar offers Ram a drug-laced drink that induces Ram to conjure figures from the riot scene in Calcutta, as well as heightening his sexual interest in Mythili. Seducing her away from a dance performance, he leads Mythili to their room. As they begin to make love, we see her morph into an enormous gun with Ram stroking its barrel. This is a heavy-handed metaphoric substitution that carries a banal psychoanalytical association: the woman replaces the gun in a way that demands we understand how the libidinal drive severs itself from object identification. Clearly, the excesses of the scene lead us to recognise how morphing showcases digital technology, providing only a tangential link to the narrative. Nevertheless, another reading also obtains here, taking us down a different road. Blinding us with technological prowess, *Hey! Ram* uses morphing to veil its relationship to censorship regulations. Instead of including a sexually explicit scene that may provoke the ire of the Board of Censors, the altered image allows us to view the scene through metaphoric substitution, a substitution that reconfigures the temporality of censorship. In its extreme form, popular films simply substitute the love-making scene with pastoral evocations, cut to a song and dance sequence to regulate the overflow of passion, or push the envelope to the limit. In all three possibilities available in the pre-digital era, we confront a linear unfolding of the narrative where a cut directs us to the next image. Morphing, on the other hand, maintains intact an old-fashioned relationship to censorship while distracting us with a showstopping spectacle that morphs objects within the frame – a spatial transformation rather than a temporal one. Cushioned in a visit that highlights Ram's political conversion, morphing in this sequence overdetermines the connectives between political and sexual desire, an overlap that the film underscores during a secret meeting in the maharaja's palace, when from Ram's point of view we see the maharaja's face morph into Aparna's. In other words, morphing allows a film such as *Hey! Ram* to push the limits of what is permissible on the Indian screen through metaphoric substitution, a substitution that inverts the relationship between space and time between frames.

The second spectacular scene of morphing occurs soon after Ram's visit to Maharashtra, detouring through scenes of riots in 1996 composed in monochromatic colours mimicking black-and-white documentary footage – a burst of red fire undercuts the documentary gesture, moving it towards the diegesis of the film. These excursions to the monochromatic footage focus on an ailing Ram in the care of his grandson. Escorting Ram to hospital through streets littered with signs of the communal riots that marked the anniversary of the demolition of the Babri Masjid in December 1992, his grandson is halted by the police and escorted to the safety of a bunker. From an extreme close-up shot of Ram's left pupil, the film dissolves into a digitally produced target. On the soundtrack we hear the police officer's command to shoot – a sound bridge connecting the two images. In the digitally produced scene, we see a muscular Ram at target practice; his attire is clearly that of a Brahmin man and includes the sacred thread flying across his bare chest, an image that cannot completely sever its relationship to the real – Ram converts the handgun to a rifle by attaching a shoulder rest. This short scene of target practice celebrating the morphed, muscular Brahmin body gives way to a simulated storm that sweeps over the entire screen. Undeterred by the ferocity of the storm, he stands his ground.

Poised to function as an explanatory segment, morphing actualises Ram's meta-

Saket Ram morphs into a
muscular male: *Hey! Ram*

morphosis from a reluctant spectator into a fully fledged member of a right-wing militant Hindu political party. Clearly, the digital simulation of a muscular body adds further credence to popular representations of militant masculinities that surface in Amar Chitra Katha comic books and on cable television.[18] In a compelling reading of masculinity and morphing in *Forrest Gump* (1994), Joseba Gabilondo suggests that in the 1990s representations of morphing on screen usher in a different kind of masculinity, a resolutely heterosexual masculinity, constructed after or in response to both gay and feminist politics.[19] Rather than the hard masculinities of the 1980s, according to him we find a masculinity that is self-involved, more narcissistic, and more openly engaged with gayness, without being gay.[20] Its response to feminism, however, has involved usurping reproduction not through duplication, but by inverting – masculinity reclaims fatherhood as well as motherhood. This shift in representations, mobilised by morphing, equally effects the conventional sado-masochism underlying masculinity: 'The morphed and reproductive masculinity of the 1990s shows a new arrangement of this sadomasochistic economy: masochism becomes *avowed* by traditional filmic means (narrative and camera) while sadism is *disavowed* through morphing' (p. 197).

Although great differences separate the unwilling male protagonist who suffers in *Forrest Gump* from the very deliberate action-oriented hero in *Hey! Ram*, both films engage with narratives of placing the common man in history, official and marginal. Here, too, we find the sections preceding the morphing segment ripe with masculine inability: Ram helplessly watches his wife Aparna being raped; bows to family pressures by marrying again; and even bears a sentimental attachment to women, home, and domesticity. The communal riots do not immediately transform him into a militant Hindu nationalist. Rather, the narrative derives sufficient pleasure in his suffering. The conventions of realism deployed in the film combine with the pressures of the star system. In several Tamil films starring Kamal Haasan, we find masochistic scenes that provide the rationale for his actions: frontal shots of a bruised body by the police in *Nayakan* (1987) and *Guna* (1991); unrelenting masochistic narrative of the suffering male in *Mahanadhi* (1993); and so on. Morphing, on the other hand, provides the space to articulate a sadistic masculinity that is set in motion after Abhiyankar's death when Saket Ram is chosen to assassinate Gandhi. Although we find a fair share of masochism in the scene, morphing nevertheless constructs a hyperreal space outside the conventions of realism, allowing his passage from being subjected to being a subject, from victim to agent. The narrative decisively moves towards action and resolution soon after the morphing segment: he leaves his wife and begins his participation in the assassination scheme. At its closure, the film renders the excesses of militant masculinity as a futile excursion, choosing instead to close on a male subject whose place in history is assured after a journey through sadism.

Saket Ram somersaults over
the piano

Using the sadistic possibilities offered by the morphing segment, the film
redresses the masochistic suffering incurred by Ram in an earlier scene, a scene that
the film cannot forget. I refer to the notorious rape scene that serves as a foundational moment for the masculine narrative of conversion. Much against Aparna's
warnings about the volatile situation in Calcutta, Ram ventures into the city to buy
food. Running into marauding men who are distinctly marked as Muslim, Ram saves
a young Sikh woman and returns home. As he enters the building he notices that it
has not been spared from looting and killing. His own apartment has been broken
into and a group of men is beating down the bedroom door to gain access to Aparna.
As he enters, a couple of marauders knock him down and tie him to the piano, leaving his body splayed open like an animal for slaughter. Thus immobilised, Ram fails
to save his wife from being raped. Although we catch glimpses of Aparna's face a
couple of times in the bedroom mirror, her rape takes place in an off-screen space.
We hear her screams on the soundtrack as the men troop in one by one. On the
screen, we see the man guarding Ram sexually fondling him. Although he is tied
down, Ram manages to somersault over the piano, landing on the keyboard and in
the process kicking his guard in the groin. Pretending to be cooperative towards his
captor, Ram succeeds in getting the guard to untie his ropes. This, of course, turns
out to be a clever ruse, allowing Ram to regain control over the situation. Grabbing
a hockey stick he swings it at the intruder and eventually pushes him off the balcony. He loads and shoots his gun at Aparna's attackers, but they rush out of the
apartment after fatally slitting her throat.

The visual arrangement of this scene borrows liberally from rape–revenge narratives in Hindi popular films by relying on our sadomasochistic identification with

the screen.[21] However, there is an important difference. Feeding into Hindu communal fantasies of Muslim men as predators and sexually violent, the segment depicts men marked as Muslim as a marauding crowd that preys on Hindu and Sikh women. Whereas this image of Muslim men may circulate in the dominant popular Hindu imaginary, it is worth bearing in mind that popular cinema has generally been reluctant to indulge in these stereotypes. For instance, in Mani Ratnam's *Bombay* we find several scenes of Muslim men as predators, but the film maintains a distance from sexualising violence, particularly sexual violence against women.

By contrast, *Hey! Ram* sexualises communal violence by returning to stock cinematic representations of rape that structure the avenging women genre. Like the visual configuration of rape in this genre, we witness the scene with censorship regulations clearly in place: Aparna's rape takes place in an off-screen space, but her screams dominate the soundtrack; we see her reflected a couple of times in the bedroom mirror, and towards the end of the segment we are privy to her brutal death. Additionally, like other aspects of this genre, we do not witness her rape in a continuous sequence like the gang rape in *Bandit Queen*, but rather see it through the logic of intercutting shots that relies on other images as stand-ins for the horrifying image of rape.

In *Hey! Ram*, the image on screen simulating the off-screen rape is Saket Ram's body lying across the piano after being tied down. Initially two men hold him down, but one of them joins the gang rape in the bedroom. We see the other intruder fondling Saket Ram. When he outsmarts his attacker by asking him to untie him, his first physical reaction is a full-bodied kick at the latter's crotch. We cannot underestimate the aggressive display of homophobia in this scene that functions as a stand-in for Aparna's rape, a display that personifies the fear of miscegenation in a heterosexual paradigm. Ram's vulnerable body is the one holding centre stage in this rape scenario, the one that is hit and held down for fondling. Aparna's screams on the soundtrack feminise the scene, playing on the gendered formulation of the relationship between image and sound in narrative cinema: sound is subservient to the image, joining image and context. By foregrounding the distressed male body on the screen, at least one narrative strand of the film borrows from the logic of the rape–revenge narrative. In other words, Saket Ram avenges not his wife's rape, but his own.

By introducing the distressed male body into the composition of the rape scenario, the film initiates a shift in Hindu nationalist narratives that routinely use women as bearers of tradition and community. Undoubtedly, the Muslim man as the predator maintains a fixity of representation in *Hey! Ram*, but this is a defensive ruse that cannot completely account for the image of the vulnerable Hindu male body facing a sexual threat. The film manages this threat by mobilizing an avenging narrative that literally takes apart this *mise en scène* and reconfigures its constituents.

Ram and Aparna share a moment of intimacy and peace at the piano

Let me elaborate. The intruders lay Saket Ram on top of the piano in the living room, a prop that the film has established as an integral part of the heterosexual *mise en scène*: on his return to Calcutta, Ram and Aparna playfully flirt by the piano, and in a post-coital scene he sits and plays a few notes. As the central prop in the first song and dance sequence at the club in Karachi, the film establishes the piano's association with both Westernisation and modernity. Besides these signifiers within the text, *Hey! Ram* calls on our familiarity with the piano as a standard prop in Hindi and Tamil films. Typically, a male protagonist will use the piano to express desire, however tortured the consequences turn out to be: Raj Kapoor by the piano in *Sangam* (1964) singing the virtues of male friendship; heterosexual love in *Kati Patang* (1970); Sivaji Ganesan in *Pudiya Paravai* (1964); Gemini Ganesh in *Missamma* (1955).[22] Although I associate the piano with men, a more careful inventory points to female protagonists using the piano in very similar settings: Madhuri Dixit in *Saajan* (1991), Rakhee in *Muqaddar Ka Sikandar* (1978), Zeenat Aman in *Dhund* (1973). Whereas the piano signifies modernity and Westernisation in general, its recurrence in masculine melodramas as a prop underscores the feminisation of a male protagonist. The most extreme form of this assertion obtains in American Westerns, where we see the piano as a signifier of civilisation drawing the men away from anarchic frontier violence. The piano in *Hey! Ram* also recalls the piano in Buñuel's *Un Chien Andalou*, which Linda Williams adeptly reads as signifying bourgeois conventions that Buñuel mocks by loading it with a dead donkey; or the piano in Jane Campion's *The Piano* as a sign of civilisation in recently settled New Zealand.[23]

Athough the piano in the *mise en scène* draws us into a wide range of intertextual references, Ram's near rape is the traumatic foundational scene that the film tries to regulate, but cannot completely manage. In a surrealist scene after his second marriage, Ram mistakes Mythili's scream at seeing a lizard for Aparna's rape and subsequently sees different characters from the riots in Calcutta morph in the bathroom. One would think that we are being directed to read Aparna's rape as serving as the foundational moment explaining Ram's conversion. However, the film returns to the male body spread out on the piano in a way that is no different from recalling a traumatic event: we recall fragmented moments of the scene.

Although the film cannot ever fully recall Ram's vulnerable body on the piano, other aspects of the scene periodically enter the film to emphasise the extent of the trauma. After the riots, we see Saket getting ready to leave Calcutta. Standing at the entrance of his apartment building, he watches the removal men lower the piano from the balcony. The weight of the piano makes it slip the pulley and it comes crashing down. Although we see Ram rushing off in a taxi before the final crash of the piano hitting the ground, the film returns him to this scene when he returns to Calcutta after marrying Mythili. In a flood of nostalgia, Ram looks up at the balcony of his apartment in Calcutta and imagines Aparna gesturing to him in slow motion. Her image dissolves into the piano crashing down. Both images connote the end of a modern secular imaginary associated with Ram's career as an archaeologist, leading us to make sense of his political conversion.

After the riots in Calcutta, the film seems invested in restoring several aspects of the *mise en scène* before the onset of the communal riots that disrupted the domestic scene. Nowhere is this impulse more evident than in the love-making scene at the palace in Maharashtra. As I noted earlier, the film plays with metaphoric substitution by morphing Mythili into a gun to counter the censorship regulations regarding sexually explicit scenes. However, a different kind of censorship is also

A post-coital Ram at the piano in Maharashtra

at work here that directs us to Calcutta before and after the riots. We first see Aparna holding a gun as Ram sneaks into his apartment on his return from the archaeological dig. That condensed image of her with the gun, I suggest, seeks reinstitution by displacing it on to a morphing scene in Maharashtra: a large gun replaces Mythili. Later, in the post-coital scene in the palace, we see Ram playing the piano. Recalling several elements from the *mise en scène* of the apartment in Calcutta, the film restores Ram's brutalised body without forgetting the traumatic aspects of the initial scene.

Although *Hey! Ram* converts Kamal Haasan, the star, into a spectacular digital image that exceeds the star ideal, it is the not the first film to do so. We find a more benign version of this digital simulation in *Magalir Mattum/Ladies Only* (1994), also starring Kamal Haasan. Frustrated by sexism at work, the women office workers conjure a computer-simulated image of an ideal man who turns out to be the star Kamal Haasan. Whereas *Magalir Mattum* unabashedly celebrates the star's image as the ideal pin-up for women office workers, *Hey! Ram* accentuates this available image by severing its purchase to an indexical referent: the digital image is a vastly improved version of the star's body. However, the muscular body in the digital space does not abdicate its commitment to other referents, but seeks to find its purpose within an older regime of filmic representation that continues to battle with notions of the real. In other words, the muscular, militant body in the film services the cause of the ideal male image in Hindu nationalism and not a simulated battle on the screen. Yet Gabilondo's proposal that 'masculinity's masochistic renunciation of reality also represents a Utopian possibility for other subject positionalities' (p. 201) provides us with a way to imagine possibilities offered by hyperreal digital images in *Hey! Ram*.

Distinctly placed to highlight spectacular aspects of the masculine body's conversion, this segment borrows the spectacular aspects of the song and dance sequences. With little prompting, the film literally ruptures the diegesis by cutting into a digitally simulated space rife with anachronisms; the sudden breaks in narrative temporality are not dissimilar to the onset of song and dance interruptions. Focusing on the singular male body in focus, the morphing segment, too, cannot help the exhibitionistic impulse that similarly infuses this interruption. In short, I suggest that by resorting to morphing the film seems to acknowledge the fetishising of the male body that is usually reserved for female protagonists in heterosexual world cinema. Even if this shift recasts our conversations about the masculine subject's place in nationalist narratives, the hyperreal scenario does hold out the possibility of deploying morphing for other struggles of representation.

Tied closely to modernity and nationalism, the dominant form of narrative cinema retains a commitment to realism and indexicality, a commitment that is under threat with the arrival of digital technologies. Of course, I am exaggerating the large-scale shifts promised by digital technologies considering the ways in which they are already harnessed into realist narratives. But just as the early years of cinema enjoyed a space outside routinised narratives, digital technologies with their excessive specularity promise different Utopias heralded through the violent manipulation of space and time. Even in one of its most aggressive forms, it returns us to the myriad possibilities offered by cinema in its early years of development that were systematically foreclosed by the domination of a particular form of narrative cinema.

I cannot but help mourn the passing of celluloid – most recently literalised at my local theatre during a screening of *You Can Count On Me* (2001), when the credit sequence started slowly burning because of careless projection conditions, an event that reminded me that, despite film's promises of posterity, its material conditions were always vulnerable to degradation and combustibility. This memory of a world of spinning celluloid and dark theatres now seems a distant image for those of us working on popular cinemas in the diaspora who have long been accustomed to videos and now DVDs. Our memory of filmic images transformed into other forms has been the only avenue available when both private capital and state interest in the preservation of popular films barely exist. Inadvertently, our viewing practices of watching films on video and DVD have affected their production, a relay that imagines a compression between production and consumption time.

Wall poster for *Daud* (courtesy of the National Film Archive, Pune)

At this point I wish I could offer grand proclamations for the future of Indian cinema, but I would rather return to the cinephiliac urge that opened this book by returning to another film by Ram Gopal Varma – *Daud/Run* (1997). After having made a clean getaway from the police, our protagonists Bhavani and Nandu ride through a rain-drenched landscape to be finally alone. In yet another flamboyant homage to *Sholay*, Varma has them riding a motorcycle with a sidecar: she is in the sidecar and he is on the motorcycle. Exasperated by his wild cornering she asks him, 'What do you intend to do now?' Without missing a beat he responds, 'Sing a song.' The film abruptly cuts to New Zealand, where we find our favourite couple slowly sauntering to 'O bhanwr ... dekho hum deewanon ko'/'O bee! Look at us drunk with happiness'. A lesson from the annals of *Daud*: when in doubt, break into a song. Cut away. Let the song and dance begin.

Notes

1. David Desser (1992), 'Toward a Structural Analysis of the Postwar Samuari Film', in Arthur Nolletti Jr and David Desser (eds), *Deframing Japanese Cinema: Authorship, Genre, History*, Bloomington and Indianapolis: Indiana University Press, pp. 145–64.

2. See the essays in Mahnaz Afkhami and Erika Friedl (eds) (1994), *In the Eye of the Storm: Women in Postrevolutionary Iranian Cinema*, London and New York: I. B. Taurus and Syracuse University Press.

3. Among the books written recently on Eastern Europe, see Dina Iordanova (2001), *Cinema of Flames: Balkan Film, Culture and Media*, London: BFI. For a comprehensive discussion of the changing face of transnational film production and reception, see Robert Stam and Ella Habiba Shohat, 'Film Theory and Spectatorship in the Age of the "Post"', in Christine Gledhill and Linda Williams (eds) (2000), *Reinventing Film Studies*, London: Arnold. On film-making practices in the diaspora, see Hamid Naficy (2001), *An Accented Cinema: Exilic and Diasporic Filmmaking*, Princeton, NJ: Princeton University Press.

4. Siegfried Zielinski suggests these editing programs point to the hybrid nature of current audiovisual production. He expands in the following manner:

For the filmic illusion of motion, digital non-linear editing marks the transition from a horizontal to a vertical method of working. The process of montage no longer takes place between the horizontally positioned feed and take-up plates of an editing machine or a video console. Now, it is more a kind of expanded data-processing operation. After conversion into digital form, the film material is then available in the form of files, documents, and data lists, which can be moved around or combined at will without the film or video material having to be touched at all. Only after the complete construction has been assembled in the computer – on the more complex machines, this includes montage, processing effects and sound – comes the step back to the realm of what is perceived by the senses. The package of data is brought together with the coded original material and edited and woven together according to the given structure of instructions. Possible inordinate extravagance (in the shooting) and predictable calculation (in the post-production) enter into a symbiosis.

Siegfried Zielinski (1999), 'Conclusion: Good Machines, Bad Machines for Living Hetereogeneity in the Arts of Picture and Sound – Against *Psychopathia Medialis*', in *Audiovisions: Cinema and Television as Entr'Actes*, Amsterdam: Amsterdam University Press.

5. The four-day digital film festival was organised by Digital Talkies, a production outfit formed by film director Shekhar Kapur.

6. Michelle Pierson (1999), 'CGI Effects in Hollywood Science-fiction Cinema, 1989–95: The Wonder Years', *Screen*, vol. 40, no. 2, pp. 158–77.

7. For the special effects in his film Kamal Haasan used the Mantra digital facility at Ramoji Film City in Hyderabad, an outfit that has now emerged as the major post-production centre in India.

8. For a similar overlap between heterosexual union and nations, see Doris Sommer (1991), *Foundational Fictions: The National Romances of Latin America*, Berkeley: University of California Press.

9. However, it is important to bear in mind that in *Mouna Ragam* the problem delaying the happy marriage is the wife's past, which the film narrates as a flashback at a later point in the film.

10. Karan Johar's *Kuch Kuch Hota Hai* uses the structure of the flashback to reunite a college romance. At the same time, the flashback maintains the sanctity of the original romantic unit, but allows us in a *Rashomon* fashion to reassess the past.

11. *Buffalo 66* plays with the frame within a frame to suggest the progressive breakdown of family dynamics.

12. Lynne Kirby (1997), *Parallel Tracks: The Railroad and Silent Cinema*, Durham, NC: Duke University Press.

13. See Madhava Prasad's fine reading of this declaration in English that abounds in Hindi films. He suggests that the transgressive act of love finds its match in an English utterance that conveys modern sentiments while maintaining its forbidden status within the diegesis. Madhava Prasad (1998), *Ideology of the Hindi Film: A Historical Construction*, Delhi: Oxford University Press.

14. Mikhail Iampolski (1998), *The Memory of Tiresias: Intertextuality and Film* (tr. Harsha Ram), Berkeley: University of California Press.

15. Mantra, the digital facility at Ramoji Film City in Hyderabad, won the National Award for Special Effects in *Hey! Ram*.

16. See the collection of essays in Vivian Sobchack (ed.) (2000), *Metamorphing: Visual Transformation and the Culture of Quick-Change*, Minneapolis: University of Minnesota Press.

17. On the coincidence between cinema and military technologies, see Paul Virilio (1989), *War and Cinema: the Logistics of Perception*, London and New York: Verso.

18. See Anand Patwardhan's film *Father, Son, and Holy War* for a thorough investigation of masculinity in the Indian public sphere. See also Arvind Rajagopal (2001), *Politics after Television: Religious Nationalism and the Reshaping of the Indian Public*, Cambridge: Cambridge University Press.

19. Joseba Gabilondo (2000), 'Morphing Saint Sebastian', in Vivian Sobchack (ed.), *Metamorphing*.

20. Gabilondo engages extensively with Susan Jeffords's argument that there is a definite shift in representations of masculinity in the Reagan era. See Susan Jefford (1994), *Hard Bodies: Hollywood Masculinity in the Reagan Era*, New Brunswick: Rutgers University Press.

21. See Chapter 2, 'Avenging Women in Indian Cinema', for a fuller treatment of this genre.

22. I wish to thank Murali Gopalan for generously sharing with me his cinephiliac knowledge of pianos in Indian films.

23. Linda Williams (1981), 'Un Chien Andalou', in *Figures of Desire: A Theory and Analysis of Surrealist Film*, Berkeley: University of California Press.

Bibliography

Abraham, Itty (1998), *The Making of the Indian Atomic Bomb: Science, Secrecy and the Postcolonial State*, London: Zed Books.

Adams, Parveen (1998), 'Per Os(cillation)', *Camera Obsucura*, May, pp. 7–30.

Altman, Rick (1989), *The American Film Musical*, Bloomington: Indiana University Press.

Anderson, Benedict (1991), *Imagined Communities*, London: Verso (rev. edn).

Asher, Catherine and Thomas Metcalf (eds) (1994), *Perceptions of South Asia's Visual Past*, New Delhi: Oxford University Press and IBH.

Aumont, Jacques, Alain Bergala, Michel Marie, and Marc Vernet (1992), *Aesthetics of Film*, Austin: Texas University Press.

Bal, Mieke (1997), *Narratology*, Toronto: University of Toronto Press.

Barnow, Erik and S. Krishnaswamy (1980), *Indian Film*, New York: Oxford University Press.

Baskaran, Theodore S. (1996), 'Songs in Tamil Cinema', in *The Eye of the Serpent*, Madras: East–West Books, pp. 38–61.

Bazin, André (1967), *What Is Cinema?*, vol. I (tr. Hugh Gray), Berkeley: University of California Press.

Benjamin, Walter (1969), 'The Work of Art in the Age of Mechanical Reproduction', in Hannah Arendt (ed.), *Illuminations*, New York: Schocken.

Berger, Maurice, Brian Wallis, and Simon Watson (eds) (1995), *Constructing Masculinity*, New York: Routledge.

Bergstrom, Janet (1979), 'Alternation, Segmentation, Hypnosis', *Camera Obscura*, pp. 3–4.

Bhabha, Homi (1994), 'DissemiNation: Time, Narrative and the Margins of the Modern Nation', in *The Location of Culture*, London and New York: Routledge.

Bingham, Dennis (1994), *Acting Male: Masculinities in the Film of James Stewart, Jack Nicholson, and Clint Eastwood*, New Brunswick: Rutgers University Press.

Bliss, Michael (ed.) (1994), *Doing It Right*, Carbondale: Southern Illinois University Press.

Bordwell, David and Kristin Thompson (1993), *Film Art*, New York: McGraw-Hill.

Bordwell, David, Kristin Thompson, and Janet Staiger (1985), *The Classical Hollywood Cinema Narrative: Film Style and Mode of Production to 1960*, London: Routledge.

Bourdieu, Pierre (1984), *Distinctions: A Social Critique of the Judgement of Taste* (tr. Richard Nice), Cambridge, Mass.: Harvard University Press.

Branigan, Edward (1992), *Stagecoach*, London BFI.

Caughie, John (ed.) (1981), *Theories of Authorship*, London: Routledge & Kegan Paul.

Chabria, Subresh (1992), 'Images of Rural India in Post-Independence Cinema', in Alok
    Bhalla and Peter Bumke (eds), *Images of Rural India in the Twentieth Century*, New
    Delhi: Sterling.

Chakravarthy, Sumita (1993), *National Identity and Indian Popular Cinema*, Austin:
    University of Texas Press.

Chakravarthy, Venkatesh (1999), 'Eliminating Dissent: the Political Films of Mani Ratham',
    The Toronto Review, vol. 17, no. 3, Summer, pp. 19–32.

Chopra, Anupama (1997), 'Southern Invasion', *India Today*, 13 October, pp. 38–40.

Clarke, David B. (ed.) (1997), *The Cinematic City*, London: Routledge.

Clover, Carol J. (1992), *Men, Women, and Chain Saws: Gender in the Modern Horror Film*,
    Princeton: Princeton University Press.

Cohan, Steven and Ina Rae Hark (eds) (1993), *Screening the Male: Exploring Masculinities
    in Hollywood Cinema*, New York: Routledge.

Corrigan, Timothy (1991), *A Cinema without Walls. Movies and Culture after Vietnam*, New
    Brunswick: Rutgers University Press, p. 4.

Creekmur, Corey K (1995), 'Acting Like a Man: Masculine Performance in *My Darling
    Clementine*', in Corey K. Creekmur and Alexander Doty (eds), *Out in Culture: Gay,
    Lesbian and Queer Essays on Popular Culture*, Durham, NC: Duke University Press,
    pp. 167–82.

Cubitt, Sean (1999), 'Introduction. Le Reel, c'est l'impossible: the Sublime Time of Special
    Effects', *Screen*, vol. 40, no. 2, Summer, pp. 123–30.

Daniel, Valentine (1998), *Charred Lullabies: Chapters in an Anthropography of Violence*,
    Berkeley: University of California Press.

Das, Veena (1992), Introduction, in Veena Das (ed.), *Mirrors of Violence: Communities and
    Survivors in South Asia*, Delhi: Oxford University Press.

De, Aditi. 'How He Gives "Force" to his Drawings', from Thotta Tharani's personal library.

Desser, David (1992), 'Toward a Structural Analysis of the Postwar Samurai film', in Arthur
    Nolletti Jr. and David Desser (eds), *Reframing Japanese Cinema: Authorship, Genre,
    History*, Bloomington and Indianapolis: Indiana University Press, pp. 145–64.

Dhareshwar, Vivek and Tejaswini Niranjana (1996), '*Kaadalan* and the Politics of
    Resignification: Fashion, Violence, and the Body', *Journal of Arts and Ideas*, no. 29,
    January.

Dhondy, Farrukh (1990), *Bombay Duck*, London: Cape.

Dimendberg, Edward (1995), 'The Will to Motorization: Cinema, Highways, and
    Modernity', *October*, no. 73, Summer, pp. 91–137.

Dissanayake, Wimal and Malti Sahai (1992), *Sholay: A Cultural Reading*, New Delhi: Wiley
    Eastern.

Doane, Mary Ann (1991), *Femmes Fatales*, New York: Routledge.

Doctor, Geeta (n.d.), 'One Artist, Two Lives', from Tharani's personal library.

Doriaswammy, Rashmi (1995), 'Hindi Commercial Cinema: Changing Narrative

Strategies', in Aruna Vasudev (ed.), *Frames of Mind: Reflections of Indian Cinema*, New Delhi: UBS.

Duara, Ajit (1989), 'Where are the "Mother Indias" of Today?', *Cinema in India,* vol. 3, no. 4, October–December.

Dutta, J. P. (1986), Interview, *Filmfare,* 1–15 December.

——— (1997), Interview, *Indian Express*, 9 May.

——— (2000), Interview with Subhash K. Jha, *Filmfare*, June, pp. 82–5.

Dyer, Richard (1992), *Only Entertainment*, London and New York: Routledge.

Edelman, Lee (1994), *Homographesis: Essays in Gay Literary and Cultural Theory*, New York: Routledge.

Eisenstein, Sergei M. (1997), 'The Montage of Film Attractions', in Peter Lehman (ed.), *Defining Cinema*, New Brunswick: Rutgers University Press, pp. 17–36.

Eitzen, Dirk (1991), 'Evolution, Functionalism, and the Study of American Cinema', *The Velvet Light Trap*, no. 28, Fall, pp. 82–3.

Feuer, Jane (1993), *The Hollywood Musical*, Bloomington: Indiana University Press.

Fletcher, John (1988), 'Versions of Masquerade', *Screen*, vol. 29, no. 3, pp. 43–70.

Freud, Sigmund (1919), 'Fetishism', in James Strachey (tr. and ed., 1987), *On Sexuality*, New York: Viking Penguin, pp. 345–57.

Freud, Sigmund (1919), '"A Child Is Being Beaten" (A Contribution to the Study of the Origin of Sexual Perversions)', in James Strachey (tr. and ed., 1987), *On Psychopathology*, New York: Viking Penguin, pp. 159–93.

Friedberg, Anne (1994), *Window Shopping: Cinema and the Postmodern*, Berkeley: University of California Press.

Gabilondo, Joseph (2000), 'Morphing Saint Sebastian', in Vivian Sobchack (ed.), *Metamorphing: Visual Transformation and the Culture of Quick-Change*, Minneapolis: University of Minnesota Press.

Gallop, Jane (1982), *The Daughter's Seduction: Feminism and Psychoanalysis*, London: Macmillan.

Gallagher, Tag (1995), 'Shoot-out at the Genre Corral', in Barry Grant (ed.), *Film Genre Reader II*, Austin: University of Texas Press.

Gangar, Amrit (1995), 'Films from the City of Dreams', in Sujata Patel and Alice Thorner (eds), *Bombay: Mosaic of Modern Culture*, Bombay: Oxford University Press.

Gaudreault, Andre (1990), 'Detours in Film Narrative: The Development of Cross-Cutting', in Thomas Elsaesser and Adam Barker (eds), *Early Cinema: Space, Frame, Narrative*, London: BFI, pp. 133–50.

Genette, Gerard (1972), *Desire, Deceit, and the Novel: Self and Other in Literary Structure*, (tr. Yvonne Freccero), Baltimore: Johns Hopkins University Press.

Ghosh, Shohini (1996), 'Deviant Pleasures and Disorderly Women', in Ratna Kapur (ed.), *Feminist Terrains and Legal Domains: Interdisciplinary Essays on Women and Law in India*, New Delhi: Kali for Women.

Gopal, Priyamvada (1999), 'Of Victims and Vigilantes: The *Bandit Queen* Controversy', in Rajeshwari Sunder Rajan (ed.), *Signposts: Gender Issues in Post-Independence India*, New Delhi: Kali, pp. 292–330.

Gopalan, Lalitha (1997), '*Coitus Interruptus* and Love Story in Indian Cinema', in Vidya Dehejia (ed.), *Representing the Body: Gender Issues in Indian Art*, New Delhi: Kali for Women, pp. 124–39.

—— (1997), 'Avenging Women in Indian Cinema', *Screen*, vol. 38, no. 1, pp. 42–59.

Grewal, Inderpal (1999), 'Traveling Barbie: Indian Transnationalism and the Global Consumer', *Positions*, vol. 7, no. 3, Winter.

Gunning, Tom (1990), ' "Primitive" Cinema: A Frame-Up? Or the Trick's on Us', in Thomas Elsaesser and Adam Barker (eds), *Early Cinema: Space, Frame, Narrative*, London: BFI, pp. 95–103.

—— (1990), 'Non-continuity, Continuity, Discontinuity: A Theory of Genres in Early Films' and 'The Cinema of Attractions: Early Film, its Spectator and the Avant-garde', in Thomas Elsaesser and Adam Barker (eds), *Early Cinema: Space, Frame, Narrative*, London: BFI, pp. 86–94.

—— (1991), 'Heard over the Phone: *The Lonely Villa* and the De Lord Tradition of the Terrors of Technology', *Screen*, vol. 32, no. 2, Summer, pp. 184–96.

—— (2000), *The Films of Fritz Lang: Allegories of Vision and Modernity*, London: BFI.

Haasan, Kamal (1994), 'Our World, Their World', *Sunday Times of India*, 2 October.

Hall, Stuart (1996), 'When was "Post Colonial" Thinking at the Limit?', in Iain Chambers and Lidia Curti (eds), *Post Colonial Question: Common Skies, Divided Horizons*, London: Routledge.

Hansen, Miriam (1987), 'Benjamin, Cinema and Experience, "The Blue Flower in the Land of Technology"', *New German Critique*, 40, Winter, pp. 179–224.

—— (1991), *Babel and Babylon: Spectatorship in American Silent Film*, Cambridge, Mass.: Harvard University Press.

Hariharan, K. (1995), 'The Structural Relationships between *Thalapathi* and the *Mahabharata*', Philadelphia, March.

Hart, Lynda (1994), *Fatal Women: Lesbian Sexuality and the Mark of Aggression*, Princeton: Princeton University Press.

Hayward, Susan (1996), 'Auteur Theory', in *Key Concepts in Cinema Studies*, London: Routledge.

Heath, Stephen (1975), 'Film and System: Terms of Analysis, I', *Screen*, vol. 16, no. 1, Spring.

The Indian Cinematograph Code (1982), Hyderabad, Cinematograph Laws Research Institute.

'Imagining You', *Illustrated Weekly of India*, 29 May–4 June 1993, pp. 24–37.

Iyer, Pico (1988), *Video Nights in Kathmandu: Reports from the Not-So-Far East*, New York: .

Jaymanne, Laleen (1992), 'Sri Lankan Family Melodrama: A Cinema of Primitive Attractions', *Screen*, vol. 33, no. 2, Summer.

Jenkins, Henry (1995), 'Historical Poetics', in Joanne Hollows and Mark Janovich (eds), *Approaches to Popular Film*, Manchester: Manchester University Press.

Jha, Subhash K. (2000), 'That Gut Feeling', *Filmfare*, June, pp. 82–5.

Joseph, Ammu and Kalpana Sharma (1994), 'Rape: A Campaign Is Born', in Ammu Joseph and Kalpana Sharma (eds), *Whose News?: The Media and Women's Issues*, New Delhi: Sage, pp. 43–50.

Kasebekar, Asha (1999), 'An Introduction to Indian Cinema', in Jill Nelmes (ed.), *An Introduction to Film Studies*, London: Routledge (rev. edn).

Khan, Salim (1988), Interview, *Screen*, 11 November; also published in Rafique Baghdadi and Rajiv Rao (eds) (1995), *Talking Films*, New Delhi: HarperCollins India, pp. 127–37.

Khanna, Anil Ranvir (1993), 'That's Style', *Filmfare,* February, pp. 46–9.

Kirby, Lynne (1997), *Parallel Tracks: The Railroad and Silent Cinema*, Durham, NC: Duke University Press.

Konstantarakos, Myrto (ed.) (2000), *Spaces in European Cinema*, Exeter: Exeter Intellect.

Kracauer, Siegfried (1995), 'Cult of Distraction', in Thomas Y. Levin (tr. and ed.), *The Mass Ornament: Weimar Essays*, Cambridge, Mass.: Harvard University Press, pp. 323–8.

Krutinik, Frank (1991), *In a Lonely Street: Film Noir, Genre, Masculinity*, London: Routledge.

Kuntzel, Thierry (1980), 'Film Work, 2', *Camera Obscura*, 5, pp. 6–69.

Lapsley and Lipset (1998), *Film Theory: An Introduction*, Manchester: Manchester University Press.

Leach, Edmund (1964), 'Anthropological Aspects of Language: Animal Categories and Verbal Abuse', in Eric H. Lenneberg (ed.), *New Directions in the Study of Language*, Cambridge, Mass.: MIT Press, p. 23.

Lehman, Peter (1993), *Running Scared: Masculinity and the Representation of the Male Body*, Philadelphia: Temple University Press.

Leutrat, Jean-Louis and Suzanne Liandrat-Guigues (1998), 'John Ford and Monument Valley', in Edward Buscombe and Roberta E. Pearson (eds), *Back in the Saddle Again: New Essays on the Western*, London: BFI.

Lévi-Strauss, Claude (1969), *The Elementary Structures of Kinship* (tr. James Harle Bell, John Richard con Sturner, and Rodney Needham), Boston: Beacon.

McCabe, Colin (1986), 'Defining Popular Culture', in Colin McCabe (ed.), *High Theory/Low Culture: Analyzing Popular Television and Film*, New York: St Martin's Press, pp. 1–10.

Malik, Farhad (1981), 'Fact and Fiction', *Cinema in India,* August, pp. 5–8.

Mankekar, Purnima (1999), *Screening Culture, Viewing Politics: An Ethnography of Television, Womanhood, and Nation in Postcolonial India*, Durham, NC: Duke University Press.

Martin, Adrian (1998), *Once Upon a Time in America*, London: BFI.

Masud, Iqbal (1989), 'The Pillars Are Borrowed', *Cinema in India,* October–December, pp. 16–17.

———— (1997), *Dream Merchants, Politicians and Partition: Memoirs of an Indian Muslim*, New Delhi: HarperCollins India, p. 133.

Mayne, Judith (1993), *Cinema and Spectatorship*, London: Routledge.

———— (1994), *Directed by Dorothy Arzner*, Bloomington: Indiana University Press.

Menon, A. G. Krishna (1997), 'Imagining the Indian City', *Economic and Political Weekly*, 15 November.

Metcalf, Thomas (1989), *An Imperial Vision: Indian Architecture and Britain's Raj*, Berkeley: University of California Press.

Metz, Christian (1982), *The Imaginary Signifier: Psychoanalyisis and the Cinema* (tr. Celia Britton, Annwyl Williams, Ben Brewster, and Alfred Guzzetti), Bloomington: Indiana University Press.

———— (1985), 'Story/Discourse: Notes on Two Kinds of Voyeurism', in Bill Nichols, *Movies and Methods*, Berkeley: University of California Press.

Michelson, Annette (1984), Introduction, in Annete Michelson (ed.), *Kino-Eye: The Writings of Dziga Vertoy* (tr. Kevin O'Brien), Berkeley: University of California Press.

Mohamed, Khalid (1986), 'Apocalypse Now', *Filmfare,* 1–15 December.

Mulvey, Laura (1975), Visual Pleasure and Narrative Cinema, *Screen*, vol. 16, no. 3.

———— (1988), 'Visual Pleasure and Narrative Cinema', in Constance Penley (ed.), *Feminism and Film Theory*, New York: Routledge, pp. 57–68.

———— (1993), 'Some Thoughts on Theories of Fetishism in the Context of Contemporary Culture', *October*, no. 65, Summer, pp. 3–20.

Neale, Steve (1991), 'Aspects of Ideology and Narrative Form in the American War Film', *Screen*, vol. 32, no. 1, Spring, pp. 35–57.

———— (1990), 'Questions of Genre', *Screen*, vol. 31, no. 1. pp. 45–66.

———— (1992), *Genre*, London: BFI (rev. edn).

———— (1993), 'Masculinity as Spectacle: Reflections on Men and Mainstream Cinema', in Steven Cohan and Ina Rae Hark (eds), *Screening the Male: Exploring Masculinities in Hollywood Cinema*, London: Routledge.

———— (2000), *Genre and Hollywood*, London and New York: Routledge.

Neale, Steve and Murray Smith (eds) (1998), *Contemporary Hollywood Cinema*, London and New York: Routledge.

Neupert, Richard (1995), *The End: Narration and Closure in the Cinema*, Detroit: Wayne State University Press.

Pandian, M. S. S. and Venkash Chakravarthy (1996), '*Iruvar*: Transforming History into Commodity', *Economic and Political Weekly*, 21 December.

Pendakur, Manjunath (1990), 'India', in John A. Lent (ed.), *The Asian Film Industry*, Austin: Texas University Press.

——— (1995), 'Dynamics of Cultural Policy Making: The US Film Industry in India', *Journal of Communication*, Autumn, pp. 52–72.

Pfeil, Fred (1995), *White Guys: Studies in Postmodern Domination and Difference*, London: Verso.

Pierson, Michelle (1999),'CGI effects in Hollywood Science-Fiction Cinema 1989–95: The Wonder Years', *Screen*, vol. 40, no. 2, pp. 158–77.

Pinney, Christopher (1997), *Camera Indica: The Social Indian Photographs*, Chicago: University of Chicago Press.

Prasad, M. Madhava (1990), *Ideology of the Hindi Film: A Historical Construction*, Delhi: Oxford University Press.

Raghvendra, M. K. (1992), 'Generic Elements and the Conglomerate Narrative', *Deep Focus* vol. IV, no. 2.

Rahman, M. (1998), 'Women Strike Back', *India Today*, 15 July, pp. 80–2.

Rajadhyaksha, Ashish and Paul Willemen (eds) (1999), *Encyclopaedia of Indian Cinema*, London: BFI (rev. edn).

Ram, K. (n.d.), Profile: 'Through the Lens, Darkly…', *Aside*, P. C. Sriram's personal library.

Ramusack, Barbara N. (1995), 'The Indian Princes as Fantasy: Palace Hotels, Palace Museums and Palace on Wheels', in *Consuming Modernity: Public Culture in a South Asian World*, Minneapolis: University of Minnesota Press.

Rangoonwala, Firoze (1993), 'The Age of Violence', *Illustrated Weekly of India*, 4–10 September, pp. 27–9.

Rao, Maithili (1998), 'Victims in Vigilante Clothing', *Cinema in India*, October–December, pp. 24–6.

Rathnam, Mani (n.d.), Interview, *Aside*, no. 36.

Razdan, C. K. (ed.) (1975), *Bare Breasts and Bare Bottoms*, Bombay: Jaico.

Reid, David and Jayne L. Walker (1993), 'Strange Pursuit: Cornell Woolrich and the Abandoned City of the Forties', in Joan Copjec (ed.), *Shades of Noir*, London: Verso.

Riviere, Joan (1986), 'Womanliness as a Masquerade', in Victor Burgin, James Donald, and Cora Kaplan (eds), *Formations of Fantasy*, London: Methuen, p. 35.

Ronell, Avital (1991), Interview, *Re/Search*, no. 13, p. 127.

Rosen, Philip (1993), 'Document and Documentary: On the Persistence of Historical Concepts', in Michael Renov (ed.), *Theorizing Documentary*, New York: Routledge, pp. 58–89.

Ross, Kristin (1995), *Fast Cars, Clean Bodies: Decolonization and the Recording of French Culture*, Cambridge, Mass.: MIT Press.

Routt, William D. (1989), 'Todorov among the Gangsters', *Art and Text*, no. 34, Spring, pp. 109–26.

Sanghvi, Malavika Rajbans (1998), 'Where Doubles Dare', *Sunday*, 13–18 November, pp. 76–80.

Sarhadi, Sagar (1988), Interview, *Screen*, 11 November; also published in Rafique Baghadi and Rajiv Rao (eds) (1995), *Talking Films*, New Delhi: HarperCollins India, pp. 155–61.

Sarkar, Kobita (1982), *You Can't Please Everyone: Film Censorship, the Inside Story*, Bombay: IBH.

Schor, Naomi (1987), *Reading in Detail: Aesthetics and the Feminine*, New York: Methuen.

Sealy, Allan (1990), *Hero*, Delhi: Viking India.

Sedgwick, Eve Kofosky (1985), *Between Men: English Literature and Male Homosocial Desire*, New York: Columbia University Press.

Seydor, Paul (1980), *Peckinpah: The Western Films*, Champaign: University of Illinois Press.

Shah, Naseeruddin (1998), Interview, *Filmfare,* May.

Shahini, Kumar (1986), 'Myths for Sale', *Framework*, 30–31, pp. 71–8.

Shetty, Manmohan (1994), 'Trends in Film Processing', *Lensight,* vol. 3, no. 4, October.

Shivkumar, S. (1999), Interview, *Stardust*, February, pp. 54–61.

Sinclair, Iain (1999), *Crash: David Cronenberg's Post Mortem on J. G. Ballard's 'Trajectory of Fate'*, London: BFI.

Singh, Madan Gopal (1983), 'Technique as an Ideological Weapon', in Aruna Vasudev and Phillipe Lenglet (eds), *Indian Cinema Superbazaar*, Delhi: Vikas, pp. 119–25.

Singh, R. Bhagwan (1990), 'Myth and Magic', *Sunday*, 25–31 March.

Smith, Murray (1996), *Boys: Masculinity in Contemporary Culture*, Boulder: Westview.

——— (1998), 'Thesis on the Philosophy of Hollywood History', in *Contemporary Hollywood Cinema*, London and New York: Routledge.

Smith, Paul (1993), *Clint Eastwood: A Cultural Production*, Minneapolis: University of Minnesota Press.

Sommer, Dorris (1991), *Foundational Fictions: The National Romances of Latin America*, Berkeley: University of California Press.

Sriram, P. C. (1988), Interview, *The Hindu,* 22 July, p. 7.

Staiger, Janet (1985), 'The Hollywood Mode of Production, 1930–60', in *Classical Hollywood Cinema: Film Style and Mode of Production to 1960*, New York: Columbia University Press.

Stern, Lesley (1995), *The Scorsese Connection*, London: BFI.

Stringer, Julian. '"Your Tender Smiles Give Me Strength": Paradigms of Masculinity in John Woo's *A Better Tomorrow* and *The Killer*', *Screen*, vol. 38, no. 1, Spring, pp. 25–41.

Subramaniam, Babu (1990), 'Whirlpool', *Deep Focus*, vol. 3, no. 1, pp. 97–8.

Bahadur, Satish (1969), 'Towards a National Cinema', *Movement*, p. 4.

Turim, Maureen (1989), 'Disjunction in the Modernist Flashback', in *Flashbacks in Film: Memory and History*, New York: Routledge.

Vanaik, Achin (1991), *The Painful Transition*, New York: Verso.

Vasudev, Aruna (1978), *Liberty and Licence in Indian Cinema*, Delhi: Vikas.

Vasudevan, Ravi (1996), 'Bombay and Its Public', *Journal of Arts and Ideas*, vol. 29, January, pp. 44–65.

Vernet, Marc (1983), 'The Filmic Transaction: On the Openings of Film Noirs', *The Velvet Light Trap*, no. 20, Summer, pp. 2–9.

Wattal, P. K. (1958), *Population Problem in India: A Census Study*, Delhi: Minerva Bookshop.

White, Mimi (1998), Paper presented at the Annual Conference of the Society of Cinema Studies, Ottawa, July.

Willemen, Paul (1994), 'Through the Glass Darkly: Cinephelia Reconsidered', in *Looks and Frictions: Essays in Cultural Studies and Film Theory*, Bloomington: Indiana University Press.

Williams, Linda (1981), *Figures of Desire: A Theory and Analysis of Surrealist Film*, Berkeley: University of California Press, pp. 56–105.

———— (1989), *Hard Core: Power, Pleasure, and the 'Frenzy of the Visible'*, Berkeley: University of California Press.

Willis, Sharon (1997), 'Combative Femininity: *Thelma and Louise* and *Terminator 2*', in *Race and Gender in Contemporary Hollywood Film*, Durham, NC: Duke University Press.

———— (1998), *High Contrast*, Durham, NC: Duke University Press.

Wilson, Rob and Wimal Dissanayake (eds) (1996), *Global/Local: Cultural Production and the Transnational Imaginary*, Durham, NC: Duke University Press.

Wlaschin, Ken (1996), 'Birth of the "Curry" Western: Bombay 1976', *Film and Filming*, vol. 22, no. 7, April, pp. 20–3.

Wollen, Peter (1982), 'Godard and Counter Cinema: *Vent d'Est*', in *Readings and Writings: Semiotic Counter-Strategies*, London: Verso.

———— (1998), 'The Auteur Theory', in *Signs and Meaning in the Cinema*, London: BFI (rev. edn).

Wyatt, Justin (1994), *High Concept: Movies and Marketing in Hollywood*, Austin: University of Texas Press.

Žižek, Slavoj (1989), 'Looking Awry', *October*, no. 50, pp. 31–55.

———— (1992), 'In His Bold Gaze My Ruin is Writ Large', in Slavoj Zizek (ed.), *Everything You Always Wanted to Know About Lacan (But Were Afraid to Ask Hitchcock)*, London: Verso, pp. 211–72.

Index

Notes: *Italicised* page numbers denote illustrations or extensively illustrated sequences; *n* = endnote (indexed only for background information, not citations)